THE LETTERS OF

Richard Brinsley Sheridan

RICHARD BRINSLEY SHERIDAN

From the engraving by Hall after the painting by Sir Joshua Reynolds

THE LETTERS OF
Richard Brinsley Sheridan

EDITED BY

CECIL PRICE

VOLUME II

OXFORD
AT THE CLARENDON PRESS
1966

Oxford University Press, Ely House, London W. 1
GLASGOW NEW YORK TORONTO MELBOURNE WELLINGTON
CAPE TOWN SALISBURY IBADAN NAIROBI LUSAKA ADDIS ABABA
BOMBAY CALCUTTA MADRAS KARACHI LAHORE DACCA
KUALA LUMPUR HONG KONG

PRINTED IN GREAT BRITAIN

CONTENTS

VOLUME II

VOLUME III

200. To Henry Holland

Gilmore MS. *Address*: H. Holland Esq. *Dock.*: Sienesi 14 Yrs. from | Mr. 93 at £65— | price is £2400[1]

[1794?]
T.R.D.L. Thursday

My Dear Sir,

I have a particular engagement that will keep me out of Town tomorrow but I want so earnestly that we should have an hour together that if it is not practicable for us to meet on saturday I will return tomorrow and I leave a servant in Town to wait for your answer. I will meet you punctually at half past one on saturday and then we will decide everything. | Yours ever | R B Sheridan

I have just seen the Prince—but I have left the Riding house in your hands.

201. To William Adam

Adam MS. *Address*: W. Adam | Lincolns-Inn-Square | London *Pm.*: BATH *Dock.*: Mr. Sheridan | January | 1794

Jan. 1794

Dear Adam,

If it is true that M.[2] and P.[3] are to be sent off on saturday

[1] A reference to premises leased by Samuel Wegge to Pio Sienesi, a pawnbroker.

[2] Thomas Muir (1765–98), parliamentary reformer, was found guilty of leasing-making and sentenced on 30 Aug. 1793 at Edinburgh to fourteen years' transportation. He was brought (with T. F. Palmer) to Woolwich on 1 Dec., and was visited by S. and Lauderdale, who then waited on Dundas to suggest that the sentences on both Muir and Palmer were illegal and ought not to be put into execution until after the meeting of parliament. On 15 Jan. 1794 the King signed an Order in Council for transportation. See *The Berry Papers* (ed. Melville, 1914), pp. 119–20; *The Times*, 1 and 24 Jan. 1794; *Newcastle Courant*, 18 Jan. 1794. For the subsequent attempts by S. and Adam to prove the illegality of the sentences, see *Speeches*, iii. 251–6, 260; P. Mackenzie, *The Life of Thomas Muir* (Glasgow, 1831), pp. 27, 135–6, 147–9; *Caledonian Mercury*, 15 and 17 Mar. 1794. For late and unexpected support for the basic point of view of S. and Adam, see *Colchester Corr.* i. 50.

[3] Thomas Fyshe Palmer (1747–1802), unitarian minister and parliamentary reformer, was convicted at Perth of sedition.

surely surely the Hab. Corp. should be tried. | Yours ever | R B S.

202. [To the Duchess of Devonshire][1]

Harvard MS.

[*17 Jan. 1794*]
Wansted Friday

I am vex'd beyond measure at having been disappointed Day after Day of the Books,[2] but I am solemnly promised them on monday. Pray pray believe that nothing but the helplessness of our present situation could have made me disappoint you. But on monday by a Hook or a crook it shall be.

I find I could have sent you a great deal of news last week —but I thought your Sun[3] would have had it all much sooner. To Day I have nothing for I write from Wansted, where Tom is returned after destroying a great many Pheasants and winning Golden Opinions in Norfolk.[4] I shan't go to Town 'till Monday unless I find the meeting is tomorrow of our numerous and uncombined Army to settle the *moderation* of Tuesday next.[5] As *Friends of the People* we are going to do as rash and ill-timed a thing as possible. It has made Lord Lauderdale[6] mad and Mrs. Bouverie cry, but I hope we shall reconsider the matter.

I believe the Government will avow the strongest determination of Persevering in the War. The Prospect of success is certainly less than ever. The cause of the Royalists

[1] The Duchess was at Bath with Lady E. Foster. See *Georgiana*, p. 204.

[2] The word has been altered and may possibly be 'Boots' or 'Notes'.

[3] *The Sun*, edited by John Heriot, began publication in Oct. 1792 and supported the government.

[4] W. Fraser Rae prints (in 'Sheridan's Sons', *Temple Bar*, cxvi (1899), p. 411) a letter (from Fox to S.) which he thinks belongs to 2 Jan. 1794. Fox promises to take Tom S. with him to Lord Petre's and to Holkham, but intends to return to London on 16 Jan.

[5] The King's speech to Parliament on 21 Jan. stated, 'It only remains for us to persevere in our united exertions'. In the debate that followed, S. declared that the Government had forced the war on France, and he went on to denounce the blunders of the campaign. See *Speeches*, iii. 182–222.

[6] Fox stated that Lauderdale was 'the sole cause of' this association. See Add. MS. 47569, f. 14.

irreparably over—Lord Rawdons[1] expedition totally given up—his Troops going into Hospitall at Southampton and the Isle of Wight—the French Army in West Flanders multiplying daily to attack Cobourgh[2] on the 24th. The King of Prussia has certainly written for a Subsidy and a loan of *£3 million 700,000* and certainly has written that he is not bound by his *Defensive Alliance* with us as we *were the Attackers* in our present war with France[3] by sending away Chauvelin[4] etc. We shall try to have this Paper produced. There are certainly notwithstanding the confused List in the Gazette *15* Sail of the Line saved to the French.[5] I have talk'd an hour with Sir Sidney Smith[6] and have seen many private Letters. Sir James St. Clair[7] thank God is safe!—He only tumbled into the Water. If any further Delay interposes I suppose he will come over like Leander. The Duke of Grafton[8] is said to Waver again. I can send no late news and I must send this to Town directly or it will miss the Post. | bless you Ma'am *for all* | R B S.

I hope there may be some good news that may reach you

[1] Wind and weather had prevented Rawdon from assisting the Royalists. When he arrived on the west coast of France on 2 Dec. he received no signals from them and he eventually returned home. S. said in Parliament that the expedition was 'talked of so long as to deliver over all the unhappy royalists on the coast to massacre' (*Speeches*, iii. 221).

[2] Prince Frederick Josias of Saxe-Coburg-Saalfeld (1737–1815), general in the service of the Austrian emperor. His troops attacked the French near Marolles on 16 Jan.

[3] See *Speeches*, iii. 199. Frederick-William II, King of Prussia (1734–97), agreed in the following April to continue to assist the allies in return for large subsidies.

[4] François-Bernard, Marquis de Chauvelin (1766–1832), was the French envoy in London from Apr. 1792 to Jan. 1793.

[5] See *Speeches*, iii. 221. The *London Gazette*, 17 Jan. 1794, lists nine ships burnt at Toulon, four sent to other French ports, one burnt at Leghorn, and one remaining at Toulon. Cf. J. H. Rose, *Lord Hood and the Defence of Toulon* (Cambridge, 1922), p. 80.

[6] Sir William Sidney Smith (1764–1840) set fire to the French fleet at Toulon on 18 Dec. 1793, just before the British evacuation. He arrived in London, with Hood's dispatches of 20 Dec., on 15 Jan. 1794.

[7] Sir James St. Clair-Erskine (1762–1837) succeeded his father as 6th baronet in 1765; married Mrs. Bouverie's daughter, Henrietta, in 1789; and became 2nd Earl of Rosslyn in 1805. He was Adjutant-General at Toulon.

[8] Grafton was expected to support Fox on the question of ending the war, but *The Times*, 25 Jan. 1794, wrote: 'We are glad to hear, that the Duke of Grafton's good sense has convinced him of the imprudence of moving to make peace with France.' In its issue of 19 Feb., however, *The Times* (commenting on the debate of 17 Feb.) noted that Grafton's advocacy of peace did not include any mention of how it might be brought about.

with this—Lady E and Mrs. St. John[1] might be sure I should have written sooner if there had been any *comfortable* intelligence to send.

203. To J. Bluett[2]

Pub.: *The World*, 22 February 1794, quoting *The True Briton*, 19 February 1794. *Address*: London, January 29th, 1794 | Mr. J. Bluett, | Falmouth. *Fr.*: Free.—R. B. Sheridan.[3]

29 Jan. 1794

Sir,

I am much obliged by your Communication respecting *Halifax*. I mentioned the subject in the house the first day of the Session, and I since find your intelligence confirmed in every particular. I shall be happy at all times to be favored with any Intelligence which you may think may be made use of for the advantage of the Country. | I am, Sir, | Your obedient Servant, | R. B. Sheridan.

Lower Grosvenor Street, Jan. 29th.

204. To Henry Holland

Gilmore MS. *Address*: H. Holland Esq. | Sloane-St: *Dock.*: Mr. Sheridan | Feb. 17. 1794 | Recd. Feby. 17th. 1794 | after the work was done

17 Feb. 1794

My Dear Sir,

I hope to be able to get to the Theatre tomorrow or

[1] John St. John (1746 ?–93) dramatist and member of the Devonshire House circle, did not marry; but his elder brother, Henry (1738–1818), afterwards a Major-General, married Barbara Bladen in 1771.

[2] S. had received an anonymous letter on the inadequate defences of Halifax, Nova Scotia, the British naval and military centre in America, and had spoken vigorously on the subject in the Commons on 31 Jan. 1794 (*Speeches*, iii. 230–3). On the first day of the session, however, he had made a long speech on the nepotism, corruption, and general inefficiency of the administration (ibid. iii. 184–222). The above letter appeared in the Government paper, the *True Briton*, with the statement that Bluett was a 15-year-old midshipman and that the original anonymous letter was a hoax on S. He took up the matter in parliament on 21 Feb. (*Speeches*, iii. 237–8), and said that he had fifty other letters on the same subject, that his note was to Blewitt, a merchant at Falmouth, and that to print it was to degrade Englishmen into eavesdroppers and informers (*Salopian Journal*, 5 Mar. 1794).

[3] *The True Briton*, 20 Jan. 1794, quoted in *Speeches*, iii. 238.

Thursday—and then the two Principal things I have reserved the Division of the Private Boxes and the fixing the pay offices shall be decided—a very few Days work will finish them. | yours truly | R B Sheridan.

Monday.

205. To Henry Holland

Gilmore MS. *Address*: H. Holland Esq | Sloane-St: *Dock.*: Mr. Sheridan | March 16. 1794

16 Mar. 1794

My Dear Sir,

I could not get to you on Friday, and you see we had another late Day in the House.[1] I was there yesterday—and *most peremptorily fix'd* our first Play for *Saturday sen'-night.*[2] And all have promised so you must be in the way for a Crown of Laurel.

I was glad to see the Decorations going on—I will be at the Theatre all tuesday morning. I wrote such a Letter to White and another to Allan[3]—as I think have completely silenced their Battery. | yours ever | R B S.

Sunday morning

I find the approbation of the Theatre increases.

206. 'To the Right Honourable Henry Dundass[4] One of His Majesty's Principal Secretaries of State'

Osborn MS. Draft. *Dock.*: [in Thomas Moore's hand] Letter to Dundas on the affair of Stone—must examine whether this has ever been published.

[*9 May 1794*]

Sir,

On the Ground of Mr. Stone,[5] and whom your Letter

[1] D.L.Th.? S. spoke in the Commons in 14 Mar.: see *Speeches*, iii. 268–73.

[2] Plays were not given at the new D.L.Th. until 21 Apr. *The Times*, 5 Apr. 1794, announced they were 'unavoidably postponed on account of the extent of the Preparations for compleating the Scenery and Machinery, in a stile suitable to the Theatre.'

[3] Attorney. He bought one-eighth share in C.G.Th. in Apr. 1790, 'for a client'.

[4] Henry Dundas, afterwards 1st Viscount Melville (1742–1841), was Home Secretary, 1791–4.

[5] William Stone, brother of John Hurford Stone (1763–1818), was committed to Newgate on a charge of high

states to have been apprehended on suspicion of High Treason having in the course of his examination referr'd to a conversation which He states himself to have [had] with me I thought it incumbent on me yesterday[1] to give the information required relative to that conversation which but for the Reference to Mr. Stone himself I should have thought it incumbent on me to have refused unless summon'd as a witness in the Trial in case of such an even[t] taking Place and having given that information I think it right and proper to comply with your suggestion of putting it upon Paper, and verifying it upon oath. The following is as accurate a statement of all the circumstances that came within my knowledge relative to that conversation as my recollection can furnish which was at the time not considered by me as a matter of any importance or seriousness. Some time since, I find it must have been on the second or Third of March I received a Note from Mr. Richard Wilson,[2] proposing to call on me the next morning with a Gentleman who had something to propose which He conceived would be for [the] advantage of the Public and that Lord Lauderdale and Major Maitland[3] would meet them at my House. I know nothing of the origin of the appointment but I understand since that it originated accidentally at the Whig Club[4] where I was not present the evening before. The next morning I found that Lord Lauderdale and Major Maitland as well as Mr. Wilson and Mr. Stone had call'd before I was up and had gone away. Soon after Mr. Wilson and Mr. Stone returned. I learn since yesterday by enquiry from my

treason, on 10 May 1794; but was tried and acquitted in Jan. 1796. S. gave evidence then: cf. Moore, ii. 267–9.

[1] S. was examined at the Secretary of State's office on 8 May 1794, and so were Lauderdale, Maitland, William Smith, and Benjamin Vaughan, about disclosures made by William Stone. S., Lauderdale, and Vaughan were also questioned by the Cabinet on the following day. See *The Times*, 9–10 May 1794.

[2] 'Mr. Wilson of Bartlett's-Buildings, was Stone's Solicitor and in that capacity' was also examined on 8 May. Richard Wilson (1759–1834) was a shrewd attorney known as 'Morpeth Dick', and the friend of Joseph Richardson. See *Notes and Queries*, 12th Ser., ii (1916), 74–75.

[3] Hon. (afterwards Sir) Thomas Maitland (1759?–1834), a member of the committee of the Friends of the People, and M.P. for Haddington Burghs.

[4] The Whig Club met at the London Tavern on 3 Mar. under the chairmanship of the Duke of Norfolk. A toast to S. ('and may genius and talents ever triumph over prejudice') was drunk then. See *Morn. Chron.* 5 Mar. 1794.

Servants that Mr. Wilson and Stone had call'd first and finding they could not see me had left a message to request that Lord Lauderdale and Major Maitland might be directed to find them at Hudson's Coffee [House] in Bond St: On Mr. Wilson's recommending [?] Mr. Stone to me I enquired for Lord Lauderdale and Major Maitland and was informed that they had just parted with them having communicated the business to them which they came now to communicate to me. Of Mr. Wilson I had considerable knowledge, to Mr. Stone I was an entire Stranger. I may have been in a room with him and it is probable that I have but to my knowledge I never saw or spoke to him before in my Life. After some Preface Mr. Stone begg'd my attention to what he had been stating to the Gentlem[en] he had parted from, as He had before to others, whom I think he named. He said He thought He had an opportunity of being of signal service to his country but that He wanted the authority and opinion of Persons of more might to assist his idea.

The substance of what He then proceeded to state was according to my best recollection accurately as follows. An american Gentleman[1] a great Friend of his Brothers had lately arrived in London, He was a very proper Person to consult respecting the means by which any channel for Peace might be opened—this Mr. Stone soon pass'd from—and said his great object was to assist in preventing the French from persevering in their idea of invading this country. He was well assured they had such a Determination. His Brother had even advised him to sell his House and Property. He found the Resolution of men in Power in France in this respect was found'd entirely on a Notion that the Discontents in this Country were so great and the People so ripe for insurrection that a great majority of the Nation would second such an attempt. That he knew the fallacy of such an idea, and that He thought he had an opportunity of equally convincing Those in Power in France, and proving to them that all Parties would instantly unite with equal

[1] Lauderdale made it clear at William Stone's trial in Jan. 1796 that the 'American' was actually the Irish revolutionary, William Jackson 1737?–95).

zeal in case of such an event. The attempt however tho' unsuccessful would be a great calamity. He thought it would be highly meritorious to prevent it. He wish'd therefore to fortify himself with the Opinions of Those men adverse to the Principle of the War and to the measures of the Minister. For this Purpose He had applied to Mr. Vaughan[1] who thought it would be extremely fortunate if the French could be undeceived as to any expectations from this country. He had even given him his[2] Thoughts in writing with that view. Here Mr. Stone read a Paper which in most Parts appears to be in substance the same or to the same purpose as that I saw yesterday in the office—but I also think that Paper differs in others—as to the identity of the Paper I can say nothing. I never look'd at the Handwriting touch'd the Paper or made any observation on it. But I should imagine it could not be the same I saw yesterday for I read quickly and fluently and that appear'd scratch'd and interlin'd.

Here ended his statement and I rather think I did not even wait to hear out the whole of this Paper—I am confident I avoided making any comment upon it, resolving in my own mind to speak to Mr. Vaughan respecting it. I told him shortly that tho' I did not doubt the goodness of his intentions it was a subject I would by no means meddle in and that he would do well to have nothing more to say to it. I express'd my surprise at his corresponding in the manner he said with his Brother one of whose Letters he had read or quoted. He said he had been with Mr. Pitt I think a few Days before and as I understood on this subject or on some suspicions which had reach'd Government respecting his conduct. I advised him then to see Mr. Dundass and acquaint him with the present object—that he might be sure that He would not carry any conceal'd correspondence on such a subject, and that if I was in office[3] I should certainly

[1] Benjamin Vaughan (1751–1835), a protégé of Shelburne and M.P. for Calne. His letter, apparently intended for J. H. Stone, was found on William Stone. Vaughan fled to France after the interrogation. See J. G. Alger, *Englishmen in the French Revolution* (1889), pp. 89–90.

[2] Vaughan's.

[3] In his evidence at William Stone's trial in 1796, S. said, 'I had been in office as under Secretary of State once and that I should have thought it my duty to intercept that communication.'

think it my Duty to watch very narrowly any intercourse between Persons in this country and a Person in the situation which his Brother had chosen in France. Mr. Stone seem'd dispos'd to give up all further idea of the business—but He did not seem to consider his Brother's Friend at all as an agent from the French Government, but as an American Gentleman who had a right to go and form his opinions as [and] where he pleased and whom Government could not meddle with—and I think said something of his being seen to go to Scotland or Ireland—on this I more gravely (for I had not treated the matter with much seriousness before) gave my opinion that He had better have nothing more to say to him, and that his Friend whatever he profess'd to be seem'd very likely to get into [a] scrape. In this advice Mr. Wilson very strongly join'd. And from what Mr. Stone answer'd when They took their leave they certainly gave me the impression that Mr. Stone meant either instantly to break all intercourse with the American Gentleman or act with the knowledge of Government.

Before they left the Room I think some Person must have come on and that I must have taken Mr. Wilson aside for I recollect perfectly asking him how He who was a man of sense and discretion could think of bringing a man to me on such a foolish errand—and Mr. Wilson apologised and said He was sure the Intentions of Mr. Stone were good—but that He saw the matter in the light I did and would by all means advise him to meddle no further—if this did not pass then it must have been on meeting Wilson very soon after tho' I do not recollect where

On the same Day I am pretty confident I met Mr. Vaughan in the House of Common and told him whom I had seen—observing that tho' Stone probably meant well, I was sure He did not [think] it was very discreet to leave a Paper in hands, Parts of which as they hastily trench[?] very near[?] might be liable to misconstruction—which might possibly turn it to an ill use. Mr. Vaughan express'd surprise at the Paper's having been shewn to me, and said I think that it was intended for no other use than to be read to a Person, with a view which He thought meritorious, and might be serviceable to the Country—a few Days after in passing thro' the Lobby He thank'd me for the Hint I had given him and as I understood said He had got the Paper back again.

The first time I met Lord Lauderdale we mention'd this subject and both argued that Stone seem'd a very weak and idle man tho' He appear'd to mean well. And I perfectly remember his saying that either He or the Major had [written] or would write to him and advise him to see Mr. Dundass. About a Fortnight after as I guess I heard it in Mr. Debret's Shop, and Persons jesting at it, that Stone was boasting everywhere that He had saved the Kingdom from an Invasion—and I found that the Story of his going about to us and of the Paper was a thing as Public as if it had been in the Gazette.

After this I never heard or thought more of the subject or of the Parties—till common rumour inform'd me that a Mr. Stone was taken up.

The above tho' I can by no means be sure of Phrases or expressions which Mr. Wilson who was present at the whole conversation with Mr. Stone may perhaps remember better is I am confident accurately the substance of everything that has come within my knowledge on this subject—and on the whole I think it but just to add that tho' Mr. Stone appeared to me a very weak man yet that he appear'd really and zealously convinced that he was endeavouring at a Public Benefit.

Under the circumstances in which the application has been made to me I have thought it equally a matter of respect to myself as well as of justice to the Person under suspicion to give this Relation more in Detail than at first perhaps might appear necessary. My own conduct in the matter not being in Question I can only say that were a similar case to occur I think I should act in every circumstance possibly in the manner I [acted] on this occasion.[1]

[1] Lord Holland told Thomas Moore that S. 'behaved very well in this business.' He also said that Vaughan was 'the author of a pamphlet called "The Calm Observer" ', and S. at the same time, 'I should be sorry poor Vaughan was hanged, because it would sound so awkward when he was dangling in the air for people to say, "There hangs the Calm Observer".' (Widener MS.)

207. To Lord Kenyon[1]

The Lord Kenyon MS. *Pub.*: H.M.C., *Kenyon MSS.* (1894), iv. 541. *Address*: Rt. Honble. | Lord Chief Justice Kenyon | etc. etc. etc. *Fr.*: R. B. *Sheridan Dock.*: 12 May 1794

[*11*] *May 1794*

My Lord,

I must trust to your indulgence to excuse the Liberty I take in troubling you with a few Lines respecting the appointment of the next Day of sitting for the Trial after tomorrow (monday).[2] I would by no means wish a single hour to be lost in the week, but if it be intended to miss one Day, and as I am informed that tuesday is the least convenient Day for the attendance of the Judges I have presumed to suggest that from particular circumstances it would be a material accommodation to me to speak on wednesday instead of tuesday and my reply will certainly be confined to that one Day.

I have only again to apologize to your Lordship, not meaning to be in Town tomorrow, for directly addressing myself to your Lordship, as I apprehended any other mode of application might be too late. | I have the Honor to be | My Lord, | with the greatest Respect | your Lordship's | obedient Servant | R B Sheridan

Wansted.
Sunday Night

208. To Mrs. Almon

Huntington MS. HM 24045. [Ph.]

[*1794?*]

Madam,

I expect Lord Rt. Spencer[3] in Town to Night or to-

[1] Lloyd Kenyon, 1st Lord Kenyon (1732–1802), was Lord Chief Justice from 1788 to 1802.

[2] Smyth describes (p. 31) S.'s hurried preparations to speak at the trial of Hastings and his need for time: S. sent 'a letter to Lord Kenyon, to implore him to give him a further interval of two or three days, in which to prepare himself. This was granted.' For the speech on 14 May, see Add. MS. 24246, ff. 161–233, and Rae, ii. 383–434.

[3] Lord Robert Spencer (1747–1831) was the third son of Charles, 3rd Duke of

morrow it is impossible for me to do anything for Mr. A. 'till he comes[1]—you had better call or send on sunday | Yrs | R B Sheridan

209. To J. W. Payne

Windsor MS. 38938–9.

28 June [*1794*]

Dear Payne,

If ever there was a Lad formed to play the Devil with the French at Sea it is the Bearer James Goddard.

He is a Stafford connexion of mine and will not be perswaded to think of anything but the Sea to which his Father has at last consented. I don't know the regular way of getting him made a Midshipman but He is so impatient that tho Grey has promised his Brother[2] shall provide for him when He returns in the Boyne He will not wait nor miss the sailing of the Fleet from Portsmouth. I have therefore consented to recommend him to you I am sure He will not disgrace your Patronage, and as I wish very much to serve him, you will oblige me extremely by placing him in a proper situation. I wish you joy of the Victory, and of your own Lawrels[3]—we shall get the poor mens widows above a thousand Pounds by the Theatrical Benefit which I am doing all I can for.[4] | yours ever | R B Sheridan

June 28th

Marlborough, and Foxite M.P. for Wareham.

[1] Almon had been paid by the Opposition for inserting propaganda in the *General Advertiser*, and the money had been doled out by Lord Robert Spencer but had fallen into arrears. Almon claimed the balance in a letter to the Duke of Portland of 21 July 1794, in which he wrote: 'Mr. Sheridan allows this state of the fact to be exact, for I had the honour to see him on the subject before I waited on Lord Robert. . . .' (P.R.O., H.O. 42/32; and A. Aspinall, *Politics and the Press*, 1949, pp. 271–2.) Almon appears to have begun a suit against the Duke for the money: see S.C. 5 June 1899, lot 19.

[2] George Grey (1767–1828), third son of Sir Charles Grey, 1st Earl Grey, was a Post Captain in Sir John Jervis's flagship, the *Boyne*.

[3] Payne was given a gold medal for his command of the *Russell* in the naval battle of 1 June 1794.

[4] The first performance of *The Glorious First of June* was given at D.L.Th. on 2 July. Cobb wrote part of it, but S. also 'gave the dialogue on scraps of paper out of the boxes during rehearsal' (Moore, *Journal*, ii. 303). S. paid £1,310 into Angerstein's bank for the widows' fund: see Winston, 1793–7.

210. To His Son Tom

Pub.: Smyth, p. 45.

[*Autumn 1794*]

My Dear Tom,

Meet me at dinner at six o'clock on Wednesday next, at Guilford. I forget the inn. I want particularly to speak to you.[1] | Ever your affectionate Father, | R. B. S.

211. To Richard Peake

McAdam MS. *Dock.*: R B S. *Wm.*: 1794

[*c. 1794*]

Private

Dear Peake,

You must contrive to do this one more Jobb for me, and pay the *£100* into the Hands of *Sir Robt. Herries*[2] in the name of the *Duchess of Devonshire* it is for a Purpose of mine of the *greatest consequence*, and must be done to *Day* or *to-morrow* | Yrs ever | R B S.

I hope you are better. I return Friday and will explain about the accounts.

212. To Henry Holland

Gilmore MS. *Address*: H. Holland Esq. *Dock.*: Decr. 28th. 1794 | Mr. Sheridan on the | private Boxes

28 December 1794
Sunday morning

My Dear Sir,

I have corrected the Estimate, and if you approve it I think it *perfect* and *unanswerable* (which is pretty conceited of me) and I am sure it will bring us in the money—

[1] Smyth recounts how S. characteristically forgot the appointment. He wanted to speak to his son about his (S.'s) intention of marrying Hester Jane Ogle, daughter of the Dean of Winchester. After various delays (described by Sichel, ii. 264–5), the wedding took place on 27 Apr. 1795.

[2] Banker. Cf. *Georgiana*, pp. 64, 171.

If you adopt it, and have a clerk who could *immediately* copy it—it would be *invaluable* to me to have it ten minutes before *five o'clock to Day* when I am to meet *Coutts* with *Adam*, and then *Lord Derby*[1] at Dinner.—If not practicable pray write to me to the following Purport—(assuming the Result to be your opinion)—viz. 'That you have no Copy of the Estimate made out for the Trustees which you can send me to Day but if it answers as well you can inform me that the result is for the reasons given in your Answer[2] that the Trustees cannot demand less for each of the Orchestra Boxes nearest the Stage[3] than the sum of £2399 for a Lease of fourteen years to commence from the opening of next season. And that you have directed a copy of the Particulars to be sent to me tomorrow morning.—

Your's
H. H. '[4]

Westley take[s] this

you will find me neither abating in my alacrity or punctuality—

Pray write a memorandum of what you observed last Night. | yours | R B S.

213. [To Thomas Smyth?][5]

Maine Historical Society MS. [Ph.]

[*1795?*]

Sir,

I have forwarded the Letter to Mr. Smyth and shall be happy at all times to be honor'd with your commands. Your writing to me required no apology but my present intrusion[6]

[1] Edward Stanley, 12th Earl of Derby (1752–1834), a Whig peer. The Sheridans visited him at Knowsley in Sept. 1785.

[2] Holland replied to the trustees on 28 Dec., to say that boxes were of greater value if left open: they then held nine persons, but if they were partitioned they accommodated only six.

[3] There were four of them.

[4] Holland duly sent a copy of the letter as directed by S.

[5] Father of William Smyth (1765–1849), Tom S.'s tutor. He was a partner in the Liverpool banking firm of Charles Caldwall & Co., which went bankrupt (as a consequence of the war with France) in 1793. See Smyth, p. 11; and *Europ. Mag.* xxiii (1793), 490.

[6] The government refused to consider making peace until a counter revolution had taken place in France, so Fox declared (2 Jan. 1795) that 'Petitions ought to be attempted

on you certainly does: yet I will risk it without further excuse or Preface.

I understand there is to be a Meeting at Liverpool on wednesday next with a view to a Petition to the Crown on the Subject of Peace, and I have just read the Draught of a very moderate Petition which I am informed will be proposed. I believe I may presume to consider you as a very zealous wellwisher to the object proposed. At the same time to fail in the attempt to get such a Petition, or to procure such a one as could not fairly be stated to speak the Sense of the Majority of the People of Liverpool would have a very bad effect for as this would be the first Step of the kind attempted by Friends to Peace the Failure would discourage the measure in other Places where I am confident it may, if we are not too hasty, be carried with almost general consent.

Of course I do not mean to offer any opinion to you on the subject who are every way enabled to judge so much better of it, but being requested to write to Liverpool instead of addressing myself to some with whom I might have taken that Liberty I have addressed myself where I think a suggestion if well founded might be most useful altho' I have not the Pretence of personal acquaintance to excuse me.

I shall be happy to know that you excuse the Liberty I have taken and have the Honor to be | with great Respect | Sir | Your obedient Servant | R B Sheridan.

214. To Vanhutchison[1]

Osborn MS. *Address*: – Vanhutchison Esq. | Gray's-Inn-Gardens *Dock.*: 27 Feby. | Shedredan *Wm.*: 1794

27 Feb. [*1795*]

Sir,

At a meeting of the Trustees for Drury Lane Theatre

wherever they are likely to be successful' (Add. MS. 47569, f. 52). At Liverpool the Mayor refused to call a public meeting to address the King on the unhappy consequences of the war and the 'dangers which threaten the commerce of the Kingdom'. The supporters of Fox therefore decided, at a meeting on 2 Feb., to sign a petition for peace; and this was duly presented in the Commons by General Tarleton (*Gore's Liverpool General Advertiser*, 5 and 26 Feb. 1795).

[1] Richard Van Heythuysen, Mrs. Garrick's attorney?

this morning to consider of the speediest method of paying the remaining mortgage due to the Estate of Mr. Garrick it was judged that the business might be much expedited, if Mr. Hammer[s]ley and myself could have the Pleasure of seeing you in the course of tomorrow. If you will name any time the most convenient to you we will attend an appointment where you please— | I am, Sir, | Your obedient | R B Sheridan

Old-Burlington-St:
Friday
27th: Feby.

215. To Ozias Humphry

Bodleian Library, Western MS. 25436, f. 38. *Address*: Mr. Ozias Humphry | Old Bond St.

[*1795*][1]

My Dear Sir,

If you have no better engagement to Day will you eat a mutton chop with the Linleys in Old Burlington? | Yours truly | R B Sheridan.

Tuesday morning

216. [To Edward Jerningham][2]

Huntington MS. HM 2949. [Ph.] *Dock.*: Mr. B. Sheridan.

[*Before 17 Apr. 1795*]

My Dear Sir,

Another Delay! but 'till tuesday only and the last peremptorily. Mrs. Jordan[3] is going now to qualify herself for your play— | Yours trul[y] | R B Sheridan

Sunday morning

[1] S. lived in Old Burlington Street in 1795, when Humphry lived in Old Bond Street.

[2] Edward Jerningham (1737–1812) was the author of a farce called *The Welch Heiress*, given at D.L.Th. on 17 Apr. 1795.

[3] Dorothy Jordan (1762–1816), brilliant comic actress, played Miss Plinlimmon.

217. To His Wife

Price MS. *Address*: Mrs. Sheridan | Hertford-St.[1] | May-Fair

[*1795?*]

My Soul's beloved, my Heart's dear Hecca—

I find the nasty House of Commons will not let me see your lovely eyes so soon as I hoped—and me thinks of you so that I must send to get a Line from you to tell me that you are well and that you don't *depise* Dan.—[2]

218. To Samuel Ireland

Add. MS. 30348, f. 3. Copy. *Dock.*: Correspondence with Sheridan etc. relative to [*Vortigern*]

9 June 1795

The Proprietors of Drury Lane Theatre wish to deal in the most liberal Manner with Mr. Ireland and are ready to leave to Mr. Wallis's arbitration the terms on which the play of Vortigern should be produced.[3] They conceive that the fairest and most honourable grounds to proceed on will be to assign to Mr. Ireland a proportion of the first forty Nights receipts.[4] The compensation will then be contingent on the success and if that answers present expectation it will be [a] most considerable sum | R B S

June 9: 95

[1] S. purchased Burgoyne's house there, in Feb. 1795, for £4,000: see the *True Briton*, 10 Feb. 1795.

[2] Her pet name for him.

[3] The 'finding' of an unknown play, said to be by Shakespeare, created much interest. Albany Wallis (Ireland's neighbour in Norfolk Street) acted as intermediary with the managers of D.L.Th., and wrote to S. on 2 June (Dufferin MS.) complaining of his inattention. On 9 June he was able to report to Ireland (Add. MS. 30348, f. 2) that he had at last seen S.

[4] The play, *Vortigern and Rowena,* was given only one performance; but Ireland expected it to be such a great success that he demanded £500 and (minus the usual charges) six nights' receipts. See Add. MS. 30348, ff. 6, 8.

219. To Samuel Ireland

Add. MS. 30348, f. 4. *Dock.*: June 10. 95

10 June 1795
Wansted
Wednesday Night.

My Dear Sir

I fear I must put off to Saturday the Pleasure of hearing Vortigern[1] but I will take my Chance of finding you in the course of tomorrow in Norfolk-St. | Yours truly | R B S.

220. To Samuel Ireland

Add. MS. 30348, f. 7. *Dock.*: July 8. 95

[*8 July 1795*]

Dear Sir

As I must dine out of Town tomorrow and am particularly engaged in the morning I will call on you at ten this evening as I have miss'd you now[2] | Yours | R B S.

221. To Samuel Ireland

Add. MS. 30348, f. 11. *Dock.*: July 14. 95[3]

[*13 July 1795*]
Southampton[4]
Monday

My Dear Sir

By some mistake I was not met on the road and so am

[1] S. and Richardson inspected the play at Ireland's, and S. was not entirely satisfied that it was by Shakespeare. See *The Confessions of William Henry Ireland* (1805), p. 138.

[2] Ireland complained on 17 June and 24 July that S. had failed to meet him as agreed on several occasions (Add. MS. 30348, ff. 6, 17).

[3] A Tuesday and presumably the day the letter was received.

[4] David Kent's letter (Salt MS.) begging a loan of twenty guineas was readdressed to S. at St. Mary's, Southampton, and stamped JY 15 95.

come on to this Place and cannot be in Town till wednesday —the moment I come I will call or send to you[1] | Yours truly | R B Sheridan

222. To Samuel Ireland

Add. MS. 30348, f. 15. *Dock.*: July 24: 95

24 July 1795
Friday Night

Dear Sir,

I shall return to Town tomorrow and will call in Norfolk St.—if you see Mr. Troward you will find there has been no delay on my Part,[2] for considering the matter settled I only waited for the agreement which he twice promised to send me. I suppose there has been some mistake for I certainly have never yet seen it. | Yours truly | R B S.

223. To Richard Troward

Harvard MS.

6 Aug. [*1795*]

Dear Troward,

Since you spoke to me on the subject of a Theatrical arrangement with Mr. Grubb,[3] I have had a good deal of conversation on that matter with Mr. Shaw[4] which has ended in his taking a Proposition from me to that Gentleman and going himself with it to Margate.[5] It will be unnecessary therefore for me to trouble you in the way I had in-

[1] This appointment was not kept (Add. MS. 30348, f. 17).

[2] This letter is a reply to Ireland's of the same date (Add. MS. 30348, f. 17) complaining of broken appointments and asking what S.'s intentions really were about signing the agreement for the production of *Vortigern*.

[3] John Grubb had money in the Margate Theatre and was keenly interested in acting. He played Sir Toby Belch in the private performance of *Twelfth Night* at the Margravine of Anspach's theatre in Jan. 1796 (A. M. Broadley and Lewis Melville, *The Beautiful Lady Craven* (1916), i. xciv).

[4] Thomas Shaw was conductor of the band at D.L.Th. until 1809. He was also a proprietor of the Margate Theatre 1782–1813 (P. and S. C., 6 June 1859, lot 299).

[5] Troward wrote to Grubb on 6 Aug. 1795, enclosing the above letter and stating, 'I have had frequent conversations with Mr. Sheridan since you left Town on the subject of the Theatre and

tended. But the more I have considered the subject and the more I have learn'd of Mr. Grubb's character and Disposition the more I am convinced that an arrangement both creditable and profitable to him and greatly for the advantage of the Theatre might be made between us. Of course therefore as I have not the pleasure of knowing him your future interposition who are so much master of the whole subject must be serviceable. I think it probable that I shall see Mr. Grubb myself—as Time presses and I wish to have a discussion with him before I renew the negotiation with the Parties you know of.[1] | Your's truly | R B Sheridan.

Hertford St:
August 6th:

224. To Samuel Ireland

Add. MS. 30348, f. 20. *Dock.*: Augt. 8; 95.

8 Aug. 1795

My Dear Sir,

I have been disappointed this morning, but I am confident I shall not fail tomorrow when I will be with you by one. | Your's truly | R B Sheridan.

Saturday 2 o'clock

225. [To John Grubb]

Harvard MS.

Thursday
August 20th: [*1795*]

Dear Sir,

There is a Spell I think on my punctuality with you. But

in consequence of it I understand he has conversed with Mr. Shaw whom you have by this time probably seen' (Harvard MS.).

[1] Thomas Linley, S.'s partner, was a sick man and died on 19 Nov. 1795. S. had sought financial help from several people and had offered a share in the management in return. The *True Briton*, 15 May 1795, mentioned that the new management would be made up of Richardson, Kemble, Westley, and Storace, but added on 24 June that this arrangement was laid aside. By 2 Aug. S.'s need for money was so great that Shaw was sent to approach various other people but they were all 'either from home or out of town' (Dufferin MS.). On 17 Aug., S. gave Grubb a bond for £1,000 (Garrick Club MS.).

the case is I have been detain'd ever since in Town,[1] and am obliged to join Mrs. S. and see her safe at Bognor[2] which if I were to leave again on Sunday she would think me lost for ever.

I hope a change of Day will be no inconvenience to you. The Friday following would suit me best. And if agreeable to you I will be punctually at five in Lincoln's Inn.[3] | Dear Sir Your truly | R B Sheridan

We yesterday made a scrap from our List of £130 per week.[4]

226. To Richard Peake[5]

McAdam MS. *Address*: Chichester August twenty fourth | 1795 | Rd. Peake Esqr. | Brompton-Row | Near London *Fr.*: Free | R B Sheridan *Dock.*: R B S

24 Aug. 1795
Bognor
Monday

Dear Peake,

I am sure you always mean for the best, but faith it was very unlucky you were so confident about the £500. I understand you to have settled something certain with Shaw,[6] or I would not have left Town without getting that Note done somehow.[7] But I still Trust you will have made some Stand

[1] Winston, 1793–7, includes a note (dated 12 Aug. 1795) that S. 'is now almost daily at the theatre'.

[2] S. introduced his wife to the Prince of Wales at Brighton on 22 Aug. (*Hampshire Chronicle*, 7 Sept. 1795). Mrs. Chapone heard that the Sheridans now lived in extravagant style at Bognor in the company of the Duchess of Devonshire. See A. G. C. Gaussen, *A Later Pepys* (1904), i. 416; *Leveson Gower Corr.* i. 116.

[3] Grubb's home.

[4] The *True Briton*, 29 Aug. 1795, reported that forty-two members of staff had been dismissed from D.L.Th.

[5] Peake was the fourth son of Samuel Peake of Stafford; he spent forty years in the treasury of D.L.Th.

[6] Thomas Shaw reported in a letter to S. of 2 Aug. (Dufferin MS.) that he had approached a Dr. Pearson to assist him with £500 on the security of a D.L.Th. share, and had made other unsuccessful efforts to obtain money for S.

[7] Cf. *Monthly Mirror*, i (1795–6), 244, where it is alleged (Feb. 1796) that the managers of D.L.Th. deal 'in nothing but *promissory notes*'.

for monday. I shall not fail being in Town at the Time. | yours ever, | R B S.

I write to Troward, yet I wish you to see Franco.[1]

—pray write by this Post to Kelly[2] to stay and say I have directed to him at the Post Office Scarbro'.

write what you mean by a sequestration in the Theatre—see Troward.

227. To His Wife

Osborn MS.

[*Aug. 1795?*][3]
London Saturday Night

I stay'd too long at Mrs. Wilmot's[4] to have it in my Power to write to you or even to send what I had written by this Day's Post—and the provoking thing is that no Post goes tomorrow so that you will be three Day's—*saturday sunday* and *monday* without a Line from me! and I believe I have never miss'd a Day since first you permitted me to write to you. I ought by the bye to ask—do I not tire you? or do you like that I should write at such unconscionable Length?—Well—I found Mrs. Wilmot at breakfast. There was an Aunt and a Lady Stewart.[5] Mr. Wilmot in Town where He has been these two months without having been once at Farnborough![6] How very justly you seem to have estimated his Character—and indeed how justly in my opinion, notwithstanding you

[1] Raphael Franco bequeathed Lacy's mortgage to Jacob Franco, junior, his eldest son, who filed a bill of complaint against S. The order is dated 19 Dec. 1794 (P.R.O., Chanc. Procs., C 12/197/7).

[2] Michael Kelly (1763–1826), singer and composer, was on a visit to the north with his mistress, Anna Maria Crouch (1763–1805). They sang in *Lionel and Clarissa* at Cawdell's theatre in Scarborough on 22 Aug.: see Folger MS. T. a. 141.

[3] Apart from its lack of endearments, this has all the appearance of an early letter. Its date is conjectured from the Duchess of Devonshire's long stay in London (May–Aug. 1795) and S.'s visit to Southampton in mid-July. The Duchess went to Bognor in August. See *Georgiana*, p. 214. There are no letters at Chatsworth between the Duchess and Mrs. Wilmot.

[4] Barbarina, fourth daughter of Admiral Sir Chaloner Ogle, 1st baronet, was born on 27 May 1767 and married Valentine Henry Wilmot of Farnborough Place in 1789 (Ogle, p. 153). She was a beauty and a wit and delighted in riding horses and modelling them.

[5] Elizabeth (later Inge, d. 1855)?

[6] Wilmot was Clerk of the Letters Patent in the Examiner's Office of the High Court of Chancery (*The Royal Kalendar* (1793), p. 171).

are such a *novice* and *your mind* such a *Sheet of blank Paper*, do you always appear to observe on the character of all whom I have heard you notice. As for Mrs. Wilmot I think her a Divinity. I was always disposed to think so. I cannot conceive how Sukey[1] could have had a different notion of my opinion of her. I talk'd to her a great deal and said nothing I think you would not have entirely approved of. You are a thousand times more like each other in a thousand respects than either of you imagine. She has the greatest opinion of you and the greatest affection for you—a way of thinking that certainly did not diminish my idea of her Perfection. I liked everything she did or said—her Frankness, her good-nature, her good sense her account of herself, her observations on others, her way of sitting down on the hearth, her manner of bounding on her Horse, her Del[i]cacy, her robustness, her Drawings, her Boots, her Figures in short *herself* altogether.—But the Truth is that I am more than ever convinced that you are a most extraordinary Breed. What was said of the *Hervey's* might with more truth be said of your race—that the world consists of Three Descriptions of Inhabitants—*Men*, *Women* and *Ogles*. Only that in applying this to *Herveys* it meant only that they differ'd from their fellow mortals, not that they surpass'd them. I find the Duchess of Devonshire did not stop at Farnborough. She staid in Town so long Mrs. W. had been obliged to send to put her off while I was at Southampton, so that *a Talk* which I thought must have pass'd between them had not taken Place. This made my speaking to her auk[w]ard at first but we parted very good Friends and I am to write to her and she vows to you *her everlasting Love*.

I saw the Colonel[2] at the Play to Night. And He ask'd me in a suspecting Tone rather *where I had been*? He said Lady Grey[3] had a Letter from Sukey to *Morocco*[4] which He

[1] Mrs. S.'s eldest sister, Susannah Ogle (1762–1825). For her recollections of S., see Moore, *Journal*, ii. 298–9.

[2] Possibly Sir Charles Grey, later General and created 1st Earl Grey of Howick (1729–1807). He was Colonel of the 7th Dragoon Guards, 1789–95; and of the 20th Light Dragoons, 1795–7.

[3] Elizabeth, wife of Sir Charles Grey. She died in 1822.

[4] Mrs. Wilmot? 'Lord Grey always called her Cousin Barbary' (Barbarina, Lady Grey, *A Family Chronicle* (ed. G. Lyster), 1908, p. 18).

had left with her to be shewn to me—but added—I had probably since *seen* Sukey herself. I turned his suspicions aside perfectly well by avowing that I had been to Mrs. Wilmots as C. Grey had advised. I could not gather the Purport of the Letter from him, but He assured me there was nothing in it that would vex me but quite He thought the contrary. Good Night my Dearest Hester—what are you thinking about at this moment? What are you doing?—I see—reading the 2d. volume of the French novel you brought from Town—go to bed directly.

228. To Samuel Ireland

Add. MS. 30348, f. 39.

[*1795*]
Pall-Mall[1]
past two

My Dear Sir,

I find we are so circumstanced here that it must be at twelve tomorrow that we must meet and the money will be ready.[2] I assure you I have returned to Town on the business so don't accuse me of unpunctuality.

I will be exact tomorrow. Kemble is come.[3] | Yrs truly, | R B S.

229. [To John Grubb]

Harvard MS.

Bognor
Sunday September 6th: [*1795*]

My Dear Sir,

I certainly dine in Town tomorrow, but for fear I should be too late for the Post I send you a Line from Hence to beg

[1] The bankers to D.L.Th. were Ransom, Morland, & Hammersley, 57 Pall Mall.

[2] By agreement dated 9 Sept. 1795 the proprietors of D.L.Th. promised to pay Ireland £250 for *Vortigern*. See Add. MS. 30348, ff. 36–37.

[3] He had been on tour, visiting Dublin and Edinburgh, but he acted at the Haymarket Theatre on 29 Aug., for the benefit of his brother, Stephen Kemble. See the *True Briton*, 31 Aug. 1795.

a Line from you by return of Post to inform me of your motions. If you can possibly come to Town on Wednesday I shall be rejoiced and will remain with Pleasure till Friday if not I shall return Wednesday morning.[1] | yours ever | R B Sheridan

230. [To John Grubb]

Harvard MS.

[*Sept. 1795*]
Petworth[2]
Friday morning

My Dear Sir,

I am on my road returning to Bognor, and have set[t]led to be in Town again on tuesday evening in order to meet you. I hope the time will suit you and you will find me and Richardson and a cold chicken at the Crown and Anchor Tavern at *half past nine*. I will also send to Troward. You will see that I have advertised the opening[3] and laid a claim to reform the Free-List. What makes it most pressing that we should meet on tuesday is that Kemble taking advantage of the near approach of the season and the Delay in settling the new management[4] is advancing some such unreasonable claims that my Patience is nearly exhausted. This between ourselves. He not only demands an increase of his own Salary,

[1] The Duchess of Devonshire described the Sheridan party at Bognor on 2 Sept. 1795 as composed of 'Mrs. Sheridan, her old blind mother Mrs. Ogle, two Miss Ogles and poor Tickells boys. Sheridan is down occasionally for a day but the new arrangement of the Theatre keeps him in London' (Chatsworth MS. 1305).

[2] The seat of George Wyndham, 3rd Earl of Egremont (1751–1837). Lady Bessborough stayed there on 20 Aug. on her way to Bognor, and described it as 'a charming place and very pleasant' (*Leveson Gower Corr.* i. 115).

[3] The *True Briton*, 14 Sept. 1795, advertised that D.L.Th. would open on 17 Sept. The notice added: 'N.B. An alteration in the Property taking place in the present Season, the former Free List of the Theatre necessarily expires.'

[4] Settled on 19 Sept. 1795, when S. wrote: 'I do hereby authorize and empower Mr. John Grubb and Mr. Joseph Richardson to act with me in the Management of Drury Lane Theatre, and in my absence I shall abide by their Acts. They are each intitled to one Seventh Share of the net Profits of the Season. This Memorandum is to remain till regular Articles of a partnership can be prepared and executed . . .' (Harvard MS.). S. said later that this was contingent upon their buying up shares which remained unsold: see *Morn. Chron.*, 24 Dec. 1801.

but the renewal of his wife's[1] engagement! but of this when we meet.

I shall only add that your investigating every thing fully previous to a final arrangement will be to me most satisfactory. I certainly agree with you that a permanent and successful future connexion can only be founded on a fair and thorough understanding at the outset. | Yours my dear Sir | most sincerely | R B Sheridan.

I have Vortigern with me.

231. [To Ransom, Morland and Hammersley?]

Harvard MS. Draft.

[*Soon after 19 Sept. 1795?*]

Gentlemen,

It being decidedly our opinion that whatever confidence we may be justly disposed to place in each-other it is the surest mode of contriving a right understanding to treat all matters of business as men of business would were the[y] Trustees for others. It is our joint Desire that you will make out a correct Statement of all the acceptanc[es] enter'd into by Mr. Westley on account of the Firm directing the statement into the following three Classes. 1st: a List of all acceptances actually taken up and cancell'd specifying in whose Favour Drawn when due and where any renewal has been given 2d: such acceptances [as] are over due and unpaid, with an account of the situation and Hands they are in 3d: a List with the particulars of Bills not yet due.

Mr. Jones[2] is also requested to draw up a proper memorandum to regulate and bind this business in future untill the whole may be extinguish'd, so that Messrs. G. and R.[3] may be secured from whatever arises from former Debts—without depriving Mr. S. of the temporary use of the credit of the Theatre.[4]

[1] Priscilla Hopkins, the widow of W. Brereton, married J. P. Kemble. She retired from the stage in 1796.

[2] J. W. Jones, solicitor, of Scotland Yard.

[3] Grubb and Richardson.

[4] A note is added by S. reading: 'a copy of the said Statement to be sent to each of the Proprietors'.

232. To Richard Peake

McAdam MS. *Address*: Chichester September twenty second 1795 | Mr. Peake | Brompton Place | Near Knightsbridge | London [re-addressed to] Near Goodge St | Charlotte St | Rathbone Place *Fr.*: Free | R B Sheridan *Dock.*: R B S

22 Sept. 1795
Tuesd[a]y
Bognor

Dear Peake

I am exceedingly disappointed at not hearing from you to Day—surely Hammer[s]ly cannot have refused to advance if He has you must pay him the £600 and we *must* use the Receipts. I have not a shilling at this Place and the Bills all unpaid. I have been obliged to give Mrs. Sheridan a Draught on Hammer[s]ly's for £30. Do not fail on any account to take £30 from to Nights that it may be paid tomorrow when it will certainly be presented. To prevent mistakes I enclose a Draught[1] in the Proprietors Name for £50 tho' I hope to hear tomorrow that what I desired in my Last has been done, and then the enclosed need not be used. | yours truly | R B Sheridan

bid them begin my private account quite fresh.
pay in to Nights account as before—send me my account.

233. To John Grubb

Harvard MS. *Address*: – Grubb Esq | Great Queen St: | Lincoln's-Inn.

[*1795?*]

My dear Sir

Can you meet me at Hammersleys tomorrow at half past two or shall I find you at home at two. And may I hope that our Friend the Patriotic Christian or Jew[2] will assist in the

[1] The draft is among the Osborn MSS.; and bears Peake's note, 'This was intended as a gift but I never got the Money'.

[2] On 25 Sept. 1795, S., Grubb, and Richardson ordered Peake to pay Messrs. Hartsink £40 after every performance at D.L.Th. (Add. MS.

way I proposed or even partially, and I assure you press'd for time as I am I shall consider it a serious obligation. | Your's truly | R B Sheridan

Hertford St:
Sunday Evening.

234. [To John Grubb]

Harvard MS. *Wm.*: 1794

London October 7th [*1795*][1]

My Dear Sir,

A Mistake of Richardson's led me to hope for the Pleasure of meeting you in Town. I am now obliged to leave it again for a week. But I am glad I came as I have not been idle and tho' much Imposition must be submitted to this Season I see the Prospect of future Prosperity clear and certain.[2] I will send you some remarks on the S[t]ate of Things in [a] Day or two. I only send this Line at present for fear you should hurry yourself on the idea of finding me here. I leave Richardson on guard till your arrival. I am very sorry to hear you have been unwell. | yours ever, | R B Sheridan.

35118, f. 69). Hartsink's patriotism is alluded to in a long article in *The Times*, 6 Jan. 1797, which mentioned 'that he is *still* the Minister Plenipotentiary of the legitimate Sovereign of the United Provinces, to the Princes of the Circle of Lower Saxony, and one of the Hans Towns . . .'. See also *The Impostor Unmasked* (1806), p. 13.

[1] Dated from Shaw's letter to Grubb, of 3 Oct. 1795: 'Mr. Sheridan is now at my elbow, he says that he came to Town on Purpose to meet you, and the disappointment distresses Him and the Theatre. He begs you will give him the meeting here before Wednesday next, as he must leave Town on that day. . . . There is something brewing by K[emble] your Presence is absolutely necessary. . . .' (Harvard MS.)

[2] Westley's note (Harvard MS.) of the receipts of the first ten nights of the season (to 6 Oct.) showed that the average takings were £332. 10*s*. 0*d*. a night. The new proprietors were to take a seventh of the clear profits. A note by S. describes the general change as 'one calculated to increase the stock of public amusement, to secure the interest of all concerned in the Property and to ensure the completion of a building which may fairly be styled a National Ornament and advantage' (Salt MS.).

235. To Thomas Shaw

Harvard MS. *Dock.*: Letter from Mr. Sheridan to Mr. Shaw.

[*Oct. 1795*]
Chiddingstone[1]
Near Penshurst

My Dear Sir,

It is my intention to pay Margate a Visit towards the end of this month, as I have resolved to curtail my Bognor Plan, but I wish very much to have a few hours talk with Mr. Grubb and you as soon as possible. I could slip away from this Place tomorrow where I am with Mrs. S. at her Sister's, and, as it would be extremely convenient to me, could wish to meet you and Mr. Grubb at *Canterbury* where I will be punctually at *four o'clock*, and propose staying all Night. I make this Proposition in the hope that Mr. Grubb's Touch of the Gout will have disappear'd so as to be no impediment, because I have appointed to meet Kemble in Town on *Sunday evening*.[2] I received the enclosed on wednesday but I left Town in the evening and was glad to put off present discussion. If it should be very inconvenient to Mr. Grubb to meet me at Canterbury, I will come on to Margate. Tho' independent of my being press'd for time I doubt our meeting there and my stopping for a Day only may make a premature talking about our business. If my Plan is approved my Servant, whom I send with this, is to order us a Dinner at four at Canterbury. At all events He is to meet me there | Yours truly | R B Sheridan.

Storace[3] is in Town and much puzzled at my not staying to meet Kemble

[1] Mrs. S.'s sister, Elizabeth Catherine Ogle (died 1821), married Henry Streatfeild of Chiddingstone on 6 June 1782 (Ogle, p. 140).

[2] Shaw's letter of 3 Oct. 1795 (Harvard MS.) mentions that S. would leave London on Wed., 7 Oct.

[3] Stephen Storace (1763–96), composer, was mentioned earlier in the year as one of those who might form the new management. When this scheme broke down, S. approached him alone. In a letter from Berwick Street on 'Saturday afternoon' (Osborn MS.), Storace refused the partnership and commented on 'the absurdity of my entering into any engagement with you *singly*'. He was willing, however, to consider buying the twenty-nine or thirty-seven shares S. could put forward, if a proposal could be worked out that would be agreeable to Kemble and Richardson, 'without whose concurrence I should feel it dishonourable to make any new arrangement'.

236. To Thomas Greenwood[1]

Folger MS. Ireland's copy (Add. MS. 30348, f. 53) is dated 'Novr. 18: 95'. *Address*: Mr. Greenwood.

18 Nov. 1795

Sir,

I wish you to forward the Scenery of Vortigern as speedily as possible it is certainly to be represented at D. L. Theatre and that without Delay.[2] | Yours | R B S.

Novr: 18th;

237. [To Willoughby Lacy]

Shuttleworth MS.

[19 Nov. 1795?]

My Dear Sir

I am waiting now for Peake but He is so surrounded with claims and Duns that I am afraid of going to him. I will not however leave the House without getting the means of assisting you[3] I dine *in the Theatre* with Mr. Grubb—so that you will be sure of me at six o'clock | Yours | R B S.

238. To Henry Holland, John Grubb, Joseph Richardson, and Tom Sheridan

Gilmore MS. *Dock.*: Decr. 5th, 1795.

5 Dec. 1795
Wansted, past 5

To Messrs. Holland, Grubb, Richardson and Tom—greeting

your memorialist penetrated with the deepest affliction

[1] Thomas Greenwood, senior, scene painter at D.L.Th., died in 1797.

[2] Ireland saw S. on 13 Nov. and was told he might call on Greenwood and 'renew the order for the Scenery of Vortigern agreeable to his [S.'s] order delivered to you at the Theatre three months ago. The Play is by agreement to be brought out in Decr.' (Add. MS. 30348, f. 46). Ireland blamed Kemble for the delay. *Vortigern* was presented on 2 Apr. 1796.

[3] The D.L.Th. account book (Add. MS. 29710, f. 51) notes, under 19 Nov. 1795, 'Lacy Jun 10.10.[0].'

that it is not in his Power to join the congress now sitting in Sloane-St:[1] earnestly entreats your favourable consideration of the causes of his absence. Since this Day Fortnight your memorialist occupied unceasingly on the Public business[2] or the secret committee[3] has not been able to dine once with his Family notwithstanding which your memorialist particularly anxious to attend the Party this Day in Sloane-St: determined to return from Wansted where He was indispensably compell'd to go in the morning—but owing to re-iterated delays, notwithstanding the known early hours of your memorialist He finds himself arrived on his morning visit at this Place just as it is Dark, and altho' He could dispatch his business here in a short time He submits to High Mightinesses,[4] and if any doubt arises He appeals to the Ladies of the Family in Sloane-St: whether under the *existing Circumstances*[5] It would be prudent to risk Mrs. Sheridan's returning on so Dark an evening on such a Road. Agreeing therefore to whatever your High-mightinesses may in your Wisdom and wine judge proper to determine on your memorialist concludes in the sanguine Hope that his apology will be accepted. | Health and Fraternity | R B Sheridan.

239. To Henry Holland

Gilmore MS. *Address*: H. Holland Esq. | Sloane-St: *Wm.*: 1794

Monday morning Decr. 28th: [*1795*]

My Dear Sir,

You could not find me because I had nearly lost myself—but now to sober business let's advance—I am in Town to Day and shall be at the Play the whole evening with Mrs. S. The best of all things would be your making it convenient

[1] At Henry Holland's house.

[2] S. presented petitions and spoke against the Treason and Sedition Bills on 23, 24, 27 Nov. and 3 Dec.; and also led the attack on the 'Libel on the Constitution' of 26 Nov. See *Speeches*, iv. 137–89.

[3] Of the House of Commons. It secured information and proceeded against conspirators.

[4] The conventional form used in addressing members of the States-General of the Netherlands.

[5] Mrs. S.'s pregnancy.

to look in. If not I am at your service and as early as you will tomorrow morning. | yours ever | R B Sheridan

P.S. Still maintaining the conscience of Juries.

240. To William Capon[1]

Amy A. C. Montague and Gilbert H. Montague MS., New York Public Library. *Pub.*: Myers Catalogue 214 (1917), item 179. *Dock.*: 1796—while preparing for Iron Chest

24 Feb. 1796

Mr. Sheridan begs Mr. Capon will get immediately whatever assistance is necessary for the Library Scene in Mr. Coleman's Piece[2]—but to attempt no more than can be finish'd by *Saturday sen'night* on which Day the Piece will positively come out.

Wednesday Feb 24th.

241. To John Grubb

Harvard MS. *Address*: J. Grubb *Dock.*: S. with Harris's Letter as to the score of Artaxerxes.

17 Apr. 1796

My Dear Sir

I have just got the enclosed.[3] I think it not worth refusing —only I would give notice that we may want them ourselves—but do as you please—and give directions accordingly— | Yrs ev[er] | R B S.

[1] Architect and scene painter (1757–1827). See J. Boaden, *Memoirs of . . . Kemble* (1825), ii. 101–2.

[2] The first performance of *The Iron Chest*, a melodrama by George Colman the Younger (1762–1836), was given at D.L.Th. on 12 Mar. 1796.

[3] It is a note from Thomas Harris, manager of the C.G.Th., and is dated 'Saty. April 16th'. It reads: 'Dear Sheridan | We are going to do Artaxerxes for three Nights and Madm. Mara wishes to have the Drury Lane recitatives instead of the Original, which we have (tho' I understand ours is decidedly the best) so must beg you wil[l] be so good as to give an order by Brandon for the delivery of Yours | Ever etc etc | T Harris' (Harvard MS.).

Sunday Evening

How soon could your new Farce[1] come forward—I wish we could shew a particular Vigour of exertion just now

Since folding this up I have also the enclosed from Bensley[2] —but pray speak of it to no one 'till we meet, and keep this Letter.

242. [To John Grubb]

Harvard MS.

[c. 17 Apr. 1796]

Private

My Dear Sir,

There has been a Cabal and intrigue which I will explain to you when we meet which has deprived us of having Mara in Artaxerxes[3] with Braham,[4] which I should otherwise have settled. I still think we may try it a Night or two in case the Opera should not succeed on my Plan as *one Piece* of *three*—(the bad parts omitted) and Salvini[5] *on Trial*, the Mandane. At the same time I wish to be civil to Harris. But in Truth in *future* Charity must begin at home, I should suggest therefore, without quoting anyone, that the best answer would be—The Truth that [we] have this Opera among the Things provided for the remainder of the Season and that we had actually treated with Mara for this Purpose

[1] John Grubb's extravaganza, *Alive and Merry*, was acted at D.L.Th. on 17 May 1796, but was criticized as containing laughable incidents 'awkwardly managed' (*Monthly Mirror*, 1st Ser., ii (1796), 51).

[2] A former officer in the marines who had played at D.L.Th. and C.G.Th. from 1765. He retired from the stage on 6 May 1796, 'not without... some motive of disgust' (*Monthly Mirror*, 1st Ser., ii. 42); 'the enclosed' probably concerned this coming event.

[3] Opera, by Thomas Arne, that was first presented in 1762.

[4] John Braham (1777–1856), tenor singer. He made his first appearance at D.L.Th. on 30 Apr. 1796, in the musical romance, *Mahmoud*, by Hoare and Storace.

[5] Signora Salvini or Salvina had formerly been Miss Plomer. Her benefit night (in connexion with Salomon's concerts) at the Hanover Square Rooms took place on 4 May; she took the part of Victoria in *The Castle of Andalusia* at C.G.Th. on 10 May. See *Morn. Chron.*, 7 Apr. 1796; *Monthly Mag.*, 1st Ser., ii. 53. She does not appear to have sung with Braham in *Artaxerxes* at D.L.Th. this season.

thro' Mr. Aik[in][1]—but that if we can spare the Recitatives they are at their service. | Yours ever | R B S.

N.B. excepting Mara the Performance at C. Garden must be execrable and I almost Doubt her being actually engaged there.[2]

with us all the other Parts would be probably well fill'd. I have already cut it, Salvini has many admirers and we want nothing of Scenes and Dresses.

243. [To John Grubb]

Harvard MS.

[*Apr.–May 1796*]

My Dear Sir

Since Siddons is notifying her Departure[3]—I should think a *Tragedy* much better than the Pirates,[4] and think Almeyda will do more than we reckon'd | Yours | R B Sheridan

244. To John Philip Kemble

Pub.: Moore, ii. 308–9.

[*Spring 1796?*][5]

Dear Kemble,

If I had not a real good opinion of your principles and

[1] James Aikin (d. 1803) became deputy manager at D.L.Th. in 1798. He was a competent actor, but a rather nervous man. His brother, F. Aikin, was also in the company and usually acted the tyrants in tragedy.

[2] She performed there on 30 Apr. 1796, as Mandane in *Artaxerxes*. She 'retains all her sweetness, but has lost much of her power' (*Monthly Mag.*, 1st Ser., ii. 53).

[3] Mrs. Siddons's benefit on 3 May 1796 (advertised as early as 18 Apr.) brought her season's engagements to an end. S. may have been referring to one of her performances in Sophia Lee's *Almeyda, Queen of Granada*, 20–23 Apr. and on 16 May. Birch and Attwood's *The Smugglers*, was the afterpiece on the first four nights.

[4] *The Pirates*, by Cobb and Storace, was first given in Nov. 1792; but S. may have been thinking of *The Smugglers*.

[5] Kemble's resignation from the post of deputy manager of D.L.Th. was noted in *Bell's W. Mess.*, 1 May 1796; and was caused by 'a variety of circumstances, among which the *personified uncertainty* of Sheridan as to money matters was the most intolerable' (T. Campbell, *Life of Mrs. Siddons* (1839), p. 271). See also C. Jerrold, *The Story of Dorothy Jordan* (1914), p. 207; and 'Tom Drury', 'The Present State of D.L.Th. Briefly Considered', *Monthly Mirror*, 1st Ser., ii (1796), 41–42.

intentions upon all subjects, and a very bad opinion of your nerves and philosophy upon some, I should take very ill indeed, the letter I received from you this evening.

That the management of the theatre is a situation capable of becoming *troublesome* is information which I do not want, and a discovery which I thought you had made long since.

I should be sorry to write to you gravely on your offer, because I must consider it as a nervous flight, which it would be as unfriendly in me to notice seriously as it would be in you seriously to have made it.

What I *am* most serious in is a determination that, while the theatre is indebted, and others, for it and for me, are so involved and pressed as they are, I will exert myself, and give every attention and judgment in my power to the establishment of its interests. In you I hoped, and do hope, to find an assistant, on principles of liberal and friendly confidence—I mean confidence that should be above touchiness and reserve, and that should trust to me to estimate the value of that assistance.

If there is anything amiss in your mind not arising from the *troublesomeness* of your situation, it is childish and unmanly not to disclose it to me. The frankness with which I have always dealt towards you entitles me to expect that you should have done so.

But I have no reason to believe this to be the case; and attributing your letter to a disorder which I know ought not to be indulged, I prescribe that you shall keep your appointment at the Piazza Coffee-house, to-morrow at five, and, taking four bottles of claret instead of three, to which in sound health you might stint yourself, forget that you ever wrote the letter, as I shall that I ever received it. | R. B. Sheridan.

245. To George Colman the Younger[1]

Harvard MS. Draft.

[*1796*]

The Proprietors of D.L. Theatre present their Compli-

[1] Colman was manager of the Haymarket Theatre, 1789–1813.

ments to Mr. Coleman. They have always been desirous to accommodate him by closing their Season much sooner than has been the Practice at the other Winter Theatre, but having been prevented this Year performing Oratorios, they cannot consistently with what is due to their Renters shut up their House till 200 Nights of Performance have been compleated—which will be on Wednesday the 15th. of June[1] but they will be extremely glad to accommodate Mr. Coleman by arranging their Performances in the manner best calculated to give his Theatre the use of such of the D.L. Performers as He may require

246. To John Grubb

Grubbe MS. *Address*: John Grubb Es | Lincoln's-Inn-Square | London *Pm.*: STAFFORD | MA 24 96 *Dock.*: S. £2500 | to Stafford. | 4 bills of 500 ea. | 24 May 1796.[2]

[*24 May 1796*]
Stafford
Tuesday[3] Evening.

My Dear Sir,

An Opposition is threaten'd[4] and indeed a Canvass attempted on behalf of a Mr. Serjeant Williams[5]—who is come from Town to try the ground—but I laugh at it—and have no doubt of being first on the Poll should there be one.—But to oppose the most invincible Front to the Enemy, I find it necessary to have a credit for £500 more in the Bankers hands. I therefore take assistance from your obliging offer and have drawn on you for another £500, which it is of the utmost consequence to my Honor as well as to my

[1] Between 1795 and 1808 the D.L.Th. season ended on 15 June only in 1796. It more frequently ended later. Colman wanted it to end on 15 May, so that his summer season would comply with the licence and be reasonably long.

[2] A note in pencil refers to a promissory note, also in Miss Grubbe's possession. It reads: '£2500 May 18th 1796 Two months after Date I promise to pay John Grubb Esre. or order the Sum of Two thousand five hundred Pounds value received R B Sheridan.'

[3] Possibly 'Sunday'.

[4] As early as Dec. 1794, subscriptions were entered into in Staffordshire to oppose S. and (at Tamworth) Courtenay. See *New M. Mag.* vi (1816), 326.

[5] John Williams, 43 Chancery Lane, was a Serjeant at law on the Oxford circuit and at the Carmarthen great sessions (*Browne's General Law List for . . . 1797*, p. 16).

election should be returned accepted by the next Post. I have drawn at two months in favour of John Wright the Banker here,[1] and I enclose in case of accidents a Memorandum for the whole sum due a few Days sooner than your Acceptances, which you may rely on being renew'd untill quite convenient to you on our final settlement to make the Payment on a connexion I trust of mutual satisfaction as well as of advantage.—

Our Election is Friday certainly, so on Sunday you will see me. | your ever sincerely | R B Sheridan

It is more than ten to one I shall bring back to return you this last £500.

247. To John Grubb

Harvard MS. *Address*: John Grubb Esq | Lincoln's-Inn-Square | London *Wm.*: 1794 *Pm.*: STAFFORD | M 25 96

25 May 1796

My Dear Sir,

I will not doubt your complying with my request of yesterday.

All opposition here is withdrawn. I shall be return'd unanimously—and see you on Sunday. | Yours | R B Sheridan

248. 'To the Worthy and Independent Electors of the Borough of Stafford'

Pub.: *Staff. Adv.*, 28 May 1796.

[*27–28 May 1796*]

Gentlemen,

The very flattering manner in which you have now a Fourth Time elected us your Representatives in Parliament,[2] calls for our warmest acknowledgements.

The proofs of steadiness of friendship, and perseverance

[1] One of the bills (undated) paid for S. by Richard Peake is from 'Mr. Jno. Wright of Stafford £200' (Harrow MS.). Cf. Sichel, i. 616.

[2] 'Yesterday the Honorable Edward Monckton and Richard Brinsley Sheridan, Esq., were re-elected Representatives for this borough without opposition on which occasion elegant entertainments were given to the inhabitants at the different inns' (*Staff. Adv.*, 28 May 1796).

in attachment, which we have both experienced, must ever excite in our minds the sincerest devotion to your interests. | We have the honour to be, | Gentlemen, | With the truest regard, | Your obedient Servants, | Edward Monckton. | Richard Brinsley Sheridan.

249. To His Wife

Osborn MS.

[*2 June 1796?*][1]
Thursday

A thousand Thanks my Heart for your Letter this morning. What a fool was I not to have been sure that you would send me an exact account of Nick.—

Indeed Ma'am I think you have gain'd the Day. But I know I shall like Nick very much—and be inclined to take Kate's Part.[2] You say nothing of Nick's hair. Pray don't think of cropping Robin[3] 'till I come—you may give Kate and Anne[4] some of his longest Locks, and amuse yourself with braiding and plaiting the rest, and combing the fore part to keep it out of his eyes. I saw Bab's filly[5] to Day—it was asleep and look'd very innocent. I have not time for another word. Bless your knees and Elbows for ever and ever | R B S.

When are the Races[6]
I enclose the Westminister Poll for the Politi[c]ians—Gardner still ahead.[7]

[1] The reference to Westminster indicates that the letter belongs to 1796, for in 1802 Fox was ahead of Gardner throughout the election: see *The Times*, 7–15 July 1802. But the allusions to braiding Robin's hair suggest that Charles Brinsley Sheridan was 6 years old rather than 4½ months. Perhaps S. was merely being whimsical on this subject, though that is not obvious.

[2] Catherine Hannah Sneyd had married Mrs. S.'s brother, the Rev. John Saville Ogle, on 14 Oct. 1794. Their son John was born on 5 Mar. 1796 (Ogle, p. 137).

[3] S.'s second son, Charles Brinsley Sheridan (1796–1843), was born on 14 Jan. 1796.

[4] Mrs. S.'s sister. Fourth daughter of Dean Ogle. See Ogle, p. 140.

[5] This can be read literally or as referring to Barbarina Wilmot's daughter, Arabella Jane Wilmot, who was born on 1 May 1796. For her see W. McKay and W. Roberts, *John Hoppner, R.A.* (1909), p. 271.

[6] At Winchester. They were the social attraction of the summer.

[7] On 2 June, Admiral Sir Alan Gardner (1742-1809) had 2,116 votes in the election of members for Westminster; Fox had 1,978; Tooke had 1,377 (*Salopian Journal*, 8 June 1796).

250. To His Wife

Osborn MS.

[*4 June 1796?*]
Saturday

My Beloved,

Forgive Dan that again He has only a moment for a single Line—

Sweet Anne, nurse my Angel and make her stout and Fat again.—scold her for the cold in her head. I can't think of Robin if anything is the matter with *her*, and pray don't you. Little Beast will take care of himself, but it should be the duty of forty Angels to guard Hecca—

My Love you shall have a long Letter tomorrow and it shall *fix* our meeting— | Your own | R B S.

The Princess at Court the Prince not.[1]

251. To——

Pub.: S.C., 1 June 1891, lot 301: 'written on the eve of Fox's election'.[2]

Tuesday Night [*June*], 1796.

For God's sake take care that there is plenty of breakfast, pigeons, etc. tomorrow and a Band of Musick. I shall come early.

252. To the Prince of Wales

Windsor MS. 39230–1. *Dock.*: Letter from Sheridan | received June 10th | 1796.

10 June 1796

Sir,

The attachment I have uniformly profess'd to your Royal Highness, the sincere and allow me to say, disinterested concern I have taken, according to the best of my Judgement, in

[1] The Prince of Wales had separated from his wife, formerly Princess Caroline of Brunswick-Wolfenbüttel (1768–1821), shortly after the birth of his daughter, Charlotte, on 7 Jan. 1796. The Prince went to Grange on 31 May, and sent a letter apologizing for his absence from the King's birthday celebrations on 4 June. The Princess was at these celebrations. See *Bell's W. Mess.*, 5 June 1796.

[2] Fox was elected as M.P. for Westminster, with Gardner, on 13 June.

whatever related to your Interests, and the unaffected Respect I have always felt for your Royal Highness's great and amiable Qualities—all suggest to me rather to risk incurring your Royal Highness's Displeasure by the appearance of intrusion than not to offer at this critical juncture in your Royal Highness's *public* Situation[1] the humble and sincere opinion of one who thinks He has the means of judging not incorrectly, and who is sure that judgement is guided by the truest anxiety for your Royal Highness's real Honor and Happiness.

Passing almost by the Door[2] of your Royal Highness in my way to Southampton, I have presumed to send this forward only to say that I am in readiness to obey any commands of your Royal Highness.[3]

I have only to entreat your Royal Highness to forgive the Freedom I have taken, and giving me credit for the motive, to believe me at all events—with every sentiment of Duty and attachment | Your Royal Highness's | very faithful Servant | R B Sheridan.

Friday morning
June 10th.

[1] Much public sympathy was felt for the Princess over the estrangement from her husband. The Prince's behaviour was thought to be dictated by Lady Jersey: see *Leveson Gower Corr.* i. 123.

[2] The Grange is near Alresford, seven miles north-east of Winchester.

[3] Lord Moira had just come to the Grange on a 'conciliatory negotiation' between the Prince and Princess. His visit adds interest to the Prince's reply to S., which reads: 'Dear Sheridan, | I have just received the kind Letter which your Servant brought me and I am confident you will do me the justice to believe how truly happy I should be to see You, or any Friend who speaks so feelingly with respects to my Interests. But I will state to You with the greatest candor the real fact, and that is, that under the present existing circumstances, my family, in concert with My self have determin'd to avoid as much as possible all ministerial and even private discussion or Interference, it is therefore that I feel myself under the unpleasant necessity of declining seeing You, were we even to talk upon indifferent matters. I am sure I need not add that, under any other circumstances or at any other moment, I should have been, and always shall be very happy to see you, as you pass by when you have nothing better to do. I am dear Sheridan, | with great regard, | very sincerely Yours, | George P. | Grainge. | June 10th. | 1796. | P.S. I never knew till this moment that you was waiting on the Road for my answer but thought that you had proceeded on to Southampton. I hope I have not detain'd you long, and assure you I should have written sooner had I known that you yourself had been expecting my Letter. . . .' (Windsor MS. 42153.) Cf. *The Later Correspondence of George III* (ed. Aspinall, Cambridge, 1963), ii. 448.

253. To John Grubb

Harvard MS. *Address*: Southampton June thirteenth 1776 | John Grubb Esr. | Lincoln's Inn-Square | London *Fr.*: Free | R B Sheridan *Dock.*: S. with directions—approbn. of Management June 14 1796

13 June 1796
Monday

My dear Sir,

I know you are working for the common cause—and always will. I shall see you tomorrow or certainly early wednesday. Should anything stop me tomorrow the Post shall bring you my notion of what Palmer[1] should say and I'll meet you at Dinner or the Play. I think for strong Reasons the enclosed[2] should be up in the Green-Room tomorrow | your's ever | most sincerely | R B Sheridan

I saw Siddons[3] before I left Town.

254. To His Wife

Osborn MS. *Address*: London June eighteenth | 1796 | Mrs. Sheridan | Dean of Winchesters | St. Marys[4] | Southampton *Fr.*: Free R B Sheridan

18 June 1796
Saturday

My Dearest—one Line—and pray stop Bellman. If you do not hear from me monday I shall meet you at Winchester—

[1] In the customary speech at the last performance of the season, which took place on 14 June (*Tit for Tat* and *My Grandmother*).

[2] Many of the players went out into the provinces during the summer and took engagements individually; the enclosed note was intended to reach them before they dispersed. It read: 'Theatre Royal Drury-Lane | Tuesday June 14th 1796 | By Desire of the Proprietors All Performers not in written Articles at this Theatre and desirous to re-engage are requested to send their address within one week from the Date Here-of.' (Harvard MS.)

[3] William Siddons was greatly exasperated at S.'s delay in settling their account and thought of putting the matter in the hands of lawyers. See T. Campbell, *Life of Mrs. Siddons* (1839), p. 271. His wife acted at Liverpool on 14 June.

[4] 'The church of St. Mary is remarkable for two things, viz. the value of its benefice, said to be £1400 per annum, and the beautiful situation of its cemetery' (*Europ. Mag.* li (1807), 416).

Betsey is just come. I am sorry to say I think Harriet very ill.

R. Streatfeild[1] has been trying a Horse I want for you.

Mrs. Grey has miscarried again[2]—and is very unwell.

O Johnny[3] Johnny you are wrong—bless your eyelids my beloved | R B S

The Prince goes to your Races.[4]

255. To His Wife

Osborn MS.

[*1796?*]
Monday

My beloved my Heart—

One word to say I am settling all my business swimmingly —and one word more of more importance—to entreat my Hecca to be careful as a cat.[5] Drive on the sands my wench— and forgive my anxiety about such trifles—but in this one last absence I cannot help it. I saw Mrs. Wilmot at Janes— no letter! bless you ever and ever and all over | R B S.

I hope the pretty Miss Ogle is safe. Mrs Wilmot was ready to expire when I told her of such a Performance

[1] Richard Thomas Streatfeild of Copwood married Mrs. S.'s cousin, Jane Hester Ogle, on 6 Sept. 1792 (Ogle, p. 152). He was a keen horseman, and his MS. 'Horse Account' (in the possession of Commander and Mrs. Scarlett-Streatfeild) gives particulars of all the horses he owned between 1778 and 1802.

[2] Charles Grey married Mary Elizabeth Ponsonby, daughter of the 1st Lord Ponsonby, and had a stillborn child by her in 1795, and a first surviving child in 1797.

[3] Mrs. S.'s brother, the Rev. John Saville Ogle (1767–1853).

[4] While the negotiation between the Prince and the Court over the situation of his wife was carried on, he lived at the Duke of Clarence's in Richmond; but when this was broken off, he returned to the Grange (18 June). 'The Prince means to make his first appearance in public at Winchester Races' (*St. James's Chronicle*, 18–21 June 1796).

[5] She appears to have been a dashing rider. In a letter to S. written before their marriage, Mrs. S. remarks, 'If I *must* have a horse of your chusing, let it be excessively hot and fiery, and not too tall, with a fine crest, and be sure no Lady ever rode it' (Widener MS.).

256. To His Wife

Osborn MS. *Address*: Devizes July twenty ninth 1796 | Mrs. Sheridan | Dean of Winchester's | St. Mary's | Southampton *Fr.*: Free | R B Sheridan

29 July 1796
Friday

Beloved of Dan's Soul, I must write you a Line tho' we have parted but a very few Hours. But no Post will leave Bath[1] tomorrow and you will think me lost. I am anxious to entreat you not to forget your promise—not to drive alone and to ride; *if* ride at all, only with John and *only Pantaloon*. I rely on you, and am even afraid of some accident with these Precautions. You forgot my Note to John. Send up Tom Groom as we settled and let me find tomorrow a sweet account of yourself and Robin. Dear Anne take care of her.

Ma'am all our Liveliness is gone since you left our Party. | Yr true | R B S.

257. To His Wife

Harvard MS.

[*1–2 Aug. 1796?*]
Monday Night

O Ma'am Dan is *Lemoncholy* as a yew-tree in a Church yard. All alone—no sweet Hecca near him and no happy certainty that He can go to her in two minutes if he chose—the only feeling that can sometimes justify staying away a little. So the best I can do is to write a little to my beloved. I have been doing quantities of business to Day and I truly have been and truly will be sober as a Judge.

I have every hour some new reason to be satisfied with our Purchase.[2] Hammersley has had repeated offers of great

[1] *Bath Journal*, 1 August 1796, listing persons who had arrived at Bath during the past week, includes the names 'Mr. R. B. Sheridan; Mr. Richardson'. Possibly the purpose of the journey was to see the manager of the Bath Theatre and persuade him to release Elliston.

[2] Sir William Geary, 2nd baronet (1756–1825), of Oxenheath, Kent, spent nearly £20,000 in obtaining elec-

advantage for the Bargain. I hear of nothing but congratulations or envy at my Bargain. My negotiation for the lovely Farm adjoining[1] goes on well—and we shall have the nicest Place within a prudent distance from Town in England.[2] And sweet Hecca shall have a House after her own Fancy, and it shall be the Seat of Health and Happiness—where she shall chirp like a bird, bound like a Fawn and grow fat as little pig, and we will get rid of all the nasty Servants and have all good and do all good round us. The thought and Plan of this is my Hope and Happiness, and puts all dismal thoughts from me. and I never can visit Bath without laying in a store of them. O me it is a Place where every Spot in it and round it leads to some interesting and melancholy recollection. But you my Angel you, and you only could have done it, have brought Peace and chearfulness to a restless and harrass'd Heart.—You are its resting place and Delight —every hour more and more.—do not think it unreasonable that I should have even *unreasonable* apprehensions and cautions where everything is at risk.

Tuesday morn

A thousand Thanks my own dear Wench for your Letter just arrived—Hecca's kind words make Dan's Heart Glad.

But O you little sly Beast how you want to cajole me about your driving. So John is astonish'd at your skill is He? now you little Jade if you do nothing but drive behind and follow the Track of his Curricle, what opportunity has he of seeing your Skill!—I must beat you.—

O give sweet Robin a quantity of kisses from me. I do not long to have him in my sight to be sure—nor his Sweet

tion as member of parliament for Kent in 1796. 'To answer the demands of which the estates of the late Admiral Geary are advertised to be sold' (*Bell's W. Mess.*, 3 July 1796). The manors of Polesden Lacy and West Humble, the mansion of Polesden and its lands and pleasure grounds, made up the 341 acres advertised for sale by Spurrier and Phipps at Garraway's, Change Alley, Cornhill, on 26 July 1796. The house commanded extensive views, particularly of Box Hill, and lay in the parish of Great Bookham 'in a prime and sporting part of Surry' (*Morn. Chron.*, 4 July 1796). It cost S. £12,384, as appears in the transcript of the Polesden deeds lent me by Mr. John H. Harvey.

[1] Either Yew-Trees farm, eventually acquired in 1805, or Vinnaces (Phoenice or Venice), acquired in 1806.

[2] These four sentences are quoted by Rae, ii. 204–5.

mother. Yes Dearest give away the Dog if you think it best. Tomorrow I'll fix my coming and all my Plans.

Tuesday Night My own Hecca I could not get home in Time to get this Letter for the Post and now I am come from a sad melancholy Scene. You will be very sorry to hear that the Duchess of D. after suffering all sorts of cruel Operations will certainly lose one eye[1] *Lady B.* is half dead.[2] Heaven bless and guard my Hecca!

258. To His Wife

Osborn MS. *Address*: London August fourth 1796 | Mrs Sheridan | Deanery | Winchester[3] *Fr.*: Free R B Sheridan

4 Aug. 1796

Heart of mine—I have only a moment to say bless you—and again to beg no risks—I am now frighten'd at your account of Pantaloon.

The Duchess is a little Better and there are hopes of the eye.

Dear Dear Love bless your Days and Nights I come *Saturday*[3]— | R B S

Thursday

259. To His Wife

Osborn MS. *Address*: London August twenty second | 1796 | Mrs. Sheridan | H. Streatfeild Esqr. | Chiddingstone | Seven Oaks | Kent. *Fr.*: Free R B Sheridan

22 Aug. 1796
Monday.

My beloved, tho' I miss you more than I should my eyes I

[1] On 9 Aug. Horace Walpole wrote, 'The Duchess of Devonshire has been in great danger of losing her sight, by catching cold very indiscreetly. They have saved her eyes by almost strangling her with a handkerchief, and forcing all the blood up into her head, and then bleeding her with leeches' (*Journals and Corr. of Miss Berry* (ed. Lewis, 1865), ii. 15).

[2] See Lady Bessborough's letter ('My whole soul is fix'd on that one object') in *Leveson Gower Corr.* i. 126.

[3] They afterwards visited Southill: 'Mr. and Mrs. Sheridan have been on a visit to Mr. Whitbread' (*Morn. Post*, 20 Aug. 1796).

am very glad you are not in this red-hot Town this burning Day. I send you the account of our Boy—and another Letter and that is all I have a moment to do. I will write again this evening and kiss your green beads on Wednesday. I mean to send Edwards to convey Robin to meet us at Bognor,[1] but I'll tell you all the Plan tomorrow. Give your Heart a kiss for me. | Your | R B S

The Duchess much better[2]—I am going to dine there.

260. To His Wife

Osborn MS. *Address*: London August twenty fourth | 1796 | Mrs. Sheridan | H. Streatfeild Es | Chiddingstone | Seven-Oaks | Kent *Fr.*: Free | R B Sheridan

24 Aug. 1796
Wednesday

My Dearest one I am very unhappy at not getting a Line from you to Day—and the more so because I shall not see your eyes tomorrow. I could not leave Town to Day tho' I tried with all my might—and to Polesden I must go tomorrow. Our Coxcomb Surveyor is gone to Day, and as you will see on Thursday is to be the Sale of what I am not bound to take,[3] but a good deal of which I am told should be had. A nice account of our Treasure Boy—tho' to hear the word Small Pox frightens me.

I saw Mrs. Wilmot this morning at Jane's[4]—and these two Days she has been better. People in London are dropping in the Streets with the heat.—You never tell me about your health which is always what I want most to hear of. I must beat you. Mrs. Wilmot pass'd you on the road—

I send you the other Letters besides the enclosed. O I

[1] 'The Prince of Wales was expected last week at Bognor. Lady Jersey has been some time at Bognor, which is thronged with the most fashionable company' (*Sussex Weekly Advertiser*, 29 Aug. 1796).

[2] 'The Duchess of Devonshire will entirely recover the use and appearance of her eye' (*Morn. Post*, 26 Aug. 1796).

[3] 1 and 2 Sept., Spurrier and Phipps were to sell at Polesden the live and dead farming stock of the late Admiral Sir Francis Geary, including 149 South Down sheep, two cows, and a brood mare (*Morn. Chron.*, 24 Aug. 1796).

[4] Mrs. Richard Streatfeild.

made so cock sure that one of them must be from my Hecca. Bless you my beloved and be only as glad to meet as I shall be. | Your | S.

261. To His Wife

Osborn MS. *Wm*: 1794

[*1796?*]

My Hearts Hecca

Nothing shall prevent my setting off to Night tho the Post is just going.

This Line is to beg should it arrive at Bognors [before] me that my dear Wench will not ride out but let me find her at home—this is a superstition—but pray forgive and indulge me in it.

bless your eyes. | Yours | R B S.

Tuesday

262. [To John Grubb]

Harvard MS.

[*Sept. 1796*]

My Dear Sir,

By some confusion of that Rogue Richardson He has kept me in Town these ten Days in hopes of the Pleasure of seeing you.[1] Now I am compell'd to leave Town for a few Days,[2] and I write [to] propose postponing our meeting a Little. I return the end of the week—and have provided for the Opening, engaged Parissot[3] and hope to fix with

[1] 'Mr. Grubb is confined at Margate with a sprained ancle, which prevents his return to town' (*Morn. Post*, 10 Sept. 1796).

[2] The *True Briton*, 8 Sept. 1796, reported that S. had gone to Bognor Rocks, and (on 13 Sept.) that Richardson was there too. The *Morn. Post*, 14 Sept., noted 'Yesterday evening Mr. Sheridan set off from town for his seat in Surry, late Sir William Geary's.' The latter journey is probably the one S. alludes to, if only because the opening of D.L.Th. on 20 Sept. is first mentioned in the *Morn. Chron.*, 15 Sept. 1796.

[3] Dancer. The engagement was mentioned in the *Morn. Post*, 19 Sept. 1796, and she made her first appearance on the English stage at D.L.Th. ('by permission of the Proprietor of the King's Theatre') on 1 Oct. as Corida in the ballet, *The Triumph of Love*.

Elliston.[1]—I will write again tomorrow but fear to lose this Post | yours ever | R B Sheridan

263. To His Wife

Osborn MS.

[*20 Sept. 1796*]
Tuesday

My Life's Delight—your two sweet affectionate Letters have been my Heart's Food and Rayment. And How ungrateful I shall seem in not having written yesterday but the case was I was obliged to go out of Town to meet Mrs. Siddons and prevail on her to play on thursday.[2] My presence was very necessary in Town, and I have been worried to Death, but I am settling all the Difficulties and the Theatre will go on stoutly under the new management[3] and Dan will get all the monies in the world for Polesden and Hecca and Tom and Robin.—O my own beloved indeed you could not be more sorry at Parting than I was. I never in my Life was so nervous and oppress'd[4] as when I got up an[d] walk'd alone where I meet my wench in her Turban on Saturday Evening.

Dearest it will be Thursday I find without a Remedy before I shall see your green eyes.

I must have done | bless you bless you | R B S.

[1] R. W. Elliston (1774–1831) acted at the Haymarket Theatre that summer, and S. tried to engage him for the D.L.Th. winter season. Elliston wrote to Dr. Elliston on 8 Sept. 1796 to say, 'I mean therefore to ask Mr. Sheridan what I know he *cannot give* a £1000 . . . and a weekly stipend besides' (Pierpont Morgan Library MS.). Elliston was not engaged. See A. M. Broadley's collection (*Annals of the Haymarket*, iii. 327–29) in Westminster Public Library, and *How Do You Do?*, 10 Sept. 1796. Cf. G. Raymond, *Memoirs of . . . Elliston* (1844), i. 95.

[2] 'Mrs. Siddons has finally closed her engagement with the Proprietors of the Drury-Lane Theatre' (*Morn. Post*, 20 Sept. 1796). She took the part of Jane Shore on 22 Sept. *How Do You Do?*, 24 Sept. 1796, mentioned that she 'never used to appear till after Christmas'. She was paid twenty pounds a night.

[3] The appointment of Richard Wroughton (1748–1822) as deputy manager at D.L.Th., in place of Kemble, is mentioned in the *Morn. Post*, 30 Aug. 1796.

[4] He made over his 'Household Furniture etc.' to Hammersleys on 15 Sept. 1796, as collateral security for £6,000, interest and future sums: see the assignment in the Garrick Club Library.

264. To His Wife

Osborn MS. *Wm.*: 1794.

[*21 Sept. 1796?*]
Wednesday.

O my darling Wench how glad I am that you are not in this vile burning oven[1] where every one is dead or dying and here is misery. Tom cannot join me till tomorrow evening—and I shall not see my soul's Love 'till Friday. Believe my Hecca nothing but pressing matters would make me stay an hour from you and as you say we will part no more. Dear dear Hecca be cautious about riding till we meet—and forgive my teazing nervousness on this one subject.—I found many difficulties here to encounter—but when I set to work I easily got over them. Kemble is so unconscionable we must do without him.[2] Among other things because we did not open the House by two Days at the usual Time[3] one of the ministerial Papers asserted that we were ruin'd and couldn't. I in general only laugh at these things—but it has been thought right to bring an action against this Thief. I send you the Papers that you may know the Theatre is alive and merry—and there is every Prospect of an uncommonly successful Season.—

give two kisses to the enclosed[4] and make Robin give one —I will tell you the History of it when we meet. Tell John He and Tom may go and kill and slay at Petworth. We will settle as we come by and Dan stay with Hecca.

Tell my self that the rest of her will certainly be at Bognor so beg her not to move.

[1] Although it rained heavily on 21 Sept., the weather was sultry and did not freshen until the following day. See *Gent. Mag.* lxvi, pt. 2 (1796), p. 501.

[2] The *True Briton*, 22 Sept. 1796, reported that he had demanded £1,000 for the season and that this had retarded his engagement. The *Morn. Post*, 19 Sept. 1796, mentioned that he had 'opened a negociation for a transatlantic excursion'.

[3] 'The rumour so maliciously circulated, respecting *possession* having been taken of D.L.Th., we have done every thing in our power to repel. It originated in a Morning Paper distinguished only by the mixed malignity and falsehood of its contents' (The *True Briton*, 22 Sept. 1796). D.L.Th. opened on 20 Sept.

[4] Not with the MS.

Mrs. Ord.[1] is in Town. Tell Anne the Town is quite suffocateful.

Dear one send me a Line by return of Post altho' I mean to be off before the Post comes in Friday yet do. Bless your Heart | R B S.

265. To His Wife

Osborn MS.

[*26 Sept. 1796?*]
Monday

O my own beloved my Heart is broken into forty Bits to think of my not having been able to get to you and that I miss'd writing on Saturday. You will think Dan lost or dead or, which would be worse and more unlikely than either, unkind. Tom could not get up in time to meet me as I hoped but He [is] here now and sends his Duty. Infernal Politics have hinder'd my setting off to Day. Fox comes from Norfolk on purpose to meet me,[2] and tomorrow by Hea*ven* no Power on earth shall prevent our setting off. Tom brings 100 Dogs with him. So John and He may reckon on Sport.

O my Heart's Light and Life there is nothing makes amends for these absences and at Times all my Fits of nervous Gloom come over me—for want of my angel Hecca to brush them off with her soft white wings. But perhaps she has almost forgot me, and is quite used to do without me.

—no no— | bless you my own, bless you ever | R B S.

I will bring the Salt-sellers money etc. and John's Compass. We have re-engaged Kemble as an actor on fair Terms[3]

[1] Eleanor Brandling of Gosforth married William Ord on 4 Mar. 1779. She became Mrs. Thomas Creevey in 1802.

[2] Fox planned to be at Woburn from 6 to 13 Sept. and in Norfolk from 13 to 27 Sept. 1796 (Add. MS. 47581, f. 3). The *True Briton*, 22 Sept. 1796, mentioned that he was going to Brighton before the meeting of Parliament. He wrote to the Duke of Northumberland on 4 Sept.: 'the manner in which we should conduct ourselves when it [Parliament] does begin particularly upon the Address will I think be a matter of great importance' (Alnwick MSS., LVIII, ff. 109–10). The subject of the Address and, probably, of S.'s 'Infernal Politics' was the government's peace negotiations.

[3] His first performance that season was on 29 Sept. *The Telegraph*, 30 Sept. 1796, reported that his re-engagement was for five years, and that he was to

266. To John Grubb

Harvard MS.

[*Sept. 1796?*]
past one

My Dear Grubb,

Owing to a piece of infernal Stupidity I have but this moment got Peakes Note—I send a Servant with this—and am following as hard as possible. I shall go 20 miles round in order that I may bring £1000[1] with me, but I send this to beg you not to have one hour's despondency what has happen'd is cursed unlucky—but we have never yet thoroughly exerted ourselves and by all that's sacred on earth not one of these damn'd difficulties shall be unsettled before I leave Town again. If I arrive in the Night I will be with you in the morning | yrs | R B Sheridan

most likely I shall be with you as soon as the Servant—

267. To William Adam

Adam MS. *Dock.*: Mr. Sheridan.

[*Sept. 1796*][2]

My Dear Adam,

I am always ashamed to intrude by applying to you on trifling occasions and unworthy your interference. Here is a new instance in the case of Mrs. Jordan's withholding her assistance[3] in the commencement of the present Season. Now the Fact is I have much at stake in various matters, now *on the very point of settlement*,[4] which makes it an object

have £24 a week and £200 for his benefit. See, also, H. Baker, *John Philip Kemble* (Cambridge, Mass., 1942), pp. 226–7. Add. MS. 31973, f. 156, reveals that arrangements for the payment of his arrears were concluded on 1 Nov. 1796.

1 'Hammersley and others v. Grubb . . . 1796 Septem 28: To Bill due this day: £500 and £500. . . .' (Grubbe MS.)

2 Mr. D. E. Ginter noted that this letter was in a bundle docketed 'Sept. 1796'.

3 Mrs. Jordan had agreed on 1 Sept. 1794 to 'act, sing and perform any and every character for five years' at thirty guineas a week (Hodgson's Catalogue, 26 Apr. 1911, lot 588).

4 See p. 56, n. 2.

of the greatest consequence to me to do our best at the opening. First thanking you sincerely for your trouble with Richardson, may I ask one attempt more with this perverse Nymph. I think I understood from you that the non-payment of her arrears was the principal difficulty. She shall immediately have a Draught at a short Date on our Firm for the whole. Assuming this difficulty to be removed, it is to be observed (tho' perhaps out of the Spirit of Chivalry) that when Mrs. Jordan's *time comes*[1] to play according to the Letter of her Article she will be unfit to perform anything worth her salary. Now surely it is not *unfair* if she expects at that time the most delicate forbearance on the Part of the manager and that she is *only* to walk over the stage in a few Farces, that she should give some earlier assistance to the Theatre than she is positively bound to—and if she refuses this it cannot be *unjust* that the manager should take a similar advantage of the Letter of the article and call on her when she does come for such characters as he chuses.

I think if this *would* be delicately suggested—and the arrears settled—she could not refuse, and if she pleases she shall appear with the advantage of the first Night of *Parissot's Dance*.

Now pray excuse my again troubling you on such a subject—but if you knew all I have at stake at the present moment I know you would excuse it. | your's ever | R B Sheridan.

268. To His Wife

Osborn MS. *Wm.*: 179 |

[1796?]
Wednesday

My Sweet Beloved—Tho' your Letter was short to Day it

[1] 'Mrs. Jordan does not make her appearance until November, as she is too far advanced in her pregnancy to commence her performances at an earlier period' (*Morn. Post*, 24 Sept. 1796). She changed her mind, and the D.L.Th. advertisement (*The Telegraph*, 28 Sept.) announced that she would make her first appearance of the season on 1 Oct., as Miss Peggy in *The Country Girl*, the play that preceded *The Triumph of Love*. She continued to act until 5 Dec., though *The Telegraph*, 18 Oct., mentioned that she was 'far gone in her pregnancy'. She was the mistress of the Duke of Clarence, later William IV, and her third child (Sophia Fitzclarence) by him was born in 1796.

made my Heart glad with the assurance of your being so much better. I have had horrid nervous Fits and shall feel no stoutness of mind till I see your eyes—

O my Love I am tied by the leg here till Friday. I never in my Life was so mortified.

I am so superstitious it would make me miserable to decide about our Darling—but I think it should be in Town or we shall be again separated which wearies and worries me to Death. Pray write write. I forgot to send the money you borrow'd. Bless you Heaven.

269. To His Wife.

Osborn MS. *Wm.*: 1794

[*6 Oct. 1796?*]
Thursday
House of Commons

My Soul's Blessing—a thousand Thanks for your punctual Letters and Nasty Dan contrives always to put off writing 'till at the last moment He is caught in hurry noise and confusion and has only time to say that He loves you more and more dearly if possible every hour. Indeed I was uneasy about angelic Robin but I will not believe it possible that there ever can be such misery as his not doing well.—

Well my Heart I will not fail to be at Midhurst tomorrow to *Dinner* at six. These vile Politics shall not keep me.

So Peace is now the word—and these vile monsters of Ministers after shedding oceans of blood and breaking Thousands of Hearts are going to do what Fox proposed three years ago.[1]

tell Tom I'll bring the Warrant for shooting tomorrow. Be careful sweet Love—and be half as glad to see me as I shall to kiss your small eyes. | R B S.

[1] Parliament met on Thursday, 6 Oct. 1796, and members were informed in the speech from the throne that a minister was to be sent to Paris to open negotiations. In the subsequent debate, Fox pointed out that the government had at last adopted the course he had long recommended.

270. To——

Harvard MS.

14 Oct. [*1796?*][1]

My Dear Sir,

I did not understand from Richardson that you were leaving Town so soon or you should not have gone without the Letter I proposed to write to you, altho' I have only to repeat the Facts which I have no doubt you have already stated to Mr. Taylor and to repeat, also how extremely vexatious it is that the Good-will and Friendship which ought to subsist between Persons so long and so intimately acquainted and who have also so much of a common interest should be so frequently interrupted by one of the Parties suffering his good sense, and I sincerely add Good intentions too, to be surprised and counteracted by the most improbable Tales and suggestions, such as neither side ought for a moment to have listen'd to. I understand that Mr. Taylor has written to his old and I am sure very sincere Friend Richardson that He has proofs of the machinations of the Proprietors of Drury-Lane for the Destruction of his Property! I know that the slightest enquiry or a single half hours cool Reflexion will induce him to regret that he permitted anyone to abuse him with such an idea for an instant, but in the interval He actually engaged in the most serious Hostility to our interest. I understand it to have been asserted that we were preparing the most magnificent Series of Ballet in order to overpower the Spectacle at the Opera—it is curious how very much the contrary is the Fact. We have not even thought of a Ballet of any sort. I dont believe we have even four Figures, nor ever thought of anything more than a simple Partner for Parissot,[2] who was engaged not

[1] Dated from a note about D.L.Th. in the *Pocket Magazine*, v (1796), 194: 'Sept. 1796 . . . Madame Parisot, and other Opera House performers, are engaged for a few nights at this theatre, by permission of the Proprietors of the King's Theatre . . . which does not yet open for some time.'

[2] The *Morn. Chron.*, 4 Oct. 1796, reported that 'the new Ballet, recommended by the charms of PARISOT, was again highly applauded, and was of a kind so new to the English Stage as to have the most captivating effect on the upper regions of the house.' She was the subject of abusive verse in 1796, and her dress was denounced by the Bishop of Durham in 1798.

only with Mr. Taylor's knowledge but with his assistance. Nay so indifferent were we even about engaging *her* that after she had her Passport and her chaise at the Door it is a literal Fact that what decided both Richardson and myself was an assurance that if she went Didelot[1] would follow her, and the Opera establishment consequently be much injured should Vestris[2] not come.

With regard to Dagville[3] it ought to be unnecessary for me to declare upon my Honor that I never heard the slightest Rumour of any difference or ill conduct of his towards Mr. Taylor: we thought He had used *us* ill, and what is more extraordinary the man at whose recommendation alone He came over, I mean Thoman,[4] had been constantly abusing him beyond measure. The moment I heard of the circumstance, namely in Mr. Taylors first Letter to Mr. Richardson I sent him word that He should on no account appear on our stage untill He had apologized so as to satisfy Mr. Taylor, and I have never seen him at all nor thought about a Ballet since.

These are Facts.—Being willing to hope that nothing but some gross and scandalous misinterpretation could have induced Mr. Taylor to act so differently towards us I have taken the trouble to state them. I do not wish him to retract any service He wishes to do Covent-Garden, but I am confident He will be eager to discover the authority which Mr. Frederici[5] pretends to have from him to announce the immediate Bankruptcy of our Theatre! I believe it to be certain that Mr. Frederici has both said and written this that He could have had the authority He pretends I do not believe—

[1] Didelot was a male dancer at the King's Theatre, 1795–7.

[2] *The Telegraph*, 30 Sept. 1796, stated that the dancers of the King's Theatre were to be reinforced with L'Aborie, D'Auberval, and Vestris. Both Gaetano Vestris (1728–1808) and his son, Auguste Vestris (1760–1842), had been in this company in 1791.

[3] *The Times*, 26 Dec. 1794, reported that D'Egville had been dismissed rather cavalierly from his post as dancer at the King's Theatre. He began a lawsuit against Taylor, but lost it because 'the contract was not on a stamp' (The *True Briton*, 2 June 1795).

[4] A jeweller of 55 Spring Gardens.

[5] In the D.L.Th. ledger, *Claims and Compositions* (Folger MS.), Frederici was noted as having been paid £130. 4*s*. 0*d*. for stoves supplied by him. The other ledgers note that he was paid several sums by D.L.Th. between 1790 and 1796.

your general good will to all Parties must be my excuse for addressing this to you. | I am, Dear Sir | yours truly | R B Sheridan

Oct 14th:

271. To His Wife

Osborn MS. *Address*: London November eleventh | 1796 | Mrs. Sheridan | Dean of Winchesters | St. Mary's | Southampton *Fr.*: Free | R B Sheridan

11 Nov. 1796
Friday

O my Hecca you break Dan's Heart when you think for a moment that anything but absolute necessity could have kept me away from you. Upon my soul and honor there has not been one Day on which I could have left Town without the most ruinous consequences.[1] A business of the utmost and most critical importance has been depending—it is now brought to a conclusion and tomorrow the Deeds are to be executed[2] and that hour I set off. No Power on earth shall make me sleep in Tomorrow Night. And nothing but the thought that my Angel Hecca would be vex'd at the mischief prevented my setting off the moment I read your Letter. Hecca would only have grieved for Dan and not said one angry word if she had been over his head to have seen his situation and the difficulties he had to surmount.—

I would crawl on my Hands and knees to you rather than remain one hour from you for any slight cause—

[1] On 9 Nov. Mrs. Siddons wrote, 'I am, as you may observe, acting again; but how much difficulty to get my money! Sheridan is certainly the greatest phenomenon that Nature has produced for centuries. Our theatre is going on, to the astonishment of everybody. Very few of the actors are paid, and all are vowing to withdraw themselves; yet still we go on' (T. Campbell, *Life of Mrs. Siddons* (1839), p. 273).

[2] On 2 Dec. S. paid Garrick's executors £10,951. 14*s*. 8*d*., principal and interest on Linley's mortgage (Folger MS. Y. d. 54). Cf.: 'The Proprietors of Drury-Lane Theatre yesterday, in the presence of Mr. Hammersley, paid to Albany Walis Esq. the sum of *sixteen thousand pounds*, which, extinguishing the last mortgage of Mr. Garrick, perfects the *general trust deed*, and removes every difficulty which an expenditure of £25,000 beyond the original estimate for building the Theatre may have temporarily occasioned' (*St. James's Chronicle*, 1–3 Dec. 1796).

But you more than break my Heart when you say your cough is worse.—It is what I cannot bear to think of. O let me find it not so—

I am quite unhappy | R B S.

272. [To John Grubb]

Harvard MS. *Wm.*: 1794

[*20 Nov. 1796?*][1]

My Dear Sir,

I assure you it is no satisfaction to me to think that Messrs Still and Strong,[2] to whom I certainly never gave any cause of ill will, should wish to be unnecessarily hostile to me. I certainly may so have express'd myself, but I have no scruple in stating my authority.—Mr. Hanson[3] positively assured me, and with great appearance at least of regret, that they compell'd him to what I thought unneccessary rigour and as he understood from motives of personal or *party* Pique. In professional men of their Rank I could not but think this both extraordinary and unjustifiable. Mr. Hanson cannot venture to deny what I state—for I have it even in one of his Letters, and as certainly He must admit that He had no reason to repent the confidence he placed in me for the remainder of his Debt when he withdrew the execution.

On the present business the Delay Jack is 'till tomorrow sennight. You know that I am on the very point of making the long delay'd settlement with Mr. Wallis, which alone can enable me to fulfill engagements enter'd into in the confidence of that settlement taking Place long since—

I do not write to Mr. Smith[4] because I take it for granted He will act by his Solicitors advice. I shall be much obliged

[1] Sunday week before the settlement reported in the *St. James's Chronicle*, 1–3 Dec. 1796. See p. 56, n. 2.

[2] Peter Still and William Strong were Commissioners of Bankrupts, and attorneys, of 5 Lincoln's Inn-new-square. See *Browne's General Law List for . . . 1797*, p. 89.

[3] See Gilmore MSS. for John Hanson's bill for fire-plating and pulleys.

[4] Difficult to identify. D. Smith was owed £271. 17*s.* 6*d.* for 'Lamps and oils' (Gilmore MS.). John Smith was owed a small bill (£26. 4*s.* 8*d.*) for canvas for the theatre. On 19 May 1796 S. had ordered Richardson to pay 'Mr. Smith' £100 seven days later (Pierpont Morgan Library MS.).

if you succeed. If not Mr. Richardson will mention to you what I can scarcely state as a favour.

I shall certainly return to Town on wednesday. | yours Dear Sir | very truly | R B Sheridan

Sunday morning

273. [To John Grubb]

Harvard MS. *Wm.*: 1795

[*1796?*]

My Dear Sir,

For God's sake only pacify Still and Strong 'till thursday morning—

Mrs. Sheridan is on the Road, we dine in Town and move no more. Excuse me this Day only— | Yours ever | R B S.

274. [To John Grubb]

Harvard MS.

[*1796?*]
Wednesday Night

My Dear Sir,

Pray pray see Still and Strong—they threaten me terribly tomorrow. | your ever | R B Sheridan.

275. To John Grubb

Harvard MS. *Address*: J. Grubb

[*1796*]

My Dear Sir,

Mr. Jones, Mr. Sleigh's Partner who acts for Mr. Hammersley and who has been very active in bringing the necessary settlement to a conclusion with Wallis, is so obliging as to call himself with this—and will immediately settle what is proper to be done for Hammersley's security respecting the House which they agree to take.[1] I am going to Wallis and Trust monday will finish everything. | yours | R B Sheridan

J. Grubb Esq

276. To John Grubb

Harvard MS.

[*1796?*]

Dear Grubb,

We must all be at Sleighs tomorrow *without* fail at *Three precisely*—and all will be settled. | yours ever | R B Sheridan

Sunday Night

277. [To John Grubb]

Harvard MS.

[*1796?*]
Monday Evening

My Dear Sir,

After the most solemn assurance that everything should be ready to settle with Wallis this morning—Mr. Sleigh[2] has not been able to finish the Deeds and it stands over to *Wednesday*. This again lays me on my back about *Smith*. And I cannot apply to Still and Strong, tho' I find you must have successfully.

—You must have thought it strange that I have been three Days in Town without calling—but I really have been so worried that I never saw Richardson 'till just now for two minutes.—

I will call in the morning and hope to find all Gout gone. Once settled with Wallis and everything is settled | Yours ever | R B Sheridan

[1] Grubb's house in Lincoln's Inn Fields was accepted as security by the bankers when he became Treasurer of D.L.Th. R. Nowell's accounts (Grubbe MSS.) mention the date of the conveyance as 30 Nov. 1796.

[2] William Sleigh, attorney, of Whitehall. He was engaged in drawing up the trust deed to extinguish all the mortgage incumbrances: see Winston, 1796–7. He himself shared the tenth part in the D.L.Th. indenture of 1793 (P.R.O., Chancery Procs., C. 13/2325). Cf. iii. 272, no. 57.

278. To John Grubb

Harvard MS. *Address*: J. Grubb Esq.:

[*28 Nov. 1796?*]
Monday Night

Dear Grubb,

I think this the dirtiest Trick Farren[1] has ever yet play'd. I have not been from the House of Commons above an hour but I found a Note from her which I have answer'd and as harshly as I could.—Getting her £400 tomorrow is out of the Question. She says Shaw her attorney[2] was greatly disappointed to Day.—Therefore I suppose that Westley as usual omitted to send my Note to him.—We shall have some answer in the morning and I shall be at home to no one but you, being deep in the Bank Papers which come on tomorrow—keep the play[3] advertised of course. | Yours | R B Sheridan.

279. To John Grubb

Harvard MS. *Address*: John Grubb Esr: | Lincoln's Inn Square.

[*1796?*]
Richmond
past eight

My Dear Sir,

I am come to this Place to remove an impediment to

[1] Elizabeth Farren (1759?–1829), afterwards Countess of Derby, had been a member of the D.L.Th. company since 1778, and was particularly successful as Lady Teazle and Lady Townley. She did not appear at the theatre on 29 Nov. 1796 and, after an hour's delay, the programme was altered. The *True Briton*, 1 Dec. 1796, contained a letter signed 'Eliza Farren' that included the statement, 'the only cause of my not appearing was a considerable failure of the Managers, in performing the pecuniary part of my engagement'. This was declared a forgery in the *St. James's Chronicle*, 1–3 Dec. 1796, and the real cause of her absence was said to be illness. William Powell, the prompter, stated in a letter to the *Morn. Chron.*, 3 Dec., that the cause lay in a misunderstanding. Farington, i. 174, however, gave Lysons's authority for the statement that she had resolutely told the managers that she would not act unless her arrears were paid.

[2] R. Shawe's correspondence with S. and Grubb over £1,152. 8*s*. 8*d*. owing to Miss Farren (with a note of her wish for 'coercive measures' against them) is among the Harvard MSS.

[3] T. Holcroft's *The Force of Ridicule*. This was to have been its first performance. It was acted on 6 Dec. with Miss Farren in the lead, but was a failure.

Jordan's playing tomorrow. I think it of the greatest consequence and she does not return with her Duke[1] 'till *ten* o'clock—being gone to see her children. I have sent to Stop the Press and Bills—and as it will be so late will be with you *early in the morn.* | Yrs truly | R B Sheridan

280. 'To Mrs. Jordan'

Harvard MS. A draft.

[*Dec. 1796*]

Madam,

At the immediate desire of the Proprietors I am call'd on to observe in how very few Parts at this juncture the Theatre can be benefited by your assistance—it never being our wish to require the Performance of any Part that can be inconvenient to you.[2]—The same attention obliges us to delay the Performance of the new comedy.[3] Under these circumstances some reciprocal consideration is expected by the Proprietors—and under the unavoidable want of Novelty which such attention on their Part occasions in the entertainment of the Public it was conceived that the Part of Phillis in the Con[s]cious Lovers would be some variety and shew a disposition both on your Part and that of the Theatre to do the best under the circumstances. I hope therefore if not on Saturday the Performance of this Play will not be prevented on tuesday next. Both Proprietors and Manager hold themselves responsible to give the Public all the novelty in their Power or to assign the Reasons for with holding it. It is by no means meant to address the observation particularly to you, but the manner in which Parts have for some time Past been rejected by other Performers is what the Proprietors are determined no longer to submit

[1] The Duke of Clarence lived at Richmond in 1796. Mrs. Jordan was there with him in August (*The Telegraph*, 25 Aug. 1796), and acted at the Richmond Theatre in September (*Morn. Chron.*, 5 Sept. 1796).

[2] S. was said to be as afraid of Mrs. Jordan 'as a Mouse of a Cat' (Farington, ii. 193). She played Ophelia on 5 Dec. but did not act again that month. The cause of her absence was arrears of salary: see Farington, i. 174. She was paid £20 on 28 Nov., £120 on 1 Dec., and £10. 10*s.* 0*d.* on account on 10 Dec.: see D.L.Th. 'Receipts and Payments, 1796–7' (Folger MS.).

[3] The only new comedies that season were *The Force of Ridicule*, and F. Reynolds's *The Will and the Deed*, acted on 19 Apr. 1797.

to.[1] But equal justice must be done and equal good-will shown by all the Performers—or it is impossible the unprecedented high Salaries of this Company can be continued. At the same time where the Performer is paid by the Night, they must certainly consider *every call* for appearing in a Proper Part whether refused or not as fulfilling the contract on their Part and the Performer entitled only to Payment when they do appear.

Confident Madam, that you will see in a proper Light my executing the Duty which my situation imposes on me, and relying on your good will to the undertaking and disposition to set the necessary good example from the best authority I must flatter myself that the Public will not be disappointed of the Play of the Con[s]cious Lover[s][2] on Tuesday next—which in its present Cast will be play'd with credit and otherwise cannot be play'd at all.

I have only in addition to beg leave to remind you that as the new musical Piece will be succeeded by the Pantomine[3] you will not be call'd on to appear in any entertainments.[4] | I am

281. To John Grubb

Harvard MS. *Address*: J. Grubb Esqr:

[*28 Dec. 1796?*][5]

My Dear Sir,

Carpenter[6] has just found in my Drawer his your's and another Letter unopen'd.[7]

[1] The deputy manager, R. Wroughton, wrote to S. on 'Thursday Morning': 'I sent the Manifesto to Mrs. Jordan and have inclos'd her Answer—what's to be done?—Shall the Play of the Conscious Lovers go forward with *Decamp* for Phillis or with Miss Pope as before? or shall it be laid up in *Ordinary*?—I think Mrs. Jordan can be sooner treated with, I do not mean in this Case, by more soothing Terms. . . .' (Harvard MS.) See also *Mrs. Jordan and Her Family* (ed. A. Aspinall, 1951), p. 34.

[2] Sir Richard Steele's *The Conscious Lovers* (1722). It had not been given at D.L.Th. for twenty years. It was acted there on Tuesday, 20 Dec., with J. P. Kemble as Young Bevil, Miss Farren as Indiana, and Harriot Mellon as Phillis; but was not well received.

[3] Arnold's musical piece, *The Shipwreck*, was given with *The Conscious Lovers* on 20 Dec., but when Steele's play was repeated on 3 Jan. 1797, it was accompanied by the pantomime, *Robinson Crusoe*.

[4] Afterpieces.

[5] Dated as the Wednesday before J. W. Jones's letter to S. of 31 Dec. 1796. Jones stated '. . . after three days [*Notes 5, 6 and 7 continued on opposite page.*

The enclosed is all since settled, but I send it as a sample of a little vigour we must stand to. Tomorrow I hope both Ford and Goodenough[1] and Franco will compleat. | Your's ever | R B S.

Wednesday Evening

282. To Richard Peake

McAdam MS. *Address*: Mr. Peake | Mr. Hart's | No. 3. Stafford-Place | Pimlico.

[*After 1796*]
Wednesday 7 o'clock

Dear Peake,

Tomorrow *peremptorily* I *must* settle with *Sir W. Geary* and there is still a Purse of *ready money* deficient, which as positively I must produce by four o'clock—It has just occurr'd to me that a little Lift might be got where you are—I mean by asking Hart from me as a *most material Favour* to discount a Company's[?] Bill for *£100*. I most seriously entreat you to manage this if possible—everything shall give [way] to the punctuality of answering this exigency but by G–d the money must be raised— | Yrs ever | R B S.

283. To Anne Ogle

Pub.: Sichel, ii. 269.

[*Early 1797?*]

. . . I have made Hoppner[2] alter what you mentioned in

in explaining hammering alarming etc. etc. Dr. Goodenough and Mr. Ford have agreed, without waiting the execution of their proposed Deed, and giving up the point of having the custody of some £1 Shares. I have seen Mr. Morland. . . . The Deed is now compleat and ready for inrolment without him which I think shd. not be delayed beyond Monday. It will give life and vigour to all future matters' (Harvard MS.).

[6] Charles Carpenter, attorney, of 4 King's Arms Yard, Coleman Street.

[7] See Smyth, p. 43' for S.'s carelessness about opening letters.

[1] Dr. James Ford died on 17 Dec. 1795 and willed his interest in D.L.Th. to his son-in-law, Samuel Goodenough, D.C.L. (1743–1827), and to three sons, Thomas, James, and Richard. The last-named (1758–1806), a London magistrate, conducted negotiations with S.

[2] John Hoppner, R.A. (1758–1810). His portrait of Mrs. S. carrying a child was exhibited at the Royal Academy in

the picture, and he was quite obliged to me for the remark and saw the fault directly. It is really the loveliest thing that ever was seen—immensely admired.

284. To John Grubb

Harvard MS. *Address*: J. Grubb Esqr: *Wm.*: 1794

[*13 Jan. 1797*]
Friday

My Dear Sir

I cannot tell you how mortified I am that you should have suffer'd any apprehensions to give you the uneasiness I understand they have. Since the final tho' long retarded enrolment of the Trust-Deed rely on it nothing can hurt us. I want *tomorrow* to advertise for Every claim[1]—and I will pledge my Life and Honor on not one difficulty or discredit remaining in a month. Pray if *possible* let us meet to Night. I want the advertisement to be in tomorrow and that you should see it first. Mr. Westley Mr. Richardson and Mr. Carpenter will meet you here at nine, and I am confident on a full view of and explanation of our situation, we shall go satisfied to bed. | Yours truly | R B Sheridan

285. To——

Yale MS. *Pub.*: Moore, ii. 216–19.

26 Feb. [*1797?*]

Sir,

I am very sorry that I have been so circumstanced as to have been obliged to disappoint you respecting the Payment

1797: see W. McKay and W. Roberts, *John Hoppner, R.A.* (1909), pp. 235–6.

[1] Winston, 1793–7, includes an advertisement dated 14 Jan. 1797, and reading: 'The Trust Deed being now Enrolled, having been compleated by the extinction of all the Mortgage Incumbrances, and a new arrangement made in the property of the Theatre, any person having any unsettled demand on the same, or on the late Thomas Linley Esq. or on R. B. Sheridan Esq. is requested to send an account to Messrs Sleigh and Jones, Whitehall.'

of the 500 Guineas.[1] When I gave the Draughts on Lord Sefton[2] I had every reason to be assured He would accept them as Strangger[?][3] had also. I enclose you, as you will see by his Desire, the Letter in which He excuses his not being able to pay me this Part of a larger sum he owes me and I cannot refuse him any time He requires however inconvenient to me. I also enclose you two Draughts accepted by a Gentleman from whom the money will be due to me and on whose punctuality I can rely. I extremely regret that I cannot at this juncture command the money.

At the same time that I regret your being put to any inconvenience by this Delay, I cannot help adverting to the circumstance which perhaps misled me into the expectation that you would not unwillingly allow me any reasonable time I might want for the Payment of this Bet. The circumstance I mean, however discreditable the plea, is the total inebriety of some of the Party particularly of myself when I made this preposterous Bet. I doubt not you will remember having yourself observed on this circumstance to a common Friend the next day with an intimation that you should not object to being off. And for my Part when I was informed that I had made such a Bet and for such a sum, the first such Folly on the Face of it on my Part, and the latter so out of my Practice[4] I certainly should have proposed the cancelling it but that from the intimation reported to me I hoped the proposition might come from you.

I hope I need not for a moment beg you not to imagine that I am now alluding to these circumstances as the slightest invalidation of your due.—So much the contrary that I most perfectly admit that from your not having heard anything further from me on the subject, and especially after I might have heard that if I desired it the Bet might be off you had every reason to conclude that I was satisfied with the wager and whether made in wine or not was desirous of

[1] Shortly before 5 Jan. 1796 it was reported that 'Mr. Sheridan has taken 100 Gs. to return 500, if he does not furnish and bring out at D. L. a Comedy, an Opera and a Farce in the Course of the present Season' (Folger MS. T. a. 143).

[2] William Molyneux, 2nd Earl of Sefton (1772–1838).

[3] Carelessly written. Whitbread MS. 4123 mentions S.'s bond to R. Griffin and T. Stanger dated 10 Dec. 1800 and for £676. *7s. 6d.*

[4] But cf. Moore, ii. 215–16.

abiding by it. And this was further confirmed by my receiving soon after from you £100 on another Bet won by me.

Having I think put this Point very fairly I again repeat that my only motive for alluding to the matter was as some explanation of my seeming dilatoriness which certainly did in part arise from always conceiving that whenever I should state what was my real wish the Day after the Bet was made, you would be the more disposed to allow a little Time, the same statement admitting as it must the Bet to be as clearly and as fairly won as possible, in short as if I had insisted on it myself the next morning.

I have said more perhaps on the subject than can be necessary—but I should regret to appear negligent to an application for a just claim. | I have the Honor to be | Sir, Your obedient Servant | R B Sheridan.

Hertford-St.[1]
Feb. 26th.

286. To Richard Peake

Salt MS. *Address*: Mr. Peake | Treasury | Drury-Lane | Theatre. *Dock.*: R B S

[*1797?*]
Monday Evening

Dear Peake,

The House up unexpectedly soon—certainly *nothing looks like Peace*—Tho' Pitts Friends may try to put that contruction on his Words, and may have that effect for a Day or two. I would close *half* tomorrow at a *three Quarters* instead of one per Cent Profit. Write instead of going to *B.* but avoid using my name | Yrs | R B S.

Send my account to Night.
dont let Mrs. Linley be forgot, tell Westley she must have money to Night.[2] Beg him to return the enclosed in my account.

[1] S. did not live there until 1795, so Moore's dating (1793) for this letter is wrong.

[2] Her weekly salary as wardrobe mistress was £1. 10*s.* 0*d.*, but on 9 March 1797 she was paid £10. See Add. MS. 29710, f. 88.

287. To His Wife

Osborn MS. *Address*: London April twelfth 1797 | Mrs. Sheridan | St. Mary's | Southampton *Fr.*: Free | R B Sheridan *Pm.*: May Fair

12 Apr. 1797
Wednesday

My Beloved, I am afraid you will think me whimsical and uncertain but hear Dan out and I think you will agree with me. I find Mornit[1] very averse to the idea of travel[l]ing with Robin to so far. She describes him as very restless at Night, and in other respects so that He should not be jumbled about for fear of heating him. He is cutting these nasty double Teeth but perfectly well—now she really talk'd so sensibly about all this, that I cannot bring myself to oppose what she says. The House at St. Mary's must be crouded and his Room close, and the more fuss which I know you all would make with him might fret and heat him. I am sure you will think it best on the whole and I have desired Mornit to write herself. He goes out every Day and has the Coach and the Park all to himself. I love him better than my eyes, and there has been double caution as to anyone coming near him since you have been away—

near six

I am just returned from the Park and whom do you think I have been walking with—Robin—you would die to see him picking up dry leaves on the Grass. My sweet Hecca I meant to have written you a long Letter but I have million[s] of things to do of my own affairs, having been so much lately at that vile House morning and evening.[2] Tomorrow I will decide all my motions. Robin of course goes to Polesden—what a heavenly Day this has been—the first sweet Spring Day ma[k]es me melancholy always for particular Reasons[3]—

[1] Charles's nurse.

[2] He had made a long speech on advances to the Emperor on 4 Apr. (*Speeches*, iv. 374–96).

[3] Quoted by Rae, ii. 202.

O my idle Gypsey—you dont write me half enough what you do and how you are etc.

I must tell you something droll about the Duke of Bedford who wants me to join a Party going to Wobourn[1]—and proposes afterwards a Ladies Party and that we should bring Anne—

bless your knees.

288. To His Wife

Osborn MS.

[*1797?*]
Thursday
5 o'clock

My Soul's beloved,

I am at this moment getting into the Curricle. Pray don't leave St. Mary's—I call but for an hour at Polesden—and *by Heaven* will be with you soon after breakfast tomorrow—and on Sunday we will return. I must see St. Mary's again—and my Belle[?][2]

Bless your bones. I have done all my business. | S.

289. To John Grubb

Grubbe MS. *Address*: J. Grubb Esq *Dock.*: Sheridan to Grubb | 31.18.6[3]

[*c. 12 May 1797?*]

Dear Grubb

I have got a Person here waiting to go off at six in the morn to Polesden. Make the Deductions but for God's sake the remainder in Notes—a Draught would do me good—and you can replace | Yours ever | R B S.

[1] Fox mentioned 'a kind of annual party there in this month', in a letter to Holland from Woburn of 28 July 1795. He also wrote to him from Woburn on 6 July 1797 (Add. MS. 47572, ff. 74, 169).

[2] One word written over another.

[3] Cf. 'Grubb's Account with Sheridan: Items and Vouchers to be inquired into . . . 12 May 1797—31.8.6 qu. when paid to Sh.' (Grubbe MS.).

290. To John Grubb

Harvard MS. *Address*: J Grubb Esq | Stage Door | Drury-Lane *Fr.*: R B Sheridan

[*1797?*]

Dear Grubb.

I have settled a suspension of hostilities with the Enemy Banker (N.B. whom I will subdue) till Monday—and appointed a meeting for Saturday tomorrow I give to the House of Commons Pro Aris et Focis.[1] Pray tell Richardson to meet me there and let us spend all Saturday together | yours ever | R B S.

Pray send £10 for *subsistance*

291. To William Adam

Adam MS. *Address*: W. Adam Esq. *Dock.*: Sheridan | At the time of the proposal to make a Ministry without Fox.[2] | Summer 1797.

Summer 1797

Dear Adam,

Altho' my own business is of great importance, I want to

[1] To fight for one's prized possessions, religion and home. Possibly this refers to S.'s speech on the naval mutiny, on Friday, 2 June. See *Speeches*, iv. 424–8. D.L.Th. Nightly Accounts, 1796 and 1797 (Folger MS.) contain a note of a payment of £10 to S. on 3 June.

[2] *The Caledonian Mercury*, 8 June 1797, reported: 'A negociation, it is rumoured, was on foot through the principall part of last week, for the arrangement of a joint administration from the opposite parties, of which neither Mr. Pitt nor Mr. Fox was to form a part. It was opened under the immediate recommendation of a certain personage, through the medium of Lord Thurlow: A Parliamentary Reform, an abolition of sinecure places etc. formed the preliminary basis. The Dukes of Bedford and Northumberland, Earl Moira and Mr. Sheridan on the one side; and Earl Spencer, Lord Grenville, and Mr. Secretary Dundas on the other, had two interviews, and had proceeded to many important arrangements when the negociation suddenly broke off on the nomination of the Lord Lieutenancy of Ireland, on which the future mode of governing that Kingdom evidently turned.' Alnwick MSS., LVIII, ff. 182–230, reveal that some initiative was shown (as in the 'Armed Neutrality' of 1788) by Moira and Sinclair. Negotiations were first reported by Moira to Northumberland on 15 May (f. 182), and were declared at an end by Sinclair on 17 June (f. 230). Fox may have feared that S. would take the lead, and in a letter to Lauderdale (Add. MS. 47564, f. 14) on the day (2 June) of S.'s

talk over a Political matter of so much more consequence that I wish much you could meet me *to Night* anywhere you please in my Neighbourhood—and name your own hour. I dine at Lord Petries[1]— | yours ever | R B Sheridan

Where does Thurlow live now?[2]

292. To Richard Peake

Harvard MS. *Address*: To Mr. Peake. *Dock.*: Miss Caroline Hicks | Mr. Stidders New Street | No. 16, Brompton.

25 June 1797

Dear Sir

It is my Desire that Miss C. Hicks[3] should be engaged at our Theatre—and we are convinced Mr. Grubb will approve it—and as there is not now time to settle the Terms, she is to be considered as engaged at £1. 10 per week and the Theatre to find her instruction 'till a further arrangement shall be made | R B Sheridan | Jno. Grubb[4] | J. Richardson[4]

June 25
1797

293. To Thomas Anson[5]

The Earl of Lichfield MS. From Col. R. P. F. White's transcript. *Pub.*: J. C. Wedgwood, 'Staffordshire Members of Parliament,

conciliatory speech on the naval mutiny, suggested that Guilford, Bedford, Grey, and Lauderdale might, 'get the Government'. He added, 'you will observe that I have not named Sheridan, tho' he certainly would and ought to make part of such a system as I have mentioned; but I must confess that his mode of conduct lately convinces me that would not add much to the strength of it. What I allude to particularly is that incurable itch that he seems to have of distinguishing his conduct from that of those with whom he wishes to be supposed united.'

[1] Robert Edward, 9th Lord Petre (1742–1801). His town house was at 13 Park Lane.

[2] 13 St. James's Square, and Knight's Hill, near Dulwich.

[3] She took walk-on parts until her début (as S.'s protégée), on 25 Mar. 1802, as Perdita. See *The Oracle*, 26 Mar. 1802.

[4] Their signatures.

[5] Thomas Anson (1767–1818) 'was undoubtedly the mainstay of Whiggism in Staffordshire' (J. C. Wedgwood, op. cit., p. 4). He was created Viscount Anson of Shugborough, through Fox, in 1806.

1780–1841', *Collections for a History of Staffordshire*, 1933 (ed. William Salt Arch. Soc., Kendal, 1934), iii. 5. *Address*: T. Anson Esqr.

4 July 1797

My Dear Sir

I think you are entirely right in your decision, and the Protest on the occasion appears to me to be as well drawn up as possible. The independent interest in Staffordshire has not been tried for a long time and I have a high opinion of its strength, in the present case however I think the favourable opportunity for a Public meeting in some measure pass'd by.[1] The effects of the meeting and the existing negotiations for Peace are against us. I trust notwithstanding that you will have the Petition numerously sign'd, and under the present circumstance it *certainly* will be the preferable mode of Proceeding.

I should have been happy to have waited on you in Staffordshire, and hope to have that Pleasure some other opportunity.

I beg my Respects to Mrs. Anson and am | Dear Sir | Yours very truly | R B Sheridan

Hertford St.

July 4th. 1797.

294. To Lady Webster[2]

Holland House MS., S. 84. *Address*: Lady Webster. *Dock*.: from S. the Rivals R B Sheridan

[*Before 6 July 1797*]

I am afraid the House of Commons will preclude all

[1] S. commented on a letter addressed by Anson and his friends to the High Sheriff of Staffordshire, Sir Robert Lawley, Bart. This is printed by Wedgwood, op. cit., pp. 4–5. The Foxites complained that they had asked the High Sheriff to call a meeting of the Stafford freeholders and inhabitants to consider 'the alarming state of public affairs, and the propriety of a Petition to His Majesty, praying him to dismiss his present Ministers from his Councils for ever'; but Lawley had merely called together the noblemen, gentlemen, clergymen, and freeholders, and omitted any summons to the general inhabitants.

[2] Elizabeth Vassall married Sir Godfrey Webster in 1786, but parted from him in 1795. This marriage was annulled on 4 July 1797, and she married Lord Holland two days later. She 'made friends' with S. in autumn 1793, but noted that he had behaved 'abominably' to her two years earlier. See *The Journal of Elizabeth Lady Holland* (ed. the Earl of Ilchester, 1908), i. 98.

chance of my seeing you to Night. I had rather you would not listen to the Play,[1] from my good will to the Author, and yet I would not have your attention otherwise engaged

Monday

295. To Richard Peake

McAdam MS. *Address*: Mr. Peake *Dock.*: Cook Piazza Order

[*Summer 1797?*]

Dear Peake

Mr. Kemble must be settled with before He goes. The least we can do is a bill with interest payable the moment the House opens. See Mr. Grubb immediately He will give the proper directions to Westley and send a messenger this Day to Hampstead for the acceptance. | Yours | R B Sheridan

Sunday morning

I have given him a Draught for fifty guineas[2] dated 13th:

296. To John Grubb, Richard Wroughton, and Richard Peake

Harvard MS. *Address*: Messrs: Grubb | Wroughton | and | Peake *Wm.*: 1795

[*July 1797?*]

O most uncertain! Here is one Letter from Peake *assuring* me you *will come to Polesden*[3] and desiring my chaise to meet you at Mitcham, and here is another from Richardson assuring me you are to dine at the *Percy*[4] and that I must come to you! both are of the same Date and neither reach'd

[1] *The Rivals*, from the docketing.

[2] The D.L.Th. ledger, Receipts and Payments, 1797–8 (Folger MS.), notes under the date, 3 Oct. 1797: 'Mr. Kemble for Mr. Sheridan's Draft arrears £52. 10. 0. . . .'

[3] D.L.Th. Nightly Accounts, 1796 and 1797 (Folger MS.) records the payment of £1. 13*s.* 0*d.* on 16 July 1797 for 'Chaise hire Mr. G., Mr. W. and Peake to Polsdon'.

[4] Percy Coffee-House, Rathbone Place.

me till this morning. What can I decide? I think Peake the steadier authority, so I send the chaise. If that does not find you, I shall come to Town in the Evening, for meet we must tho here would be so much pleasanter. | yours | R B S

297. To His Wife

Harvard MS.

[*July 1797?*]
Wooburn
Friday Night

My pretty Wench, now are you fast asleep—your green eyes closed—and your arm under one of your rosy cheeks—but we really keep such good Hours here that my best Time to write to you is when we separate at Night. In the morning there is plenty to do—and we dine at half past four—and always walk out before coffee—and the Post goes at six. Then I have been playing every Day at Tennis[1]—tho' I can't play the least—but all strong exercise agrees with me.—In short the Party is certainly very well put together; and I see a number of old Friends in very good spirits and apparently very glad at my coming—and as to wine I assure you we are moderation itself, and I am particularly well—and should like it all very well if I had Hecca under the roof. Yet either I or They are alter'd for it is not to me anything really Jolly or pleasant. I must tell you, whom we consist of—1. C. Fox 2. Fitzpatrick 3. Hare[2] 4. Lord John Townshend (all pleasant as possible) 5. Sheridan (stupid) 6. Erskine (in great spirits) 7. Francis (laugh'd at)[3] 8. Lord Thurlow (first Question after Robin which I told him I should write you word of) 9. Richardson 10. Adair,[4] 11. Lord John Russell (my particular Favourite)[5]

[1] The largest tennis court in England was completed at Woburn in Aug. 1792. See *The Oracle*, 27 Aug. 1792.

[2] James Hare (1747–1804), wit. M.P. for Knaresborough, 1781–1804.

[3] Philip Francis (1740–1818). He was at Woburn in July 1798, July 1799, and July 1801. See *The Francis Letters* (ed. B. Francis and E. Keary, n.d.), ii. 443, 451, 483; and J. Parkes and H. Merivale, *Memoirs of Sir Philip Francis* (1867), ii. 315.

[4] Robert Adair (1763–1855), a warm friend of Fox.

[5] 1766–1839. He became 6th Duke of Bedford in 1802.

12. E. Faulkner,[1] 13. Dudley North (very pl[e]asant)[2] 14. Lord R. Spencer, 15. Lord Holland 16. Duke of Bedford.[3] Then there is Riding House Tennis Court, Billiards Farm Fishing etc. etc. and if you will come on the 10th of September the Duke will have your own Party and Lady John[4] will meet you. Of course I have made no promise but He is very friendly and good-natured. Bless thy Heart my only real Pleasure on earth! Dan will go to Bed.—

London Wednesday

Here is a Hop in my Letter and yesterday I had not time to explain that as no Post went on Saturday from Wooburn I brought away my Letter with me on Sunday when I came up with the Duke in his Sociable.[5] These three Days I have been set[t]ling Theatrical matters—and tomorrow without fail I set out for Winchester and then Dearest Hecca let us not separate again—

I have millions to say to you but why do you not write my Hecca—what harm even if one Letter were to miss me on the Road—you know how unpleasant the Day is to me when I have not had a Line. I must trim you when I see you for this.

Nothing was ever more compleat than your new carriage.—
Bless you a thousand times | S.

298. To His Wife

Osborn MS. *Address*: London August twenty first 1797 | Mrs. Sheridan | Dean of Winchester's | St. Mary's | Southampton. *Fr.*: Free | R B Sheridan

21 Aug. 1797
Monday

My Life my Soul

Thanks for your loved Letters which are the only Lights

[1] Everard Fawkener, one of the Commissioners of Stamps. He died in Oct. 1803.

[2] Dudley Long-North (1748–1829), Whig M.P. for Banbury, 1790–1812.

[3] This list is quoted in Rae, ii. 223.

[4] Georgiana Byng, daughter of the 4th Viscount Torrington, married Lord John Russell in 1786. She died on 11 Oct. 1801.

[5] 'An open, four-wheeled carriage having two seats facing each other and a box-seat for the driver 1794' (*Shorter Oxford Dictionary*).

of my Days at this moment. But I shall settle everything yet—and we will be comfortable and separate no more—

On Wednesday nothing shall stop me—believe me my Heart when I shew you what has detain'd me you will say it has been inevitable.[1] Our Darling is charmingly

I fear fear about S. the curricle at all Events. The man should go first

299. To John Grubb

Harvard MS. *Address*: Chichester September tenth 1797 | John Grubb Esq | No 14, Store St. | Tottenham-Court-Road | London *Fr.*: R B Sheridan

10 Sept. 1797
Sunday

Dear Grubb,

Notwithstanding the shabby conduct of the Bankers I would keep faith by sending the Receipts as before. The £25 you will recollect is to pay a Note of yours for £1000 and with our express consent.

manage only tomorrow among you and I will work like a Horse and all shall be right. I shall be after this but a few hours— | Yours ever | R B S.

300. To John Grubb

Harvard MS.

[*1797?*]
Sunday

Dear Grubb,

I will be at the House early on tuesday morn—better not advertise till wednesday. I wish you would take an Egg and Bacon dinner with me tomorrow at Polesden. I would come on to Town but I know I shall be at the House *sooner* by

[1] He went to Southampton as promised, and postponed the important completion of the deeds for the lease and release of Polesden, until 31 Aug. See Abel Jenkins's letter from New Inn, on 26 Aug. (Harvard MS.), where Jenkins adds that he has written to S. at Southampton and to Richardson about another share in D.L.Th. to be assigned to Sir William Geary as security.

sleeping there. I find bathing so necessary for Mrs. S. that I must leave her here. Let me dine in the Theatre tuesday and not quit it 'till the Opening. I am ready for the greatest exertion | Your ever | R B S.

301. To Richard Peake

McAdam MS. *Dock.*: Recd. J R

Sept. 19th: 1797

£20

Please to pay tho' it is damn'd foolish, that Plunderer Mr. Joe Richardson twenty Pounds on my account you you were a Booby for telling him [what] you are likely to have.— | R B Sheri[1]

To Mr. Peake

302. To His Wife

Osborn MS. *Address*: London September twentieth 1797 | Mrs. Sheridan | Bognor Rocks | Chichester | Sussex *Fr.*: Free | R B Sheridan

20 Sept. 1797
Wednesday—

Only one Line my Soul's adored.—The Theatre open'd yesterday after incredible exertions[2]—and all will go on famously—

O my Wench I had only a little scrap of a Letter to Day, and by Heaven I have no other Pleasure in all the Day but in opening your *Chichester* mark'd Paper.

[1] Manuscript torn.

[2] 'With a Comedy called *The School for Scandal*' (*The Star*, 19 Sept. 1797). The announcement stated that no gifts would be permitted to servants of the theatre in future; and that a lower saloon had now been provided by the Wooburn Street entrance 'for the accommodation of frequenters of the Pit previous to opening the office doors of admission'. None of this was in the advertisement of 18 Sept., which merely announced the opening. A later report (*The Star*, 21 Sept. 1797) added that by narrowing the stage and lowering the proscenium, the proprietors had greatly improved audibility in the theatre. See, also, Add. MS. 35118, f. 73.

Yes not a bit of seal or wafer in yours yesterday,—Lord Malmsbury is now in London[1]—all Hopes of Peace gone—it will end in our coming into office[2] which I solemnly protest I hate the thought of[3]—I must see Fox in my way to Bognor. | S.

303. [To John Grubb]

Harvard MS. *Address*: J. Grubb Esq. | Store-St. | Bedford-Square | To be taken to him immediately *Fr.*: R B Sheridan *Wm.*: 1796

[*Oct. 1797?*]

My Lord Treasurer,

Having an opportunity to send a Line to Town, I wish to say that those two Lines in Cumberland's address[4] alluding to the Mutiny 'Something they ow'd their country' really ought not to be spoken on our Stage.—He may print them if He pleases—I am sure Richardson is of my mind—

I would pay the Company stoutly on *Saturday*,[5] and we will have an official committee to supply deficiencies on monday. I would put up a Notice in the Green Room 'that such Performers as chose to compliment the Charity with their Performance should send notice to the Treasury'—and their names will be known. This I would do certainly—or from the example of the last Benefit they will affect to think that they only take the money from our Pockets and not from the Charity. | Yours ever | R B S.

[1] Negotiations broke down and Malmesbury left Lille on 18 Sept., reaching London two days later.

[2] It did not, but even Burke thought that the only alternative administration to Pitt's must be provided by Bedford, Northumberland, Guilford and Lansdowne, 'under the direction of Mr. Sheridan and Mr. Fox' (*Epistolary Correspondence of . . . Burke and Dr. French Laurence* (1827), p. 212).

[3] This sentence is quoted by Rae, ii. 249–50, but misdated 1799.

[4] A benefit performance was given at D.L.Th. on 27 Oct. 1797, for the dependants of sailors killed under Viscount Duncan on 14 Feb. An address by Cumberland began:

To those immortal shades, whose vital gore
Floats on the waves that tinge Batavia's shore
We consecrate the bounties of this night

A further forty-one lines were spoken, but they contain no references to the naval mutinies at Portsmouth and the Nore in May and June 1797. See *The Star*, 30 Oct. 1797.

[5] D.L.Th. Cash Book 1797–9 and Salaries (Folger MS.) notes that on 30 Sept. 1797, Grubb handed over £195 in a 'Draft for Company'; and on 7 Oct., £300 'Cash as Dfts.'

304. To John Grubb

Harvard MS. *Address*: J Grubb Esq. *Wm.*: 1795

[*Before Nov. 1797?*]

My Dear Sir,

Mr. Wright will give you this—we cannot make out whether the man is withdrawn or not. But He is strongly of opinion that paying it would be the worst thing. I have informed him of your Friendly exertions, and the better way will be to deposit the £200 in his Hands and He will indemnify the Sheriff which will give me 'till November. I am certain then of making a different settlement with Anderson and the £200 may go to another matter. I return Tuesday and we will lay our Shoulders to the wheel in earnest.| yours ever | R B Sheridan

Tho' we parted so late I got hold of Alderman Coombe, and He will go to work for Richardson without loss of an hour.[1]

Sunday morning

305. [To John Grubb]

Harvard MS.

[*1797?*]

O most ACCURATE

Short Accounts make *long* Friends

I am a Foe to Proverbs—but this *Experience* the only true Teacher has made me a Convert to.—

I seriously wish that with Peake you would settle as exactly as possible *an account* between us.—Citizen[2]

[1] Harvey Christian Combe (*c.* 1752–1818) was M.P. for London, 1796–1817. At the meeting of the renters of D.L.Th. on 30 Nov. 1797 one of the mortgages reported as paid off was for £2,520. 15*s.* 7*d.*, in the name of 'Messrs. Skinner, Combe and others, trustees for Mr. Richardson'. See the *Monthly Mirror*, 1st Ser., iv (1797), 379.

[2] A term frequently used in the Sheridan circle in 1795–7. S. himself is called 'Citizen Sheridan' in the *True Briton*, 20 Nov. 1795.

Richardson leaves me totally in the Lurch[1] at least for some Time.—

You will see by the Papers I send by Peake that cost what it will I must risk my existence to meet the present exigency.

306. To Richard Peake

Osborn MS. *Address*: Mr. Peake *Dock.*: Mr. Sheridan about Mr. Lacy

27 Nov. [*1797*]

Pray do not deny Lacy his Pittance[2] for this week—I will pledge myself that the Board shall allow it | R B S.

Monday
Novbr. 27

307. To John Grubb

Harvard MS.

[*Shorty before 30 Nov. 1797*]

Dear Grubb—

at *five tomorrow*

— I am moving Heaven and Earth for ways and means.

I mean to attend Franco's meeting on Thursday[3]—and meet openly every attempt to discredit us— | Yrs ever | R B S

[1] In failing to purchase a share in the management of D.L.Th., according to the agreement of 19 Sept. 1795. 'The former temporary agreement between them being cancelled by mutual consent' (New York Public Library MS.: 'Assignment of twelve Debentures . . . for Mrs. S. Richardson . . .'). As early as 12 Aug. 1789, S. had conveyed a one-sixteenth share in D.L.Th. to Richardson. It was assigned to Skinner and Wilkes.

[2] D.L.Th. Receipts and Payments, 1797–8 (Folger MS.) notes payments of four guineas to Lacy on 25 Nov. and 2 Dec. 1797.

[3] Jacob Franco, as an executor of Raphael Franco and a part-sharer in the 1793 indenture, called a meeting to find out what had happened to the money subscribed for the building of the new D.L.Th. After an adjournment, the matter was discussed fully at the London Tavern, Bishopsgate Street, on 30 Nov. Richard Troward, as solicitor to the Trust, placed a complete set of accounts before the subscribers and this led to an apology by Franco for his suspicions, and to a motion expressing the warmest thanks of the meeting for 'the manly, just, and honourable conduct of R. B. Sheridan, Esq., both on the present occasion, and throughout the circumstances attending the rebuilding of the theatre' (*Monthly Mirror*, 1st Ser., iv (1797), 378–9).

308. To Richard Wilson

Fitzwilliam Museum, Cambridge: Ashcombe MS. i. 36. *Address*: R. Wilson Esq: | Bartletts-Buildings | Holbourn.

[*29 Nov. 1797?*]

My Dear Sir,

as Representative of Divers Renters-Shares[1] you will much oblige me by attending the meeting tomorrow at the London Tavern— | yours etc. | R B Sheridan

Richardson is ill or He would have call'd—

309. [To Richard Peake?]

McAdam MS.

5 Dec. 1797

If you have not another Pound in the House you must give me twenty Guineas of my money this Night. | R B Sheridan

Dec. 5th. 1797.

310. To John Grubb

Harvard MS. *Address*: J. Grubb Esqr.

[*1797–8?*]

Polesden

Sunday Evening.

My Dear Sir,

Carpenter and I are here in rather a melancholy Tête a Tête for want of you and Richardson—tho' our general Projects are very consolatory. Pray do not let the non-payment of *his* advance for me cloud the Prospect. He will give you this. Your difficulties and Richardsons as far as they are pressing may certainly be settled for £500. I must

[1] Wilson also owned five renters' shares in D.L.Th.

hope Richardson has at this moment produced means infinitely beyond this. | yours | R B Sheridan

N.B. Carpenter will be infinitely distress'd without the £600[1]

311. [To Richard Peake]

Harvard MS. *Wm.*: /96

[*1797–8?*]
near 8

I am still in chase of Franco[2]

—have Jones with [me] now and am going to meet Troward and then F. Franco[3] and Carpenter—I send the Coach and a man assure Grubb all shall go right. The present attack on him weighs heaviest on me. I'll call at Brompton tomorrow | yrs | R B S

312. To Richard Peake

N.L.I. MS. 3901, ff. 13–14. *Address*: Mr. Peake | at Mr. Sheridans *Dock.*: Mr. Sheridan *Wm.*: 1794

[*1797–8?*]

Private

Wright has settled that everything shall be suspended till twelve o'clock tomorrow He is now gone to *Graham*.[4] Most of the money will be paid to Night tell Mr. G's clerk to call

[1] The Grubbe MSS. include a note by Grubb of the securities he had given to D.L.Th. One of them (possibly given on this occasion) was 'An Eligit issued by Carpenter on the above [i.e. Grubb's Hampshire] estate being for a Sum lent to Mr. Sheridan for payment of which the Acceptance of the Proprietors was afterwards given: £500'.

[2] Jacob Franco wrote to a newspaper, from Gerrard's Cross on 2 Dec. 1797, to say that he was 'so thoroughly dissatisfied' with D.L.Th. that he was 'ready to allow a very *liberal discount* to anybody who will buy his share of the mortgage, notwithstanding Mr. Sheridan's assertion in favour of the security, and his promise of its being paid off in a month' (Winston, 1798–1801).

[3] Francis Franco.

[4] D.L.Th. Ledger, 1795 to 1799 (Folger MS.) contains twenty-six entries of payments to Wright and Graham, Sheriff's officers, between 11 Nov. 1797 and Nov. 1798, totalling £1,939. The first is for £150 'to settle Barron's action'. He was an ironmonger.

on me at 12 tomorrow. We are eating Beef-steak at your House—but wanting to see you *alone*. I will settle Shaw's business[1] in the morning— | Yrs | R B S

313. To William Adam

Adam MS. *Dock.*: Mr. Sheridan | 20th Jany. 1798

20 Jan. 1798
Theatre

My Dear Adam,

If you are still sitting I'll come to you if you think it right *directly*. But I really have been very particularly engaged by private business here. Should you be passing this way and take a Peep at Blue-beard[2]—Birchall[3] is now here—and in one moment we may settle Coutts' business[4] | Yours ever | R B S.

314. To Jonathan Sadler

Harvard MS. *Address*: Jno. Sadler Esq *Dock.*: 25 Janry. 1798 | Mr. Sheridan

Thursday
January 25th: *1798*

Sir,

Seeing you in the Place we met yesterday must certainly remind me that we ought to have no contention if it can be avoided—and Mr. Davis's statement that you are really so much press'd yourself[5] makes me very anxious that anything of the sort should be avoided. I will meet you with Mr.

[1] Thomas Shaw, the D.L.Th. band leader, noted in his 'Account rendered to R.B.S.' (Salt MS.) a payment of £18. 7*s.* 0*d.* in 1797–8, 'For a Bill of Expences paid to Wright and Laver when I was arrested on account of your not paying my demands which you promised to be answerable for.'

[2] George Colman the Younger's *Blue Beard; or, Female Curiosity* was first produced at D.L.Th. on 16 Jan. 1798.

[3] Joseph Burchell.

[4] D.L.Th. Receipts and Payments, 1798–9 (Folger MS.) notes on 6 Sept. 1798, 'Mr. Sheridan advanced to pay what was received from Messrs Coutts £2000.' Cf. iii. 267, no. 20.

[5] In a letter (Salt MS.) to S. from Lothbury, 'Saturday', Sadler asked for a draft for £200 and mentioned that he had to pay for grates. The D.L.Th. Cash Book 1797–9, and Salaries (Folger MS.) records on 19 Jan. 1799 a payment of £100 for 'Saddler's first Bill'.

Davis tomorrow or saturday and I am confident you will see by the Proposition I shall make that it is very far from my intention or wish to injure you. | Yours etc. etc. | R B Sheridan.

315. To Richard Peake

Egerton MS. 1975, ff. 77–78 *Address*: Mr. Peake *Dock*: Mr. Sheridan

[*Jan. 1798?*]
Polesden

I came to this Place only to meet you and am much disappointed—

I must *rely* on your concerting measures with Burgess[1] respecting my Taxes.[2] It is the only personal exertion and assistance I will ask of you. Whoever advances may take the first Nights receipts,[3] discounting small acceptances with a Douceur [?] must be the way— | Yours truly | R B S.

316. To S. W. Wadeson[4]

Harvard MS. *Address*: Wadeson Esq. | Austin-Friars *Wm.*: 1796

[*1798?*][5]

Dear Sir,

A Slight Cold and this villainous Day prevents my coming to you 'till the same hour tomorrow | Yours truly | R B Sheridan

Tuesday

I think there must be some mistake respecting Smith as I can't learn that I ever dealt with such a Person.

[1] Henry Burgess, solicitor, of 40 Curzon Street, became one of S.'s intimate friends and negotiators.

[2] D.L.Th. account book contains the following entry under 29 Jan. 1798: 'Taxes Hertford St Mr. Sher 22. 12. 10'. See Add. MS. 29710, f. 107.

[3] Of *The Stranger*?

[4] Samuel Wadeson was an attorney of the King's Bench and Common Pleas: see J. Hughes, *The New Law List* (1798), p. 54.

[5] A note (Harvard MS.) in Richardson's hand reads: 'Messrs. Sheridan and Richardson engage to meet Mr. Hutchinson at Mr. Waideson's in Austin Friars at ½ past one on Wednesday next March 9th. 1798.' Hutchinson was an attorney who represented Francis Hanrott, one of the renters.

317. To John Grubb

Grubbe MS. *Address*: J Grubb Esq *Wm.*: 1797

[*21 Feb. 1798*][1]
Star and Garter
Pall-Mall

Send me pray two Pound or I shall be stuck here for my reckoning.

I will be at the Theatre at nine | Yrs | R B S

318. To John Grubb

Harvard MS. *Address*: John Grubb Esq. | No. 14 Store-St. *Wm.*. 1796

[*1798?*]

Dear Grubb

For the Muse's and money's sake exert yourself in settling with Siddons[2]—£30 per week we could engage for with a Share of mine—I mean for arrears[3]—and I think Peake could [get] £500 at six months from Playfair.[4] I shall return immediately but I was obliged to go— | yours ever | R B S.

Wine totally renounced! go and do likewise

[1] 'Grubbs Account with Sheridan' includes the following item: '21 Feby 1798: £2 to Sheridan at Star and Garter Pall Mall.' (Grubbe MS.)

[2] Grubb's accounts mention payments to Mrs. Siddons only in March 1798. Between 5 and 27 March, he paid Siddons seven sums of £120 (Grubbe MSS.). On 7 January she had bewailed the fact that she could 'get no money from the theatre. My precious two thousand pounds are swallowed up in that drowning gulf, from whom no plea of right or justice can save its victims' (T. Campbell, *Life of Mrs. Siddons* (1839), p. 286). But S. was now anxious not to lose her, for she was required to play the lead in *The Stranger*.

[3] It had been agreed in the King's Bench on 17 Feb. 1797, that William Siddons had 'sustained damage' of £648. 7*s*. 6*d*. and costs of £12. 4*s*. 2*d*. from S., Grubb, and Richardson. See Add. MS. 44919, f. 67.

[4] D.L.Th. Ledger, 1795 to 1799 (Folger MS.) records on 16 Apr. 1798 a payment of £70 'To Cash on Playf. Acct.' This may be either George Playfair, attorney, Holloway; or Playfair, wax chandlers, 38 Little Eastcheap.

319. To John Grubb

Harvard MS.

[*Just before 24 Mar. 1798*]

Dear Grubb

I have reasons remarkable for deferring the Stranger[1] a few Days which I will explain to you | Yours | R B S.

320. To His Wife

Osborn MS. *Wm.*: 1797

[*Just before 24 Mar. 1798*]

My Soul's own Hecca I know you will be vex'd not to see Dan to Day but thus stands the case we are resolved to have the Stranger out on Saturday,[2] and yet if I desert it it will not be. I have to finish my song,[3] to alter an Epilogue we have got at last from Lewis[4] to be spoken by Suett[5] as a Gypsey and to touch up many things in the Play there could be no rehearsal to Day and tomorrow Mrs. Siddons and Kemble[6] have entreated me to be present, which I know I shan't be if I go to Polesden. If John and Kate stay I will come to Dinner tomorrow but if they are *dissolute* and resolved to proceed to Winchester I would wish you my Wench to come to me, as I do not think Polesden with this cold easterly wind so good for you—So I will have every thing ready for you at Brompton where there have been constant Fires, and you shall meet me at Robin's *little nest* at *half past four* to Dinner when you shall find a boil'd Lark and pitchcock'd Sprat ready for you—remember little

[1] Kotzebue's *Menschenhass und Reue* (1788) was translated by Benjamin Thompson, and, according to Thompson, altered and improved by S. This version was first acted at D.L.Th. on 24 Mar. 1798, under the title of *The Stranger*.

[2] 24 Mar.

[3] 'I have a silent sorrow here.' The air was by the Duchess of Devonshire.

[4] Matthew Gregory ('Monk') Lewis (1775–1818).

[5] Richard Suett (1755–1805), comedian. He spoke the epilogue well 'in the character of a Norwood Gipsey' (*Bell's W. Mess.*, 25 Mar. 1798).

[6] Mrs. Siddons played Mrs. Haller; Kemble, Count Walbourg, the Stranger; and Suett, Peter.

Brompton corner of Hagmore-Lane. Of course you will bring our Boy.—Upon my Life and soul I did not drink a Pint of wine yesterday,[1] nor ever will. We settled no business after all—our Party with the D. of Bedford holds for Saturday, and I have promised Lady Mary whom I met at Greys that you shall go to Burlington House on Monday and dance like a Sylph. An excellent House again last Night and not a Place to be had for Saturday. Send Charles back early in the morning with a Line from you my beloved to tell me your decision. Remember me to Shackoback and Kitty if they go—tell John I have sent an order for a private Box to Mrs. James Still[2]

Kiss for the Angel

321. To John Grubb

Harvard MS. *Address*: J. Grubb Esq *Wm.*: 1797

[*1798*]

Dear Grubb,

I have appointed that we will both be at Sleighs tomorrow at three—to settle the Pall-Mall Business.[3] I have arranged the matter with Sleigh—and also appointed Parker[4]—

For God's sake let Powell[5] be with me *directly* if above ground—I wish to God you too could call. I am doing this d——d alteration of the Stranger.[6] And pray also send Caulfield[7] to me— | Yours ever | R B S.

Sunday Evening

[1] He had been 'very drunk' at Lady Bessborough's on 15 Mar. See *Leveson Gower Corr.* i. 205.

[2] Possibly connected with Still and Strong, attorneys, who were paid £25 on 30 Mar., 'on account of Hartley' (D.L.Th. Receipts and Payments, 1798–9 (Folger MS.)).

[3] The bankers, Ransom, Morland & Hammersley, had their office at 57 Pall Mall.

[4] Solicitor for Glossop, the supplier of candles to D.L.Th. Peake was instructed on 7 July 1798 to pay Parker £120, the costs of the action between Glossop and S. See Grubbe MS.

[5] William Powell, prompter at D.L.Th. and in charge of copying.

[6] S. revised *The Stranger* after its first performance. Possibly the letter belongs to 25 March, for *Bell's W. Mess.*, 1 Apr. 1798, stated that when the play was given on 26 Mar. it was 'divested of most of his objectionable qualities. . . . Many judicious alterations and curtailments have taken place.' But it is possible that S. referred to his initial alteration of Thompson's version, or to a proposed alteration for Mrs. Siddons's benefit.

[7] Actor, but he had no part in *The Stranger*. He took his benefit with two other players on 11 June.

322. To His Wife

Harvard MS.

[*Mar.–Apr. 1798?*]
Monday

'May their pernicious Souls rot half a grain a Day'[1]—I never can again be out of the Fury I am in. There shan't be a soldier alive on the Face of the Globe in a Fortnight—I shall immediately compell the whole military of the earth to lay down their Arms. The Barracks of the world shall be levell'd to the Ground—and no such Colour as Scarlet shall exist by art or Nature. Most seriously my Beloved I am in the greatest rage and I do seriously hope Scott[2] will have complain'd of them, and got them flogg'd to Death at least. There certainly was nothing but what was perfectly proper and decent in your Dress.[3] Now my Hecca always believe my Precautions about you are not mere Acts of Discretion—but proceed from a supernatural Foresight which I am specially entrusted with by providence for your Preservation. Twas owing to this I left the distance-Post on the course when the Horse evidently commission'd by old Nick attempted your Destruction, in the same manner Holloways[4] monster who had settled to fall back upon you and crush you in five minutes more was outwitted by my Prudence. So the Chalk-Pit Grave provided by Tall for you and the Child was disappointed of its Prey. Indeed These and about seven hundred instances more wherein you have been saved by what appears to the giddy and the rash over Timidity on my Part ought to make you implicit in your Faith on this subject.—In the present case I ought not to have yielded to your desire of sending back the Servant. As to the ill-

[1] *Othello*, v. ii. 155.

[2] Anne Ogle married Henry Scott (d. 1832), a captain of the Light Infantry of South Hants, in 1798. See p. 103, n. 1.

[3] I assume that Mrs. S. had drawn the jeers of the soldiers because of some unusual garment she wore. She liked to be different from others. The *Morn Her.*, 28 Oct. 1800, mentioned that she was 'the inventor of a new fashionable cloak, which bears her name. It extends below the middle, and flies off the right shoulder; the materials are a slate coloured Persian, lined with rose colour and trimmed with bear skin.'

[4] Probably Thomas Holloway, solicitor, of 57 Chancery Lane. See Kelly, ii. 137 and 317.

looking company you left me with I saw you were frighten'd at them, and giving them some money made them stand by the Horses head while the Boy open'd the Door and put up the Step, etc. and as I got in very leisurely you were quite down the Hill, before they moved on.

My Heart I shall not be able to set out till wednesday—so send me by return of Post *Chaos's* [?] *Song*. Also specify the *Thing in Purcell* you mean, also where *I* may get the *March Kate play'd*. I will never miss writing. I was obliged to go to the House of Commons to Day about the Plot[1] etc. but the business was put off.

Notify that *I* have an order for Possession of the Cottage.[2] Bless you ever and ever | S

323. To John Grubb

Harvard MS. *Wm.*: 1794

[1 Apr. 1798?]
Polesden Sunday Night.

My Dear Grubb,

Here I am like Mrs. Haller[3] enjoying Nature and Retirement. I had forgot that this would be your only Holiday week and that of course you would be at Brompton. So Buonarparte minimus[4] will certainly not make you a visit 'till Easter week, and indeed as the Weather is I am sure the Delay is best for him.

I have written a full and *firm* tho' *conciliatory* Letter to Hammersleys House[5] and I am confident you will have no more cause of alarm from that Quarter. The more I consider our situation and our means the more afraid I feel that *if we*

[1] Fox refers to 'the Plot' in a letter of 11 March 1798, and makes it plain that he is alluding to the arrest of Arthur O'Connor (1763–1852), with others who were suspected of seeking help in England and France to overthrow the Irish government. See Add. MS. 47581, f. 14. S. made a long speech on 'traitorous correspondence' in the Commons on 26 April (*Speeches*, iv. 465–80).

[2] At Bedfont? See p. 110, n. 1.

[3] The heroine of *The Stranger*.

[4] Charles Brinsley Sheridan?

[5] The bankers were not satisfied with the way in which the proprietors of D.L.Th. discharged their debts to them. They had a man in possession at the Theatre on 27 Apr. (Add. MS. 29710, f. 113). A schedule of debts revealed that the proprietors owed £23,012. 15*s*. 9*d*. on 1 June 1798 (Grubbe MSS.).

are not wholly wanting to ourselves we shall be soon not only rescued creditably from every difficulty but have within reach the means of as much Profit as a reasonable man could wish. Something has been done towards increasing our Receipts, but as yet literally nothing towards diminishing our expences. On this subject we must be *Stout*. The Pleasure I feel in *every step* made towards *getting out of Debt*, will I know make my attention and Parsimony increase with our success. When we *owe* nothing we will talk of a more careless course and letting out a Reef or two.—Our Receipt in the next easter Fortnight OUGHT to be £6000.[1] And we must not be humbugg'd about the Benefits. Every one we buy should be mark'd in its Place therefore *Kemble* and *Wroughton* follow Mrs. Siddons[2] which is three in the week instead of one and Palmers[3] should not be 'till the week after.

I beg you will join in my order to Peake—to begin from *last Nights* Receipts to set apart *£10* for the Old Renters and *£10* interest on the unpaid Mortgages.[4] The Latter will save the whole money in Wright's Hands[5] tho' only continued 'till the Benefits, and the former will be a beginning of a Provision which must at last be made.—Our present good prospect turns my mind I own very earnestly to our affairs. It will be so excellent to have ridden out such adverse Times, and to baffle all that malice has foreboded. | yours ever | R B Sheridan

324. To Richard Peak

Add. MS. 35118, ff. 164–5. *Wm.*: 1794

1 Apr. 1798?]

Dear Peake,

These words added to the assignment to be executed by

[1] S. was, as usual, optimistic. The Theatre took £4,508 on the thirteen nights of performance after, and including, Easter Monday (9 Apr.). The programme was made up of either *The Stranger* or *The Castle Spectre* (by M. G. Lewis), with after-pieces.

[2] Her benefit performance of *The Stranger* was given on 23 Apr.

[3] His benefit night was 27 Apr.

[4] Regular payments after every night of performance are to be found in the D.L.Th. account book from Apr. 1798 onwards (Add. MS. 29710, ff. 113–15).

[5] Wright and Graham, the Sheriff's officers, had been paid £620 between 15 and 22 Jan. for executions: see Add. MS. 29710, ff. 106–7.

you will be quite sufficient 'And the said Evans[1] on his Part declares and engages for himself his Heirs Executors Administrators and Assigns that He She or they shall and will resell the said Share now assign'd by R Peake to the said—Evans to R. B. Sheridan his Heirs Executors Administrators and Assigns for and at the same Price now paid by—Evans that is to say two thousand two hundred Pounds of Lawful money of Great Britain whenever the the same shall be required.'—

Pay J. Edwards[2] £20 out of the £100, and keep the rest and the two Bills for me as the apple of your eye.

I have written to Grubb to second my order to set apart from *last Nights* Receipt £10 for the old Renters, and £10 for the interest of the unpaid Mortgages. I have good Reasons for making this beginning. I *earnestly desire* it may not be neglected. My whole mind is now in the business, and in the Pleasure of creditably paying our Debts which by God we will do. | Yrs ever | R B S.

Polesden
Sunday Night

325. To John Grubb

Harvard MS. *Address*: J. Grubb | Store-St.

[*c. 15 May 1798?*]

Dear Grubb,

In consequence of sitting with these men last Night in Carey-St.[3] hoping to bring all things round I have been so ill to Day as literally to be unable to move.

[1] D.L.Th. Nightly Accounts, 1796 and 1797 (Folger MS.) contains the note: 'Mr. Evans's Canvas Bills lie unpaid at Mr. Eves Attorney No. 3 Pump Court and unless there is not an immediate Answer Mr. E. has positive Instructions to sue for recovery.' This is dated 15 Feb. 1797, and the amount involved was £435. 19*s*. 4*d*. I take it that when the bill reached £800, S. obtained £2,200 in cash from Evans, and gave him in return a £3,000 share that entitled him to draw £1 from every performance at D.L.Th.

[2] On 1 April S. wrote to Peake: 'Pay John Edwards twenty pounds for me out of Evan's money' (Osborn MS.). Possibly this note accompanied the above letter as separate proof of authorization. Edwards was a door-keeper at D.L.Th.

[3] John Rigge wrote from Carey Street on 15 May (Grubbe MS.) to Peake to the effect that he had promised

I hope tomorrow to have means of giving essential assistance in your affairs tomorrow of which I have apprized Wright and Graham. Pray let me know if you have learn'd anything to Day? | Yours ever | R B S.

326. To William Adam

Adam MS. *Address*: W. Adam Esq. *Dock.*: Mr. Richardson[1]

[*May 1798*][2]

My Dear Adam,

We have appointed a meeting—a final consultation[3] at your House this Evening at nine—pray forgive my intrusion but every thing depends on your assistance.[4] | Your's ever | R B Sheridan

327. To John Grubb

Harvard MS.

[*21 May 1798?*]
Monday morning 10 o'clock

Dear Grubb

as the Devil will have it I must set off this moment for

Gilles, a laceman, to obtain 'your avowal in writing of the order given by the proprietors of the theatre for retaining the two pounds per night'; and that in the other case of Pulsford and Son (owed £165 by D.L.Th.), he declined hostilities against the proprietors and was ready to contribute as best he could to ease Grubb. But it is possible that the allusions are not to Rigge, Gilles, and Pulsford, but to Thomas Wright, the sheriff's officer, of 20 Carey Street, and to John Graham, as sheriff's broker, concerning pressure they had put on the proprietors of D.L.Th. for some other reason.

1 Below S.'s letter comes a note signed by Richardson: 'We are undone without you.'

2 Mr. D. E. Ginter noted that the letter was in a bundle docketed 'May 1798'.

3 'The Deed of Appointment of the Treasurer and Bankers of the Theatre and for the Application of the Nightly Receipts' was signed by S., Grubb, and Richardson, on 19 May 1798: see S.C., 25 May 1954, lot 274. John Welsh, a singer, sued D.L.Th. in the King's Bench on 26 May 1798 for £995.

4 A letter in the same bundle and from Richardson to Adam seems to refer to Richardson's buying his share in D.L.Th.: '. . . Burdett might be a useful Ally and I wished to speak to Sheridan about it. He says that B. is certainly a Man to be applied to, and is willing that the application should be strengthened by the Matter's being represented as being very useful to him (S) as to me.'

Maidstone[1] back tomorrow. I will see Sleigh first to secure you—I have written again to Burrows[2] and to Wright whom pray see if necessary with Westley | Your's ever | R B S.

328. To His Wife

Harvard MS. *Pub.*: Sichel, ii. 284–5.

[*22 May 1798*]
Maidstone.

My Heart's beloved, Knowing how anxious you will be I send [this] tho' the Trials will be over some time to Night. Matters we think look well for O Connor—but I am resolved not to be too sanguine. I got to speak to him this morning—his mind is composed—but his Nerves sadly shaken. He was greatly affected when his poor Brother[3] was brought into Court yesterday, and when the other took his Hand He burst into Tears. The usage of Roger O Connor, who is one of the finest Fellows I ever saw, has been merciless beyond example. We are all very anxious and very busy For the Counsel want assistance. Here is Fox Grey Erskine Grattan E: Moira[4] D. Norfolk, etc. etc. etc.

When I got to Wrotham[5] yesterday I was obliged to change Horses again and the intelligence there was that the Trial was nearly over and that they were all tried together, the Latter turned out to be the case, and in my Life I never spent a more miserable half hour for I believe I was not longer getting to Maidstone, but when I arrived the first

[1] The trial of Arthur O'Connor, Rev. James O'Coigley (or Quigley), and four others associated with the United Irishmen or United Englishmen, was held at Maidstone on 21 and 22 May. O'Coigley alone was condemned for high treason and executed on 7 June.

[2] The D.L.Th. account book (Add. MSS. 29710, f. 135) contains a note of the repayment of £15 on 26 March 1799, to 'Mr. Burrows of 100 lent Westley'.

[3] Roger O'Connor (1762–1834) was arrested when he came to London to assist his brother in his defence, taken to Dublin, and then brought back to London. He was 'most severely indisposed, from the effects of his long journey and rigorous confinement' (*Chester Chronicle*, 25 May 1798).

[4] The Opposition attitude to O'Connor is clearly put by Moira in his letter to Charlemont of 25 Mar. 1798. See H.M.C., *Charlemont MSS.* (1894), ii. 317.

[5] Some ten miles from Maidstone.

thing I saw was a group of my Friends who gave me a welcome that convinced me I was in Time[1]—in Fact the Crown did not finish till 12 at night. The Defence has been on since 8 this morning. You may rely on seeing me tomorrow morning—send me a Line my Soul. I was up at six Ma'am.

Shew the enclosed[2] to Mr. Streatfeild—the rest of the Letter is still more infamous. He may rely on its authenticity—it was produced in Court yesterday and made a great sensation. The Attorney General[3] behaved well and pledged himself to prosecute the writer with the utmost rigour—and Buller[4] said there was no punishment on earth to[o] much for him. He is a Clergyman and son to the agricultural Arthur Young.[5]

indeed *myself* you must wish for your poor Friend[6] O Connor, I am very sorry to learn that Mr. Streatfeild is unwell. | bless you my own wench | R B S.

Should any very pressing circumstance (which however I think very unlikely unless on O Connors account) force me to Town tomorrow I will return to Chiddingstone on Friday and stay 'till monday which perhaps would be more comfortable for on Thursday I am pledged to be in the House of Commons on the Third reading of the Land Tax bill. Or I will come to you tomorrow and back to Chiddingstone Saturday.—For it would be shabby to spend but one day with myself.

[1] S. gave evidence on his behalf, testifying that O'Connor's character was 'remarkable for its openness'. He added that he had known him for three years, and, under cross-examination, stated that 'he never met any man in his life, who so much reprobated the idea of any party in this country desiring French assistance' (*Chester Chronicle*, 1 June 1798).

[2] Clearly a copy of the letter from the Rev. Arthur Young to Gamaliel Lloyd of Bury St. Edmunds, which was read to the court. Young stated that he had dined with three yeomen who were to be jurymen at O'Connor's trial and had exerted all his eloquence 'to convince them how absolutely necessary it is, at the present moment, for the security of the realm, *that the felons should swing*...' (*Chester Chronicle*, 1 June 1798).

[3] John Scott, later Lord Eldon.

[4] Sir Francis Buller (1746–1800), Justice of the Common Pleas from 1794. His summing-up was thought too favourable to O'Connor. Mr. Justice Heath, Mr. Justice Lawrence, and Sergeant Shepard sat with him.

[5] 1741–1820. Secretary to the Board of Agriculture, and author of many important works on agricultural theory and practice. Also wrote the celebrated *Travels in France*.

[6] Sichel omits the remainder.

329. To His Wife

Osborn MS. *Wm*: 1797. *Pub.*: Sichel, ii. 285–6.

[*23 May 1798*]
Maidstone
Wednesday morn.

My Soul's Beloved, I know your green Eyes will grieve when I tell you it is indispens[a]bly necessary for me to go to Town as well for a matter of my own as on O'Connor's account, a meeting being fix'd there with Fox and Erskine etc. Your Juryman of course told at Chidingstone that O'Connor and all but Quigley[1] are acquitted—and I suppose also of the Fray that ensued on their attempting to execute a second warrant for High Treason the moment the Verdict was given. He had no thought of escaping himself,[2] but three or four injudicious Friends provoked at this unexpected second proceeding, endeavour'd to hustle him out of Court. There were many blows struck Swords drawn:[3] and when the soldiers got in I thought there would have been some serious mischief—which I was of some use in preventing for which Buller thank'd me. You may imagine that Fox and all of us were in sufficient indignation at this horrible Persecution. When O'Connor got to the Jail He entreated the under-Sheriff to [let] him see me. He applied to the High Sheriff who went to the Judges, and Buller sent me a very handsome message that tho' their commi[ssi]on was ended and

[1] A paper had been found in his clothes urging French invasion.

[2] When S. gave evidence at the trial of the Earl of Thanet and others for riot on this occasion, he said, 'As to O'Connor's leaping out of the dock, it did not strike me as any particular circumstance because I had observed a similar conduct in the prisoners at the Old Bailey when acquitted. I saw one man rush forward and it was rumoured tha the had another warrant against Mr. O'Connor . . .' (*The Oracle*, 26 Apr. 1799). But cf. C. Grey, *Life and Opinions of Charles, 2nd Earl Grey* (1861), p. 30.

[3] 'The Bow-Street officers, who, with several peace officers, rushed towards Mr. O'Connor. . . . Two swords, which were lying on the table (part of the prisoner's baggage) were drawn by some persons and several people were struck by them' (*Chester Chronicle*, 1 June 1798). O'Connor stated that since he was acquitted, he thought he was discharged, but Buller informed him that he could only be discharged when 'the gaoler had the calendar returned to him marked'.

they exceeded their authority they would direct that I might see him alone. By the Time I got to the Jail O'Connor was in Bed in the dark under a hundred Locks and Bolts the Jail full of Soldiers the Jailor who had been struck in the Fray in a furious Rage and all pretending that The[y] apprehended a Rescue at last however I got to him and was with him alone an hour. Notwithstanding his renew'd imprisonment He was in extremely good Spirits tho' He had had nothing to eat or drink the Jail was in such confusion and full of Gratitude to his Friends. I shall see him again this morning and then set off for Town where I believe we shall settle something to be done in the House of Commons tomorrow. When seized in the Court He made a very forcible appeal to the Court.[1] He saw there were Those who were determined to have his Life right or wrong and the only Favour he ask'd was to be confined in the same Dungeon with his Brother.

My Life's Heart I have not a moment more—I will write from Town and peremptorily fix the Hour when I will see your eyes at Chidingstone. We pant for a few quiet days | R B S.

Our expedition against Ostend[2] has in a great measure succeeded by destroying the Sluices and Boats—but the Retreat of our Troops was cut off, the wind rising none of them could re-embark. Some officers kill'd and wounded among the latter Coote who commanded and about 50 men all the rest about 600 made Prisoners[3]

[1] 'My lord, I am surrounded with drawn swords; I am prepared to die; and it would be better for the Court to doom me to death at once, than I should hunger out my life in gaol. Will your Lordships have the goodness to send me to the dungeon where my brother is confined, after having been acquitted on a charge of high treason in Ireland. At all events, will your Lordships order that my agent may be permitted to come to me?' (*Chester Chronicle*, 1 June 1798). The Court refused to make any order.

[2] The expedition under Sir Eyre Coote (1762–1824?) sought to 'destroy the internal navigation between Holland, Flanders, and France'.

[3] Sichel omits the postscript.

330. To William Sleigh

N.L.I. MS. 3901, f. 1. *Address*: W. Sleigh, Esq. *Dock.*: 17 June 1798 | Mr. Sheridans 2nd Letter | received between 11 and 12 at Night and answered | Sharpe No. 24 | Upper Berkeley Street | Portman Square.

17 June 1798

Dear Sir,

On my return to Town this evening I find another Letter to Mr. Grubb—I trust at least I may rely on no advertisement appearing before our meeting tomorrow.[1] I beg one Line by Bearer | yours | R B Sheridan

331. To Bryan Edwards[2]

Harvard MS. *Address*: Bryan Edwards Esq M.P. | Polygon | Southampton | if absent to be forwarded immediately *Pm.*: JU 19 98

[18] June 1798
London
Monday Evening.

My Dear Sir,

I was with Fox at St. Anne's yesterday, and He has agreed to make a last Effort and to attend the House of Commons on Friday next on a motion respecting Ireland, of which Lord G. Cavendish[3] has this Day given notice, and Lord John Russell is to second it. Recollecting your Speech respecting his secession,[4] and being convinced you will not consider a little trouble upon such an occasion I take the Liberty of apprizing you of the circumstance.—We expect a very numerous attendance.[5] | I have the Honor to be | Dear Sir | Yours truly | R B Sheridan

[1] D.L.Th. season ended on 18 June: it was 'one of the most successful within our recollection' (*Monthly Mirror*, 1st Ser., v (1798), 368). But there had been men in possession at the theatre on 27 Apr., 16 May, and 6 June (Add. MS. 29710, ff. 113, 115, 117).

[2] 1743–1800. He was a wealthy West India merchant, who became M.P. for Grampound in 1796.

[3] Lord George Cavendish (1754–1834), afterwards Earl of Burlington.

[4] Edwards lamented Fox's absence from parliament in a speech of 2 Nov. 1797. See *Parl. Reg.* iv (1798), 13–18.

[5] 'The forces of Opposition mustered

332. To John Grubb

Grubbe MS. *Address*: J Grubb Eq

[*1798?*]
Sunday

Dear Grubb.

Pray give Peake a little indispensible for me. I am gone to fetch Mrs. S. return Tuesday Evening and from that hour by Heaven I will toil in Theatricals 'till all shall be sunshine like this Day | Yours | R B S.

333. To William Sleigh

Egerton MS. 2137, ff. 170–1. *Pub.*: R. Garnett and E. Gosse, *English Literature, An Illustrated Record* (1903), iii. 370. *Address*: W. Sleigh, Esq. *Dock.*: 8th Sept. 1798 | Mr. Sheridan's Letter in answer to mine of this day.

8 Sept. 1798
Saturday morning

Dear Sir,

I am perfectly convinced how unpleasant it must be to you to write me such a Letter as I have just received containing so extraordinary and ridiculous a Threat from the Bankers—I assure you this is the first communication of the kind I have had. Mr. Grubb undoubtedly ought to give the security to the old Trustees[1] and if He does not some one must be found that will. As to the executions[2] They ought

very strong last night in the House of Commons, and almost every one of the seceders returned to their posts' (*The Times*, 23 June 1798). Cavendish's five resolutions for the more liberal treatment of Ireland were easily defeated.

[1] Their demand was so force fulthat Grubb decided to decline the office of Treasurer of D.L.Th., and one Thomas Andrews was approached to fill the vacancy. However, Grubb was persuaded to reconsider the matter, and he wrote to Troward on 21 Jan. 1799 (Harvard MS.) saying 'should I compleat my security I surely ought to be possessed of some authentic Document to regulate my Conduct without the hazard of exposing my own Property and that of my Friends to immediate disposal'.

[2] On 17 Sept. 1798, S. paid £4,284. 10*s.* 1*d.* to Hammersleys 'in discharge of so much of the debt due from the said R B Sheridan and Thomas Westley on Judgments upon which Executions have been issued against them' (Grubbe MS.).

long since to have been withdrawn in good Faith. The settling an intricate account with a Pistol at one's breast is not a Pleasant way of doing business nor I should think a satisfactory manner of having charges admitted. Everything else on our Part has been acquiesced in and done and merely my necessary attention to the Theatre and Westley's avocations have prevented this, which I must naturally be most anxious to have compleated if I considered myself only. I will do myself the Pleasure of calling on you in the course of the Day. yours truly | R B Sheridan

334. To Richard Peake

Osborn MS. *Address*: Mr. Peake Get an answer *Wm.*: 1797

[*Sept. 1798?*]
Monday morning
Polesden

Dear Peake,

See Burgess[1] *as soon as possible*. Accept that Note of £31.17 at a shorter Date—and pray lay your heads together in earnest to get me the money or I shall be sadly distress'd here to wind up my Harvest. If you cannot send by the Bearer—send Dunn[2] off early in the morning. Give *Sam Tickell*[3] a Guinea for himself and another for his journey to Winchester. He must positively go tomorrow | Your ever | R B S.

I am working here for the Theatre. Westley and I were from ten to past three yesterday at Hammerslys Desk and have completely settled the account.[4]

[1] He lent £100 to pay the company. £20 was returned to him on 13 Oct.

[2] William Dunn, Peake's assistant at D.L.Th. Treasury.

[3] 1785–1817. Second son of Richard and Mary Tickell. D.L.Th. Cash Book, 1797–9 (Folger MS.) records a payment on 5 Sept. 1798 to 'Master Tickell by Mr. S. order 2.12.6'.

[4] After paying off the executions, D.L.Th. owed Hammersleys £23,012. 15*s.* 9*d.* To reduce this balance, £110 was paid every night of performance between 18 Sept. and 17 Nov.: see Add. MS. 29710, ff. 120–4.

335. To Richard Peake

Egerton MS. 1975, f. 106. *Address*: Mr. Peake *Dock.*: Mr. Sheridan *Wm.*: 1797

[*Sept. 1798?*]

Dear Peake,

Sam Tickell will give you this. I have sent a supply to Goddard[1] for his schooling. My other note mentions that you are to tip him a Guinea. | Yours | R B S.

336. To James Aikin

Pierpont Morgan Library MS. *Address*: James Aiken Esq. | D. L. Theatre *Fr.*: R B Sheridan

[*Autumn 1798?*]
Polesden
Monday[?] morning.

My Dear Sir,

There is a Tragedy of Whalley's[2] in Mr. Siddons Hands which we are pledged to do. Pray get it from him—and the faster it is brought forward the better. Also Mr. Hoare's farce, and a Piece of Boadens.[3] I wish Johnson[4] and Greenwood had the Plots of all—There is not much expence in any of them. | Yours truly | R B Sheridan

[1] William Stanley Goddard, D.D. (1757–1845), Headmaster of Winchester College.

[2] Thomas S. Whalley's tragedy, *The Castle of Montval*, was given at D.L.Th. on 23 Apr. 1799. The Whalleys were intimate friends of Sarah and William Siddons.

[3] Prince Hoare's opera *The Captive of Spilsburg* was given at D.L.Th. on 14 Nov. 1798. James Boaden's musical drama, *Aurelio and Miranda*, was acted there on 29 Dec. 1798. Kemble noted in his diary on 14 Feb. 1798 that S. had 'promised Mr. Boaden that his play should be the first new Piece acted next Season' (Add. MS. 31973, f. 162). Cf. iii. 278.

[4] Alexander Johnson, machinist and maker of properties at D.L.Th.

337. To Richard Peake

N.L.I. MS. 3901, ff. 15–16. *Address*: Mr. Peake | Charlotte-St. | Rathbone-Place *Dock.*: Mr. Sheridan *Wm.*: 1797

[*1798?*]
Friday
past 5

Dear Peake,

I find it indispensable necessary that I should be in Town again tomorrow morning *before ten* o'clock. This [at] once gives me credit for Punctuality and pray do not fail to meet me at *Carpenter's* precisely and to a minute at eleven. And for God's sake bring the ready for one or both of those Notes.[1] | Yrs | R B Sheridan

tell Grubb I come *tomorrow*

I had wrote to G. before I knew this

338. To John Grubb

Grubbe MS. *Address*: J Grubb Esq *Dock.*: Sheridan to Grubb | for 20 Gs.

[*1798?*]

Dear Grubb,

Tho' Saturday be not *arrived* pray send me twenty guineas. We have not a shilling in the House.

I have got the Bankers in better order than any Day yet, the *State* matters make some Delay. | R B S

339. To John Graham

Price MS. *Address*: Mr. Graham | Southampton-Row[2] *Dock.*: Sheridan

[*Autumn 1798?*]

My Dear Sir,

No—you shall not be in any scrape or difficulty by

[1] Under Saturday, 29 Sept. 1798, Grubb entered a payment to Carpenter of £30 (Grubbe MS.).

[2] John Graham lived at 20 Southampton Row, so the letter is to him and not (as is sometimes stated) to Robert Graham, the Prince's Attorney-General, who lived at 6 Lincoln's Inn Stone buildings.

Heaven—. Pray meet Wright in Hertford St: tomorrow at 12 and we will discuss all Plagues.

but first let me mention a bit of good news—I have settled our job at Winchester—I will shew you Dr. Goddard's Letter tomorrow. And you must fight my battle against the Prince should it be necessary | Yours truly | R B Sheridan

Saturday

I send *Madame* a brace of Partridge

340. To John Grubb

Harvard MS.

[1798?]

Dear Grubb

I wanted much to have seen you. I am vex'd about the Receipts—which is the only thing that I ever think a real ground of Vexation. I am compell'd to Nurse my cold.—I have a hundred Plagues with me all the morning. I wish you could dine here tomorrow. | yrs | R B S.

Friday

341. To Richard Peake

McAdam MS. *Address*: Leatherhead November fifth 1798 | Mr. Peake | Charlotte-St. | Rathbone-Place | London *Fr.*: Free | R B Sheridan *Dock.*: Mr. Sheridan

5 Nov. 1798

Dear Peake,

Pray lay hands on some of Watkin's[1] Port and send it to Polesden—at any Price—I will see you tomorrow without fail | Yrs | R B S.

Monday

fix Strict[2]

[1] Probably Peake's friend, Watkins, optician and mathematical instrument maker of 5 Charing Cross. The Librarian of the Guildhall Library states that these premises were occupied from 1791, first by Jeremiah Watkins, and later by J. and W. Watkins.

[2] D.L.Th. Receipts and Payments, 1800–1 (Folger MS.) records on 7 Feb. 1801 payment of £125 to Augustus Strict, 'on account of Debt and Dft. etc.'

342. To John Grubb

Harvard MS. *Address*: John Grubb Esq *Wm.*: 1796

[*1798?*]
½ past five
Tuesday morn

Dear Grubb,

Take notice that the undersigned rises every morning at five and works three hours by Candle-light.[1] This is in other words to announce that every thing respecting the Theatre shall be set right and every difficulty got over. It is *absolutely necessary* however that we should meet as soon as possible I will dine at Spencer's[2] to Day. I wish to God you would come there | Yours ever | R B Sheridan.

The combined Enemy Threaten loudly and attempt to surround us.

You should have had this in the morn but for my forgetfulness[3]

343. 'To Commodore Nathaniel Ogle'

Osborn MS. *Address*: [In another hand] Commodore Ogle | Phaedria[4] | Southampton *Fr.*: Spencer

1 Dec. 1798

Sir

You are hereby required and directed to repair without

[1] A note among the Salt MSS. reads: 'We do hereby most solemnly engage that we will henceforth *diligently* and *punctually* attend to the affairs of the Theatre in every Department, and assiduously apply ourselves to the business of it until every embarrassment shall be removed and every Debt and demand upon it discharged and we pledge ourselves to the Performance of this Promise by every consideration that can bind men of common sense and common Honesty.' This is in S.'s hand, with his signature and that of Grubb appended. J. Aickin signs as witness. S. added to the document, 'Mr. Peake to keep this Paper. October 26th 1798'.

[2] Or 'Garrick's Head' tavern. D.L.Th. Ledger, 1799 to 1802 (Folger MS.) lists twelve payments of £10. 10*s.* 0*d.* to Spencer (through Jennings) between Nov. 1799 and May 1800.

[3] Written on the cover.

[4] A small cutter, named after the magic boat in the *Faerie Queene* and owned by Nathaniel Ogle. Moore, ii. 254, says that S. passed much of his holidays sailing about on Southampton Water in this boat.

Loss of Time to Polesden Harbour on a Christening Cruise. The Good ship Anne[1] being cut down from a First Rate in bulk and Stowage, and a tight little Schooner built out of her *waist* Timber you are required as Ships Husband to assist in naming the said s[c]hooner by breaking a few bottles of Wine against the Old Admirals Bed-post.

Given under our Hands and Seals this first of December 1798 | Hugh Seymour | T. Wallace | Arden | T. Young[2] | X (Spencer—his mark)[3] | Countersigned | R B Sheridan | H B Ogle | M A Lee[4]

On thursday at the latest fail not[5]

344. To Richard Peake

Egerton MS. 1975, ff. 51–52. *Address*: Mr. Peake. *Dock.*: Mr. Sheridan *Wm.*: 1798

[*1798?*]
at Fosbrooks

Dear Peake—

I shall be back here in half an hour, and will come to the Treasury to you. I have order'd Dinner in Hertford-St. We must pass every hour of this Day together | Yrs | R B S

[1] The *Gent. Mag.*, lxviii (1798), 83, records her marriage at Winchester to Scott on 3 Jan. 1798; but Ogle, p. 140, says they were married on 4 June 1798 by licence dated 3 Jan.

[2] Hugh Seymour (1759–1801), a Lord of the Admiralty, 1795–8; Thomas, afterwards 1st Lord Wallace (1768–1844), a Lord of the Admiralty, 1797–1800; Charles Perceval, 2nd Lord Arden (1756–1840), a Lord of the Admiralty, 1783–1801. It seems certain that the hands are not those of the persons named. This is proved by 'T. Young': the initial 'T' was usually given by S. to people whose initials were unknown to, or forgotten by, him. Here the reference is to Admiral Sir William Young (1751–1821), a Lord of the Admiralty, 1795–1801.

[3] In S.'s hand.

[4] Probably Matthew Lee, who is mentioned as 'Gigas' in the 'Rules and Regulations of the Piscatory Party' (Yale MS.). A jocular note to the letter adds that he would attend the 'christening cruise' if there were 'a fair breeze from Bond Street'.

[5] There follows in another hand an amusing list of the 'boats' that were to be present, including 'The Veteran' commanded by 'Adml. Sheridan'.

345. [To John Grubb]

Harvard MS.

[1798–9?]

O most punctilious! R.[1] and I got to the Treasury just as you left it.—I have directed Peake to send back Holloway's bond—Contrary to positive agreement I understand He has attempted to steal in another £100, which shall not be given way to. At the same time both in his case and Evan's[2] I am confident that their bringing in £100 of my private account while they give 7 months for the remainder is not an object to object to. And it is what can be easily balanced between us.

Pray let us meet tomorrow before Dinner.— | Yours truly | R B Sheridan | J Richardson[3]

Sunday Evening

346. To John Grubb

Harvard MS.

[1798–9?]
House of Commons
past nine.

Curse this Place—

we hope to be with you in half an hour—pray send to Wrights | yrs | R B S.

347. To ——

Shuttleworth MS.

[1798–1800?]
Hertford St.
Saturday Evening

Dear Sir,

I beg you a thousand Pardons for not meeting you the

[1] Richardson.

[2] D.L.Th. Ledger, 1795 to 1799 (Folger MS.) records ten payments of £20 to Thomas Holloway between 7 and 16 Feb. 1798. The volume, Receipts and Payments, 1798–9 (Folger MS.), notes that £10 was paid to Evans on 28 May 1799 as 'Expences to prevent Trial'; and a further £20 on 5 June.

[3] His signature.

other Day as we proposed. Mr. Burgess does me the favour to take this and if you should not be engaged to Dinner tomorrow I shall be very happy to see you to meet our Friend Mr. Saloman[1]—and my carriage shall return with you. Should you be engaged at home perhaps you would come to Town for an hour when Saloman will meet you and we will run thro' the Opera— | Yours very truly | R B Sheridan

348. To John Grubb

Grubbe MS. *Dock.*: From Sheredan to Grubb | Dimond £19. 10 | Dawes £17.

[*1799?*]
Monday[?] Evening

Dear Grubb,

I cannot get to the House to Night—but I have put off going out of Town and will *positively* be with you in the morning. I send the two Draughts of Trust Treasurer—and I am sure you will agree with me in treating this Trick[2] as it deserves. I have not had time to write my remarks on Sleighs alias Drewe's Draught.

Pray send me a Line to be at the Bankers by *ten* tomorrow to answer two refused Draughts of mine on which I have written this Day 'pay this R B S' one to Dimock for £19,10. The other to Dawes[3] for £17.—You may take it out of my Subsistence—and you may positively rely on my not drawing on the general Fund again. Send me a Line and the amount of the Receipt—describe the Draughts. | yrs ever | R B S.

[1] Johann Peter Salomon (1745–1815), composer and violinist.

[2] The Grubbe MSS. include a letter from Grubb to Troward of 17 Jan. 1799, in which he states that since he was '*nominated* Treasurer of the Theatre', he had 'lodged in the Bank in the names of the Trustees, a sum nearly equal to what I am informed is the stipulated Security required'. Now he understands that the Trustees have 'a Power of Attorney ready for Execution' and had met to agree to the sale of the stock transferred by Grubb, 'on some alledged Inattention' on his part.

[3] Mrs. Dawes sewed canvas at D.L.Th. for scenery.

349. To Lady Bessborough

Pub.: Leveson Gower Corr. i. 242.

[*Mar. 1799*]

Dear Traitress,

The moment Fosbrook mention'd the matter to me I desired him to do every possible thing that Lord Granville[1] wish'd. I do not care about the opposing man's Politics. I will also certainly write to Stafford tomorrow, where I have some Friends who I know have interest in Lichfield.[2] Little Monckton should be applied. By the account I have heard every exertion should be made.

I never was more pleased than when I heard the news of Grenville's Safety.[3] I want to speak to S.L.,[4] and tried to Catch her in the Park to Day.

Hecca has a cold, and I am staying with her this evening or I would come. . . .

350. To the Trustees of Drury Lane Theatre[5]

Harvard MS. Copy. *Dock.*: Copy—Letter from Mr. Sheridan demanding Copy of the Trust Deed. March 1799. *Wm.*: 1796

Hertford Street
March 1799

Gentlemen!

Notwithstanding the great Sums which I have paid for Law expences contracted by you as Trustees for Drury Lane Theatre for Drafts Deed, Copies of Deeds, Opinions, Consultations, Attendances etc. etc. etc. I have never yet

[1] Lord Granville Leveson Gower (1773–1846), afterwards 1st Earl Granville, was M.P. for Lichfield from Jan. 1795 to 1799, but stood for Staffordshire in March 1799 and was duly elected. He was a Gower Whig.

[2] Where the Gower candidate, Wrottesley, was defeated by Sir Nigel Gresley.

[3] Thomas Grenville was on his way as ambassador to Berlin, when his ship ran on to a sand-bank. He got safely ashore near Cuxhaven. See *Leveson Gower Corr.* i. 241–2, and *The Oracle*, 5 Mar. 1799.

[4] Presumably Sichel's 'T.L.', the Duchess of Devonshire. On 1 Feb. they told Grubb (Harvard MS.) they would sell 2750 3 per cent. Consols to pay arrears of £1,880 (47 nights).

been able to procure a copy of the Trust Deed itself, upon the assumed Violation of the covenants of which you have thought proper to direct your Solicitor to file a Bill against me[1] and to move in Six days.—Notice for a Receiver[2] or in other word[s], in the event to shut up the Theatre. You have rendered me sometime since a short general account of the manner in which the Sum of One hundred and fifty thousand pounds committed to your care by the Subscribers and rais'd for the purposes of paying the incumbrances in the Old Theatre and building the new one has been dissipated without effecting either of those objects. The result appears that while you have expended and paid away the whole of the Money according to the items in your Solicitors account, and that Mortgages to the amount of thirty five thousand pounds still remain'd unpaid and a Debt of £40,000 was left on the building Account. This situation it might reasonably be expected might have excited at least a sensation of regret and some feeling for me on whom this enormous defalcation was to fall, in the minds of the Trustees—but when it is considered that the three Trustees were three of the unpaid Mortgagees and that I voluntarily put into their hands new Securities for their Demands so left unliquidated but for which they could have no resource in the Trust,[3] it might further have been expected that even some feeling of gratitude and good will might have been expected both towards me and the undertaking. If I wish'd to find a proof of this in the slightest departure from the strictest execution of the Trust repos'd in them I should think myself unreasonable and unjust, but it is not much to have confided that the considerations and circumstances I have mentioned would have preceded every appearance of ungenerous or selfish proceeding on the part of any of the Trustees which would by any one be construed as stepping out of the Line of the Trust and respecting its Duties for no

[1] The Bill of Complaint was not filed in the Court of Chancery until 18 Dec. 1799. See P.R.O. Chancery Procs. C 13/2325.

[2] Troward had written to S. on 9 Mar. 1799 (Harvard MS.), to say that the trustees intended 'to move on 16 March 1799 that a proper person be appointed to receive the rents and profits etc.' of D.L.Th.

[3] As a further guarantee, Grubb gave a Treasurer's bond (Harvard MS.) of £10,000 to the Trustees on 15 Mar. 1799.

manifest object but the oppression of the Proprietors. This however is a matter not for the present discussion—all I require of you Gentlemen is that you will procure and cause to deliver to me as soon as possible a true copy of the Trust Deed authenticated to be so by your Solicitor and that he be directed to submit the original to my Counsel as being required so to do. After this shall have been done, I desire but the shortest time which my Counsel the Attorney General[1] Mr. Piggott[2] and Mr. Hargrave shall judge requisite to answer your Bill and to meet your motion. Without this I will not believe that Men of such professional Character as Mr. Mansfield[3] and Mr. Fonblanque[4] can advise you by a surprize to . . .[5] me out of the Situation I am intitled to under the Trust and inevitably to destroy all the Securities on which a large proportion of Debt independent of your Trust now depends, I enclose to each of you a Copy of my former Letter which I cannot easily believe you can have seen or [if] laid before you you can have considered, also a copy of the answer received in which instead of the gracious feeling which as I before stated I had a right to expect from the Trustees there is not the common civility due from Gentlemen to Gentlemen. I have only to add that I consider the service of this Notice and the Copy of the Bill as the first regular demand of the Arrears of the Forty pounds per Night,[6] and accordingly I give you Notice that within one Month we will make good the deficiency and that we are now and have been at all times ready to produce our Books and Accounts to be examined by the Trustees as they are authorized and directed to do by the Trust Deed before they proceed to any other measure

[1] Sir John Freeman-Mitford, afterwards 1st Baron Redesdale (1748–1830). Burgess wrote to White on 14 Mar. 1799 (Harvard MS.) to say that Wallis and Troward were 'exciting every nerve to catch' S., and had sent to retain the Attorney General but 'I had been beforehand'. In fact, retaining fees had been paid to Mitford, Pigott, and Hargrave on 18 and 19 Feb. 1799: see the D.L.Th. Ledger, 1795 to 1799 (Folger MS.).

[2] Arthur Leary Pigott (1749–1819).

[3] James Mansfield, afterwards Lord Chief Justice (1734–1821).

[4] John de Grenier Fonblanque (*c.* 1760–1837).

[5] Blank in the manuscript.

[6] By the trust deed of 19 June 1793, S. and Linley had taken the profits of D.L.Th. as long as they paid the Trustees £40 for every night of performance. In default, the Trustees had the right to appoint a person to direct the theatre and take possession of the rents and profits.

351. To James Aikin

Lee Kohns Memorial Collection MS., New York Public Library. *Address*: Mr. Aikin | to be Delivered immediately

[*12 Mar. 1799*]
Tuesday

My Dear Sir,

I will immediately see to the business myself.—

Pray take particular [attention] to *bottom in the bills of tomorrow* and make a point of having it in the Newspapers that 'Mrs. Siddons will appear in the Part of Lady Randolph in the Tragedy of Douglas on saturday next—' adding 'due notice will be given of the –th –th and –th Nights of the new Comedy of the Secret'[1]— | Yours | R B Sheridan

352. To Richard Peake

McAdam MS. *Address*: Mr. Peake

[*Mar. 1799?*]
Thursday Evening

Dear Peake,

Mrs. S. is going to Winchester tomorrow morning—by all thats good you must contrive to send me £10 to Night. I wish I could have seen Grubb to Day—but now attend to a rational Proposal to blend a little business with amusement. You talk of going to Staines tomorrow—I shall dine a few miles beyond Staines tomorrow and on Saturday morn Mrs. S. goes on with her Brother to Winchester. Now I will return and meet you and Grubb and Burgess at Dinner at Staines at half past four on Saturday—and I will order the Room and Dinner as I go by tomorrow—let us bring Letters and applications—and I will also bring Rolla[2] which if we Stay sunday I will sample if Burgess lets me dictate to him—for in this d——d Town there is not getting half

[1] Edward Morris's *The Secret* was first acted on 2 Mar. 1799. Mrs. Siddons's earliest performance in Home's *Douglas* after this date, was on Saturday, 16 Mar., by which time *The Secret* had been given on eight occasions.

[2] S.'s adaptation of Kotzebue's *Die Spanier in Peru* (1796), which was given at D.L.Th. under the title of *Pizarro*. He had been working on it from early Dec. 1798: see *Chester Chronicle*, 21 Dec. 1798.

an hour without interruption—and we will all return early on monday morning with our Plans concerted and measures settled on. | Yours | R B S

353. To His Wife

Harvard MS.

[*24–27 Mar. 1799*]
Bedfont. Sunday Evening

Here am I, my Beloved Hecca, at my little *Inn*[1] after writing all the rainy Part of the morning and walking seven miles on the Heath during two fine hours from five to seven —and then our Dinner. After I parted from you yesterday my Soul's Love I never felt more oppress'd and out of Heart. Bab walk'd with me a good way on the road and we talk'd of Hecca and *time back*—which I could not avoid doing altho' it was the recollection of Time past that had made me nervous, yet with no reflexions accompanying that recollection but such as ought to have made me chearful.—

It was more than four years and four months since I had first talk'd to her of Hecca—before Dear Hecca was mine—in *that very walk*, and assuredly I have now on proof a thousand times stronger ground to build my happiness upon, and upon experience, than Hope and Presumption could then have held out to me. Yet the memory of the past Day was oppressive to my mind. The Truth is that the Death of Time and the recollection of departed Hours, if happily spent, never can be chearful recollections. And if there is added to that the regret that those hours have not been prized enough, or all the happiness attach'd to them which might have been, the reviewing them and reflecting on them is still more painful.—

London. Tuesday Night. My own Wench—Dan left off writing to you on sunday in a melancholy mood and He did not even say that which was uppermost in his mind that He loves you more and more a thousand times than ever and you

[1] Kelly mentions (ii. 258) that S. 'had a cottage about half a mile from Hounslow Heath'. Cf. Taylor, ii. 172–3. It is just possible that S. was also referring to the Black Dog at Bedfont, 'the half way house between London and Bagshot' (*The Times*, 18 June 1798).

shall see there shall be [an] end of the least cause of Hecca's fretting. I staid[?] so long at Bedfont yesterday working like a Team of Horses that I was not in Town in Time for the Post—and to Day with my usual ill management I left my Papers at home meaning to come in before Dinner and finish my Letter, but business kept me out the whole Day so that I shall be in high Disgrace with my own good Hecca who does not neglect Dan but writes like a dear good Girl. I really have done more business as well as Rolla than you could imagine. Tomorrow I will fix to an hour my seeing you and we will undoubtedly make a short visit to Knoyle[1] and tell John I will really bring him some Plans. Bless you my Heart's Love I hope for a Line again tomorrow tho' I have been so bad—bless my Boy

Wednesday morning

Thank you my good Girl. I will send this off before I go out—I have been going over Rolla with Kemble who is just returned from Scotland.[2] All the Scenery Dresses and musick are going on.—Those are my motions. I go to my little Inn again with all-copying Burgess on Friday if the last Line of Rolla is compleat before I go to Bed I will be with you on Saturday to Dinner, if not by your own green eyes on Sunday.

Heaven thee bless and guard | S.

Indeed Sukey, I would have come sooner but it has been physically impossible

354. [To Richard Phillips][3]

Hyde MS. [Ph.]

Winchester
March 30th. [*1799*]

My Dear Sir

I am confident that no consideration would induce you

[1] John Ogle was granted the rectory and church at East Knoyle, Wiltshire, on 10 Feb. 1797 (Ogle, p. 137).

[2] Kemble acted 'during Passion week' at Edinburgh in Mar. 1799, and his benefit performance (in *Richard III*) was given there on 23 Mar. See *The Oracle*, 16 and 28 Mar. 1799.

[3] Bookseller and publisher (1767–1840). Knighted, 1808.

to spoil the first Nights effect of our Rolla by a previous publication on your Part. Therefore tho' I have paid no credit to the Rumour I trouble you with this Line. I think one of the Pieces you sent me cannot but succeed—I also wish to communicate with you respecting some manuscripts I have of Kotz[e]bue's.[1] | Yours truly | R B Sheridan

We shall be ready in a Fortnight.
I must send this to Town to be address'd

355. To John Grubb

Harvard MS.

[*1799?*]

Dear Grubb,

Woodriffe meets us to Dinner at the Shakespear.[2] For God's sake don't fail to come. They have only put off their motion 'till tomorrow—Yours ever | R B S

Friday

356. [To Henry Holland]

Gilmore MS. *Dock.*: Recd. and answered | May 13th. 1799 | saying if it[?] had come in time He would have been accommodated

17 Apr. 1799

My Dear Sir,

I must entreat you to write by return of Post to Mr. Batty to let me alone about arrears of Ground-Rent 'till *my* Play[3] appears which positively comes out on Saturday fortnight. And within four Days after that I solemnly assure you the money shall be paid. | yours truly | R B Sheridan

Wednesday
April 17th:

[1] Lady Elizabeth Foster reported on 8 Aug. 1799 that S. was adapting *The Virgin of the Sun*: see Vere Foster, *The Two Duchesses* (1898), pp. 157–8. Kotzebue thought C.G.Th. was more likely to pay him for his work: four of his plays were given there in 1799.

[2] D.L.Th. Receipts and Payments, 1798 to 1799 (Folger MS.) records on 13 April 1799 'Proprietors Bill at the Shakespear £4. 4. 0'. The Shakespeare's Head tavern was in Covent Garden, and was a favourite resort of the Foxites.

[3] *Pizarro*.

357. To Walter and James

Harvard MS. *Address*: Messrs. Walter and James.

Wednesday
April 17th: [*1799*]

Sir,

Altho' I have not the Pleasure of personally knowing you, yet I am strongly induced to hope that you will not refuse the request I now make. I understand there has been some unpunctuality in settling your account[1] for which reason the new Piece now preparing (in which I am so strongly and so personally interested) is at a Stand for want of Canvass. This Play of which I have the greatest expectations will be out in Ten Days[2] and you may positively rely on it that before it has been acted *three* Times you shall receive full Payment for whatever you supply to Mr. Johnson[3] and in the course of the season the liquidation of your former account. Your obedient Servant | R B Sheridan

358. To Richard Peake

Salt MS. *Address*: Mr. Peake to be taken to him immediately *Fr.*: R B Sheridan

[*Spring 1799?*]
Polesden
Tuesday

Dear Peake,

The blue Devils sometimes are too hard for you—Nothing shall go wrong if you will *now* work as I shall. Use every shilling of last Nights receipt—even the £40—and morrow's the same. I have written to Butlers[4] and the

[1] D.L.Th. Ledger, 1795 to 1799 (Folger MS.) reveals that they were paid £211. 13*s*. o*d*. in small sums between 5 Feb. 1798 and 5 Mar. 1799, for canvas.

[2] 'The Play of *Pizarro* will be brought forward positively after the ensuing holidays' (*Morn. Her.*, 27 Apr. 1799). S. procrastinated, as usual, and it was not presented until 24 May.

[3] 'Machinery, Decorations, and Dresses' (*The Oracle*, 25 May 1799) were under his direction.

[4] Charles Butler (1750–1832), of Lincoln's Inn. He had sent S. two draft deeds for consideration on 2 Feb. 1798

Bankers I would not take 40,000 for the two Plays[1] I am bringing with me. Pray dine with me tomorrow in H. St. at 5 precise— | Yours | R B S

my Grubb to meet you.

359. To John Grubb

Grubbe MS. *Address*: J. Grubb Esq. *Dock.*: From Sheridan to Grubb—Johnson £50 *Wm.*: 1797

[*1799?*]

Dear Grubb,

Johnson will give you this. I beseech you let him have the £50 instantly. He will explain to you that every thing is at a Stand for want of it. And every *pacer* now lost is £100 out of our Treasury | yours ever | R B S.

If Mrs. Jordan is sincere she never had such a Part on our Stage.[2]

Friday Evening

360. [To John Grubb?]

Harvard MS. *Address*: [in Grubb's hand?] J. White Esq. *Wm.*: 1796.

[*1799?*]

Shakespear
Friday Evening

Vile Absconder,

We only want you to be stout and confident and we shall trample on all difficulties. We have seen Burchell[3] Wright and Hindle Graham's[4] Partner and the alarm of this morning

(Harvard MSS.), and was associated with S. at least until 1812. His opinion of S.'s character is to be found in his *Reminiscences* (4th ed. 1824), pp. 191–3.

[1] S.'s great and justified confidence in the financial success of *Pizarro* supports the inference that it is alluded to here. The only other new plays given between 23 Apr. and the end of the season were Whalley's *Castle of Montval*; the anonymous *Trials of the Heart*; and Maria De Camp's *First Faults*.

[2] She was cast as Cora in *Pizarro*, and was very successful in the part.

[3] Joseph Burchell was solicitor to Storace's widow, and claimed money due to her from D.L.Th.

[4] Graham and Hindle were property auctioneers of 88 Chancery Lane. See *Morn. Her.*, 10 Dec. 1799.

turns out to be a mistake[1]—Our Friends Woodriffe Peake and Burgess have sign'd the Bond etc. which settles with the Trustees—we will see you tomorrow. | Yours | R B Sheridan

361. To ——

Harvard MS.

[*Apr.–May 1799?*]

My Dear Sir,

I am extremely sorry I could not keep my appointment with you to Day—but you will not fail to find me at Mr. Peakes *punctually at two tomorrow*. When we will arrange the other Benefits—about which I am very anxious. There seems to me to be a combination that my Piece should not be brought forward this year—and I am determined it shall—many of the Performers Benefits are brought unusually forward and the return they make is to occupy the whole Time of the Company etc. etc. etc.[2]—in new Plays this is really too nonsensical to be endured—and there must be an end to it | yrs ever | R B Sheridan

Tuesday Evening

362. [To Richard Phillips]

Harvard MS. *Pub.*: [R. Ryan], *Dramatic Table Talk* (1830), iii, facing 298.

2 May 1799

Mr. Sheridan will repay Mr. Phillips what he has paid Miss Plumtre[3] for The Spaniards in Peru and pay him tomorrow fifty Pounds over, Mr. S. taking the risk of publication on

[1] A note by J. Richardson to Grubb appears on the same sheet: 'The Severity of the abominable Law which threat[e]ned us today was owing to a Mistake from Burchell's office. We have laboured all day about it and have settled the thing for the present. The Affair of this Application to Chancery is also in the best Way as you by this time know.'

[2] Between 8 Apr. and 24 May there were eighteen benefit nights.

[3] Anna Plumptre (1760–1818) was paid £25 on 6 and 13 May by D.L.Th. (Add. MS. 29710, f. 139) for her translation, *The Spaniards in Peru*.

himself. Mr. Phillips is still entitled to the Preference for Publishing Mr. Thompson['s] Stranger—which Mr. Sheridan engages shall be in Mr. Phillips['s] Hands within a Fortnight from the Date of this | R B Sheridan May 2d.

Mr. Phillips is to withold the publication of Miss Plumtre's Spaniards in Peru for three weeks or till the Day after the Play call'd Pizarro shall have been performed at Drury-Lane-Theatre.

363. To John Grubb

Harvard MS.

[*May 1799?*]

Dear Grubb

I lost all yesterday by dining with Kelly,[1] and drinking wine because I liked his musick for our Piece—and I have lost this morning owing to that vile fag end of the Firm[2] calling at Kelly's just as I was going and seducing me to a Grill, and if we dine together I know I shall lose to day and to-morrow morning. I am going to Troward[3] on the great business by appointment and I am to read their Parts to Jordan and Siddons[4] this Evening—I will be with you in the morning, if I do not call in on you after Dinner | Yours ever | R B S.

364. To Richard Peake

Harvard MS.

[*8 May 1799?*]
Wednesday Evening

Dear Peake,

Nothing can equal the Distress I have been in to Day for

[1] He was musical director at D.L.Th., and composed the music for *Pizarro*. See Kelly, ii. 143–6, for his amusing account of S.'s methods and procrastination.

[2] Joseph Richardson.

[3] See p. 107, n. 2. The D.L.Th. account book records payments, on 8 and 9 May 1799, of £240 and £187. 10*s*., to Troward's partner, Albany Wallis.

[4] On 29 Apr. 1799 Mrs. Siddons's daughter stated that her mother had not yet seen her part (Elvira) in *Pizarro* (O. G. Knapp, *An Artist's Love Story* (1904), p. 191). On 14 May, *The Oracle* reported that 'Mr. Sheridan's New Play is rehearsed privately at his own house'.

the £100—I have seen Graham and the £180 will be forthcoming when ever wanted—so from to Nights Receipts (which will be plentiful) you must positively repay Storace's[1] hundred and enter it. G. Edwards will wait and bring it to me. I never got Fozard's[2] damn'd Note 'till this evening who must have £50 of it. It was directed to you

The advertisement naming the Day for Pizarro is gone[3] | Yrs | R B S.

365. To Richard Peake

Egerton MS. 1975, ff. 54–55. *Address*: Mr. Peake | Mr. Watkins, | Charing-Cross. *Dock.*: Mr. Sheridan

[*May 1799?*]

Dear Peake,

I have been disappointed where I call'd—and tomorrow is the *last* Day for the Taxes. I think your Friend Watkins would assist with £50,[4] you having authority to repay him in the first weeks etc.—pray request it.

Beg Woodriffe[5] to send to Burgess by the Bearer—advertisement I trust gone— | Yrs ever | R B S.

366. [To Willoughby Lacy?][6]

N.L.I. MS. 3901, f. 22.

[*May 1799?*]

My dear Sir,

I am very sorry I am really sorry I am so unwell this morn

[1] D.L.Th. Receipts and Payments, 1798 to 1799 (Folger MS.) notes payments to Mrs. Storace of £60 on 8 May, and £40 on account on 11 May.

[2] Probably James Fozard of Park Lane, the fashionable horse-dealer and keeper of livery stables.

[3] Advertised in *The Oracle*, 10 May 1799, for performance on 22 May. Two days before it was due to be given, an advertisement appeared in the same paper stating that the play was 'unavoidably deferred' to Friday 24 May.

[4] The D.L.Th. account book notes that Watkins lent £30 in May 1799 (Add. MS. 29710, f. 139). He was repaid on 29 June.

[5] Grubb's solicitor Robert Woodriff of Brick Court, Temple.

[6] In an undated note to Lacy (*Wm.* 1794) S. asks to be excused to Mr. Landel and promises that 'the Note shall be paid in the course of next week' (N.L.S. MS. 35218, f. 2).

I can see no one. I can get Peake to do nothing at this moment—and there is not a shilling in the Treasury but what goes to bring out our famous Piece. This infallibly comes out next week and before it has been six times acted Mr. Landell may rely on it I will settle with him | Yours | R B Sheridan

Saturday

367. 'To an Official in the Lord Chamberlain's Office'

Pub.: *A.P.C., 1914–16*, i. 141.

23 May [*1799?*][1]

I am confident you will pronounce on perusing the Piece . . . that the Form and Object of it is not only unexceptionable but such as [I] have no doubt may be honour'd with peculiar approbation.

368. To William Siddons[2]

Add. MS. 35118, f. 76. Copy.

3 June 1799

Sir,

The information you request for making up Mrs. Siddons account is in short compass—the Proprietors agreed to insure her Benefit to clear *400* Guineas by one Night of Pizarro (on Mr. Siddons engaging for her performance during its run)[3]

[1] Catalogued as '23 May 1797'; but I think the letter refers to *Pizarro*, acted on 24 May 1799. S.'s figure nine can easily be mistaken for a seven.

[2] Mrs. Siddons's husband was also her business manager. She wanted to leave D.L.Th., but Siddons persuaded her to go on acting there as the only way in which she might get the large amount of money owing to her. In spite of the above agreement, the debt was not paid. Siddons agreed in Sept. to his wife's quitting D.L.Th. and wrote claiming their money. Settlement was achieved on 21 Dec. (Mr. Robert H. Taylor's MS.), when a private box was leased to Siddons in lieu of the debt of £1,500.

[3] A note appended to the copy of the letter states, 'The parenthesis a mistake of the Proprietors'. This is probably by Siddons, but may be by Peake.

Mrs. Siddons was to put her name up as usual and Mr. Siddons to *state from his Book* the Actual money received for Tickets, if these do not amount to four hundred Guineas the difference is to be made up from the receipt of the Night | R B Sheridan | Jno. Grubb | Jos. Richardson

369. To Lady Holland

Pub.: Sichel, i. 93.[1]

July 1799

. . . The tenth of July was so delicious, something in the temperature so bewitching and tempting to go astray, [that if he were] to sit in judgment upon a cause of gallantry, if the indictment stated it as commited on the tenth of July, he would [not] go into the evidence, but instantly bring in a 'guilty by the visitation of God'.

370. To Richard Peake

Salt MS. *Address*: Mr. Peake

Wednesday morning
August 28 [*1799?*]

Dear Peake,

Pray pawn your credit once more for me, and send me by tomorrow's or Friday's conveyance a six dozen hamper of good wine viz. 4 dozen Port and two dozen Sherry, and that will set me up. I return to Town saturday | Yours ever | R B S.

we have managed Rodwell's[2] business—

[1] Sichel mentions that this letter was in the Holland House MSS., but Lord Ilchester informed me that he could not find it among them.

[2] The D.L.Th. account book (Add. MS. 29710, f. 197) contains the note of repayment: '17 Feb. 1802—Rodwell money lent to pay the company £80. 12'.

371. [To Richard Peake]

Folger MS.: D.L.Th. Salaries, 1799–1802, f. 2.

Sept. 1799

I would head the Account with '*Receipts and disbursements of Drury-Lane Theatre.*' I would then keep the Title of '1st. Office 5 Days. 2nd. Office' etc. etc. and then I would not state '5 Days Pay List—£100' or whatever it is—but recapitulate by name every individual receiving Salary. At the bottom of each Page I would leave Room for Notes and observations for the information of the Bankers, in order that they may be apprized of the Nature and exigency of many of the Payments. The whole object of this account to be so delivered and kept at the Bankers being to prove to them that if they as our principal Creditors had possession of the Theatre they could not or would not dispose of the Receipts otherwise than as disposed of by the present Proprietors, it is indispensible to his Purpose that Mr. Peake shall have a due Voucher for every Payment. | R B S.

372. To Richard Peake

Add. MS. 35118, ff. 160–1. *Address*: R. Peake Esq. *Dock.*: R B S

[*Sept. 1799?*]
Godalman
Friday morning

Dear Peake

Read the enclosed[1] and you will be master of the Line you

[1] Apparently Add. MS. 35118, f. 162. It is in S.'s hand and was written obviously for Peake to copy. It seems to be to Hammersley and is dated 'Friday'. The letter reads: 'My Dear Sir | I must entreat you will see Mr. Drewe in the course of this Day. The Paying the old Renters so early and other bills accepted has left every week in arrear to the Company—in selling the last two £500 Shares to Fosbrook Mr. Sheridan says He has exhausted every resource, and He conceives himself bound by Promise not to apply to Mr. Drewe. The overdrawing is greatly reduced to Bankers, but there is nothing for the Company tomorrow and you well know at the present moment how necessary we should be punctual with them I would have been with Mr. Drewe this morning as Mr. Sheridan sent to me, but have been quite ill and confined

are to take. *Seal* and deliver it *yourself* as *soon as possible.* About the Receipts I am *peremptory* for reasons I will shew you of the utmost benefit in future. So pledge yourself so to send the money every morning in the name of the Proprietors of D.L. Theatre. In short do everything to encourage Hammersly to assist *this on Saturday* and my Life on everything going well afterwards. Don't *croak* and press for more than £600. Our advertisement will keep back many and on the Spot if press'd they will go on a little. A Line to say you have manag'd this will make me think you a Prime Minister. | Yrs | R B S.

get Thoman's[1] money I have none

373. To John Graham

Osborn MS. *Address*: Mr: Graham | Holbourn *Dock.*: Sheridan

[*1799?*]
Thursday

Sir

I am much obliged to you and I have sent up a Person immediately on the receipt of your Letter to Mr. Carpenter. I am sure you will consult with him and prevent anything happening 'till I see you on sunday which I will *without fail.* You will find yourself perfectly safe in anything you undertake. I cannot conceive what the execution is besides Partridge's[2] which I thought there was no necessity of settling 'till the Term. I shall most readily make you amends for the risk you may run | your's truly | R B Sheridan.

all Day—will you be so good to call on Mr. Drewe. I am sure He will not under all circumstances diminish the accommodation before given, especially as the Treasury security will be lodged in the names of the Trustees tomorrow morning.' The sale to Fosbrook seems to belong to 16 Sept. 1799: see D.L.Th. Receipts and Payments, Sept. 1799 to Nov. 1799 (Folger MS.).

[1] Thoman was repaid £50 on 7 Oct. 1800. It had been lent by him to satisfy the old renters.

[2] The Grubbe MSS. contain a letter, signed by S., Grubb, and Richardson, to Peake authorizing him to accept a bill from Mr. Partridge for £100 due next season. It is dated June 1798. As early as 24 Apr. 1795, T. Wright & Co. of Henrietta Street had applied to S. (Salt MS.) for payment of two bills of £100 each, accepted by S. for Robert Partridge and discounted by Wright.

374. To Richard Peake

Egerton MS. 1975, ff. 34–35. *Address*: Mr. Peake *Dock.*: Mr. Sheridan

[*1799?*]

Dear Peake

We all come to Dinner tomorrow without fail

Burgess will give you the Receipt of Bacon for Westley[1] which enter in the Journal, and for God's sake don't fail to send me the amount by the Bearer. He must be back with me by 12, or I can not stir. I shall not leave Town again 'till all is right. | Yours ever | R B S.

Friday

375. To John Grubb

Harvard MS.

[*1799*]

Dear Grubb,

I call to make you easy about Lincoln's-Inn.—All there is safe[2]—and everything will be settled. I got there just to the moment. | Yours | R B S.

[1] D.L.Th. Nightly Accounts, 1799 to 1800 (Folger MS.) records on 7 Nov. 1799: 'Mr. Burgess for Bacon Law Expences £47. 10. 0.' The Ledger, 1799 to 1802 (Folger MS.) amplifies this on the same date naming the amount as: 'By Insurance of Mr. Westley's Life.' It also notes payments to 'Mr. Bacon Attorney' of £20 on 2 Nov., and of £71. 15*s.* 0*d.* on 27 Nov. 1799. A copy of a letter from one Bunce to Dr. S. Goodenough of 21 Nov. 1799 (Ford MS.) reveals that Westley's life had been insured for £1,800 for one year from 12 Nov., 'and in consequence of it he has been liberated'. This seems to imply that Westley had been arrested for some debt connected with D.L.Th., and had obtained his freedom by depositing the policy as a security.

[2] The Grubbe MSS. reveal that Hammersley's solicitor, Nowell, wrote on 15 Apr. 1799 that Hammersley would sell Grubb's house unless 'some arrangement would be made for the payment of the mortgage debt'. After the property had been advertised, S. stated on 16 Dec. that he had new proposals to make. Four days later, it was agreed that the sale should be postponed for a fortnight.

376. To Richard Peake

Egerton MS. 1975, ff. 67–68. *Address*: Mr. Peake *Dock*: Mr. Sheridan

[*11 Dec. 1799?*]
Shakespear

Dear Peake,

You must positively come to me here, and bring £60[1] in your Pocket—

Fear nothing. Be civil to all Claimants, for trust me in three months there will not exist one unsatisfied claimant. Shut up the Office and come here directly. | R B S.

377. [To Lord Holland]

Holland House MS. 2 (b). *Address*: [in Tom S.'s hand] Ld. Holland *Wm.*: 1798

[*Dec. 1799?*]

My dear Lord,

Knowing and much lamenting Tom's unpunctuality in answering Letters I cannot think of trusting him[2] to make my excuse and express my regret that I cannot wait on you on Saturday, as I am obliged to go out of town tomorrow Thursday Evening | Yours truly | R B S.

378. To Richard Peake

Egerton MS. 1975, f. 7. *Address*: Mr. Peake *Dock.*: Mr. Sheridan | [Then in Burgess's hand] Dear Sir | Pay Mr. Fosbrook £10 which he has lent me and send *fifty pounds* by Post *this Night* to me at the Post office Norwich [Endorsed by Peake] No. 2777 £50 26 Day of Decr. 1799 | B.N. sent to Norwich | directed to Henry Burgess | at the Post Office Norwich | Mr. Thoman 55 Spring Gardens | Tuesday.

[*25 Dec. 1799?*]

Dear Peake

See Wright and Graham and in confidence inform them

[1] D.L.Th. Nightly Accounts, 1799 to 1800 (Folger MS.) notes a payment of £60 to S. on 11 Dec. 1799.

[2] Tom S.'s letter reads: 'Seeing but scarce believing my Father's unprecedented attention in replying to an invitation, I can not think of burdening him with an excuse from me, or express how happy I shall be to wait on you on Saturday as I have postponed my going out of town till the day after—'.

what takes me out of Town. Pay Wright £85 to Night on account of £3000 Share and promise him more pray attend to both these things. Let me hear from you tomorr[ow] and later on Friday, and amount of Receipt. I shall be back saturday[1] | Yrs | R B S

379. To Richard Peake

Arthur A. Houghton, Jr. MS. [Ph.]

[*1799–1800*]

Dear Peake,

If you stop the first carriage or knock down the first man that goes past your Door you must give the Bearer of this ten Pounds. He will come to you on Horse-back It is really a matter of almost Life and Death—you must borrow of Barford[2] or any neighbour, for not a moment is to be lost | yrs | R B S.

I am making up your account another way by which much remains due to me.

380. To Richard Peake

Pub.: *A.P.C.*, 1914–16, i. 141. *Address*: Mr. Peake

[*1799–1800?*]
Sunday Evening at Wiltons[3]

I'll pledge my life on Glassissa[4] giving you back the £50 at the end of the week, but I am remin'd [?] without your

[1] The Harvard MSS. contain a note from S., Richardson, and Robert Woodriff of 17 Dec. [1799] proposing to dine with Peake at the Sugarloaf, Dunstable, on Sunday, 29 Dec. They also contain an agreement for arbitration signed there on 30 Dec. by the first three and by Burgess. To re-establish the credit of D.L.Th. they decided to refer its affairs to Pigott, Const, and Morris; and to ask Hammersley & Co. to name a fourth arbitrator.

[2] D.L.Th. Ledger, 1799 to 1802 (Folger MS.) notes a total of £65 paid to Barford between 27 Nov. 1799 and 8 Jan. 1800, as 'Cash on Account of Advance'. D.L.Th. Salaries, 1799 to 1802 (Folger MS.) shows that S. was paid £10 on 28 Dec. 1799.

[3] Wilton House, near Salisbury, the seat of the Earl of Pembroke? Or a misreading of 'Wilsons'?

[4] A misreading of 'Glossop'? He was paid £50 on 21 Oct. 1799 and on 10 Nov. 1800. See Add. MS. 29710, ff. 150, 159.

advancing it to me *early in the morning*, reserve however enough to answer for a hamper of wine *3 dozen Port and one dozen claret*—and I trust to your activity so as to provide to Night (as it is no *Wedding Day*[1]) that the said hamper shall be at my Stables BEFORE 8 tomorrow morning when my coach[2] must go off for Polesden. . . .

381. To Richard Peake

Egerton MS. 1975, ff. 114–15. *Address*: Mr. Peake | Charlotte-st. | Rathbone Place. *Dock.*: Mr. Sheridan

Sunday Jan 12th: [*1800*]

Dear Peake,

Pray call on Pratten[3] yourself and arrange with him a satisfactory mode of settling his account. His Attorney Millington well knows that He owes me £50 with many many years Interest. If He will have the fairness and Honesty to pay it to Pratten I shall think well of him. If not make Pratten assured that He shall lose no Part of his Debt—and settle certain installments with him. You know that tho' I don't think He acted rightly towards me I have employ'd no one else—for I dislike breaking with old Friends, and hate new Faces | Yrs | R B S

382. To His Wife

Whitbread MS. 4088. *Dock.*: Mr. Sheridan to Mrs. Sheridan about a Picture. *Wm.*: 18|

[*1800?*][4]
Wednesday

My Dear Hecca

I have just received a Letter from poor Gouldsmith, which begins 'Dear Sir, my errand yesterday was to learn if

[1] Probably a reference to some recent wedding as well as to Elizabeth Inchbald's *The Wedding Day*, first acted at D.L.Th. on 13 Oct. 1794.

[2] *A.P.C.* reads 'coat(?)'.

[3] D.L.Th. Nightly Accounts, 1799 to 1800 (Folger MS.) records between 11 and 13 Jan. 1800, 'Mr. Pratten for Mr. S. £10'. Pratten was a Bond Street apothecary: see Black, p. 189.

[4] D.L.Th. Nightly Accounts, 1788 to 1800 (Folger MS.) records on 14 Jan. 1800, 'Goldsmith Dft. dated 17th Mr. S. £20'.

you knew any one who would give £30 or £25 or even £20 for the Pictures it would alleviate our distress and encourage the Girl to persevere.' I send the Picture for Whitbread to look at you heard Brooks[?] said of it—if I had any money I should think it a bargain as well as a Charity—| Yours | R B S

383. [To the Editor of *The Sun* / the *Morning Post*]

Pub.: *The Sun*, 21 Jan. 1800, and the *Morn. Post*, 22 January 1800, as an 'Extract of a Letter'.

Norwich, Jan 18. [*1800*]

This city has been for some time a scene of incessant tumult and affray between the military and the town's people. As our Provincial Papers have given hasty and contradictory accounts of the transactions which have taken place, I send you a correct account of the whole business, on which you may rely.[1]

There had appeared for some time among those who are called the Democratic party, of this town, a marked antipathy to the 9th Regiment of Foot, originating, it is supposed, from their having been concerned with the Inniskillings in the tumult which took place, when Thelwall's[2] lecture-room was pulled down. I need not remind you that this regiment was engaged in the late Expedition to Holland, because its services were particularly distinguished; it lost in killed and wounded above 400 men, and nine officers. The remainder of the regiment being again unfortunately quartered at Norwich on their return, the old spirit of animosity appears to have revived with the town's-people, and

[1] The authorship of this letter is ascribed to S. by S. T. Coleridge, who states that Tom S. was concerned in the disorders at Norwich and that S. went there too. On his return S. gave Stuart, editor of the *Morn. Post*, a verbal account that completely contradicted his written version; and Coleridge claimed that, in print, S. was deliberately lying. Coleridge was friendly with Thelwall, and was angry with S. for his procrastinating attitude to the tragedy Coleridge had submitted to D.L.Th. See *The Collected Letters of S. T. Coleridge* (ed. E. L. Griggs, Oxford, 1956), i. 304, 357, 564, 603. D.L.Th. Nightly Accounts, 1799 to 1800 (Folger MS.) records a payment of £50 on 16 Jan. 1800 to 'Mr. Sheridan to Norwich'.

[2] John Thelwall (1764–1834), political reformer.

frequent disputes between them and the soldiers were the consequence; in all of which it appears that Col. Montgomery took the utmost pains to prevent riot, and promote reconciliation. Last week, however, as the Colonel and a party of Officers, who had been dining together, were returning to the barracks, they were insulted near the Market-place, and from abusive words, blows ensued; the tumult, after a short interval, became general, and a handful of officers not exceeding six or seven, seizing the bludgeons from the original rioters, dispersed their assailants, amounting to thirty or forty. In this affray, Mr. John Harper, hosier, of this city, received a blow on his hand, and a mortification it is said unexpectedly ensued; Doctor Alderson[1] and Mr. Rigby[2] having deposed upon oath that his life was in danger, Colonel Montgomery who attended on Monday with his bail, Lord Bayning[3] and Mr. Kerrison,[4] was, to the astonishment of the whole town (the magistrates having previously unanimously agreed to accept bail) committed to our city goal. Colonel Montgomery, accompanied by Lord Bayning and other friends, went there accordingly. On Wednesday night, however, about half past ten o'clock, upwards of six hundred soldiers from the baracks in St. George's assembled before the goal with a determination to rescue their Colonel. These men appear to have acted with discretion equal to their zeal. They left their arms with their comrades. They offered no insult to any person in their way to the goal. The door being opened to one of them, who requested to speak with the Colonel, a considerable number rushed in, and all defence or opposition became useless. The Colonel, however, not only intreated them to desist from so illegal and unwarrantable a proceeding, but even had recourse to the severest menaces in accomplishing his object of forcing them to retreat without the prison doors, which being properly secured, he addressed them from the window, saying he should be happy to head them in any danger in the field, but never in opposition to the civil authority of the country.

[1] Robert Alderson, a counsel on the Norwich circuit.

[2] Presumably Dr. Rigby of St. Giles's Street.

[3] Charles Townshend, 1st Lord Bayning (1728–1810).

[4] Roger Kerrison of Brooke. He was High Sheriff of Norfolk in 1800, and was knighted in June 1800.

The Colonel then entreated them to depart, assuring them that he was confident he should soon be liberated in a legal way, and the soldiers, giving three cheers, returned quietly to barracks.

The next day the surgeons, who attended Mr. Harper, testified to the Magistrates that the danger had ceased, and Colonel Montgomery[1] was in consequence admitted to bail; his brother, Sir George Montgomery,[2] and Mr. Kerrison, having entered into recognizances.—On Friday our City Quarter Sessions commenced, when Charles Harvey, Esq., the Steward, made a very pertinent speech, in which he noticed, that several bills would, it was well known, be preferred for assaults, in which the military were implicated, and that he understood each party would exhibit mutual complaints; that the Jury ought to hear both parties cases before they determined any of the bills, and in the most delicate manner touched upon the relative duties of the military and the citizens, observing, that if they found that the parties, unmindful of the services which the army had performed and the protection they had afforded to their country, had provoked a justifiable resistance; or, on the contrary, if the gentlemen of the army, without provocation, had insulted and ill-treated the inhabitants, they (the Grand Jury) would reject or find the bills from the evidence which would be brought before them. The result has been, that the indictments intended to have been preferred against Mr. J. Frewer[3] and Mr. J. Frewer, Jun. by Col. Montgomery, and against that gentleman by Messrs Frewers and Mr. Boardman,[4] were withdrawn, and the matters in dispute were referred to the determination of Aldermen Patteson[5] and Brown, with liberty to choose an umpire. This arrangement was only acceded to by Col. Montgomery, in consequence of an apology made in open Court by the Counsel, on the part of the prosecution against Col. Montgomery.

[1] Robert Montgomery was killed in a duel on 6 April 1803.

[2] Sir George Montgomery, 2nd baronet (d. 1831).

[3] J. H. Frewer, saddler and harness maker, Old Haymarket, Norwich.

[4] Presumably one of the following: R. R. and E. Boardman, woollen drapers, 22 Market Place; J. Boardman, hatter and hosier, Market Place; Ben Boardman, hatter and hosier, 33 London Lane, Norwich.

[5] J. Patteson, brewer, Barrack Street.

Before Colonel Montgomery withdrew from the Court, he was addressed by Mr. Steward Harvey in the name of the Justices who were assembled to express their sense of the firmness and propriety of his conduct in repressing the tumult of the soldiers who had attempted his rescue from confinement; especially as it had been effected by reminding them that he was amenable to the laws of his country, in whose justice he had perfect confidence. The Steward added, that he felt peculiar gratification in being called on to make this public acknowledgment of so honourable an action; and remarked, that although he must pronounce the purpose of those men to be extremely reprehensible; yet it undoubtedly bore a very flattering testimony of their esteem for the character of their Commander. He concluded by observing that he was authorized by the Magistrates of the City (and he was confident that he expressed the general feelings of the town in conveying their sentiments) to return their thanks to Colonel Montgomery for the whole of his conduct, while with his regiment in this city.

384. To Richard Peake

Egerton MS. 1975, ff. 91–92. *Address*: Mr. Peake *Dock.*: Mr. Sheridan an Account

[*1800*]

Due to Mr. S. this Season from the Theatre—up to *January* 1st.

	£		
Received by Fosbrook on my Boxes *beyond* what He has had from The Theatre at least	500	—	—
Seventy Nights Salary	367	10	0
Wrights Receipt for Rent on £3000 Share for last season	213	—	—
Ditto on the present Season	70	—	—
For the 40th Night of Pizzarro[1]	100	—	—
	1,250	10	—

[1] D.L.Th. Receipts and Payments, 1799 to 1800 (Folger MS.), records on 21 Dec. 1799 a payment to S. of £100 for the fortieth night of *Pizarro.*

Wednesday Evening

Give me tomorrow an exact account of money paid to me from the Treasury this Season—by my account there is still a great sum due to me. And including the £3000 Shares still undisposed of I could more than double the above Demand.—Burgess must have £100 for me to Night. I will meet you at the Theatre punctually at ½ past two to-morrow | yours truly | R B S.

What was the Receipt last Night—and what to Night?

385. To Richard Peake

Egerton MS. 1975, f. 113. *Address*: Mr. Peake *Fr.*: R B Sheridan *Dock.*: Mr. Sheridan *Wm.*: 1799

[*11 Mar. 1800?*]
Tuesday

Dear Peake,

On my road to Butlers I stop to give you a Line. Make up the Packets of appropriations as before, and let Dunn pay in every shilling of the Receipt as before. Borrow £15 from Dale[1] and give him a Draught for it which He may take at *one* o'clock. Pray be *exact* in all this—of course draw yourself for what you want in the course of the morning or if you can date for tuesday | Yours ever | R B S

I reckon you will have a little wine at your Egyptian Feast[2] to Day

386. To His Wife

Osborn MS. *Wm.*: 1799

[*20 Mar. 1800?*][3]
London Thursday
morn.

I got away from Farnborough only this morning at 7 o'clock

[1] Boxkeeper at D.L.Th. He died on 4 Apr. 1807. See *Annual Register . . . 1807*, p. 563. D.L.Th. Nightly Accounts, 1799 to 1800 (Folger MS.), records under 15 Mar. 1800, 'Mr. Sheridan by Dale 15.'

[2] Franklin and Florio's *The Egyptian Festival* was first acted at D.L.Th. on 11 Mar. 1800.

[3] Rae, ii. 232, dates the letter '1809', but this is unacceptable because Elizabeth (Betsy) Streatfeild, who is men-

—and was in Town by half past ten. Mrs. Bouverie and Harley went on tuesday morn. And Mrs. Wilmot press'd me so much to stay tuesday as Streatfields were not arrived that I could not refuse. They came in the Evening and a combination of circumstances kept me yesterday with the chaise waiting all Day—I'll tell you all about it when we meet. It is a most unhappy scene—*He* everything that's wrong and ungenerous thro' the whole business[1] and *She* entirely the Reverse.—Streatfield stays to Day, goes home tomorrow Betsy remains with Mrs. W. 'till monday and they go together to Chiddingstone—at least so it was settled last Night. My stopping there will cost me one Day more in Town but nothing shall prevent my being off on Saturday—half to Day I lose with the King at the Theatre where I am going to Dine and dress. The House will be immense which was not expected[2]—and so will saturday be.[3] My Dear Wench I do long to see thy eyes. Betsy told me you look remarkably well and certainly *fatter* which rejoiced the cockles of Dan's Heart. But Ma'am I don't think you write as if you cared so much about Dan's coming![4] you dip your Pen in the *cold* sea I doubt as well as your little Nob—is it so Hecca?

I hope Tom will take care of himself.[5] I am very glad He

tioned by S., died on 24 June 1801: see Ogle, p. 140. Sichel, ii. 268, suggests that it belongs to 'a year or so after' S.'s second marriage, but this is refuted by the watermark. The question turns upon the King's visit to D.L.Th. That of 5 June 1799 was the first he had paid for four years (according to the *Morn. Her.*, 6 June 1799), and there was no royal performance in the weeks before Easter in 1801. There were, however, two command performances in Mar. 1800: of *The Rivals* and *Blue Beard* on 6 Mar., and of *The Egyptian Festival* and *The Wedding Day* on 20 Mar. The reference to the nearness of Easter makes it likely that S. was referring to the performances of 20 Mar.

1 They separated because of their incompatibility of temperament; and Mrs. Wilmot agreed to visit her husband when he was paralysed in Oct. 1814 only after he had given his word of honour that it would make 'no difference to our independent circumstances' (Grey MS.).

2 D.L.Th. Nightly Accounts, 1799 to 1800 (Folger MS.), shows that receipts were £474. 13*s.* 0*d.* on 20 Mar.

3 Receipts from *Love for Love* and *Of Age Tomorrow* were £266. 13*s.* 0*d.*

4 What appears to be Mrs. S.'s reply to this is printed by Sichel, ii. 268–9. She gives S. permission to hate Wilmot as much as he likes and she adds, 'Sheridan, how much better you are than anything on earth, and how well I love you. I will hate everything you hate, and love everything you love, so God bless you.' (Osborn MS.)

5 In June he was said to be betrothed to Lady Anne Lambton, who had an income of £10,000 a year (*Monthly Mirror*, 1st Ser. (1800), ix. 369). Nothing came of this.

is away from this Vortex—next week indeed and the Easter week the Town will be deserted so we shall be only in the Fashion.

You never tell me anything about yourself or Robin or Anne or Scott—or or or—

but bless you Ma'am for all. I am rather tired—for I had no sleep last Night at all going to bed at one and being resolute to get up at five.

Kiss my child for me. Mrs. W's girl[1] is particularly improved. I have brought away the prettiest Drawing that ever was seen.

Pray tell Tom I shall bring a Book[2] for him which I am much mistaken if He will not read with Pleasure and attention tho' all over morality and Religion, and yet I think it the most argumentative logical ingenious and by far the *wittiest* performance I ever met with. For my Part I mean to die in a Hermit's cell. I met with it at Wilmots, brought there by Harley.

My Dear one write to me by return of Post. I shan't set off 'till it comes in— | S.

On the state of Things as I left them at Farnborough one word only—Streatfeild is liberal friendly and right-headed. I utterly and mortally despise and abominate Wilmot. Bouverie has been—Bouverie perfect. Arabella and Betsey everything that's amiable and proper too the Umpires most well meaning but unluckily for poor Bab duped by the coarsest craft, and Bab herself an unstrug[g]ling Victim sacrificing herself and everything for her child.

[1] Arabella Jane Wilmot, now nearly four.

[2] Possibly Johann Georg von Zimmerman's *Solitude*, published in German between 1756 and 1786, and in English from 1791. In a notice of his life and work, the *Monthly Visitor*, ii (1797), 193, 393–4 mentioned his ardour of soul, and added, 'If the style of writing known by the term wit, which was the fashion formerly, still remained so, the wit of Zimmerman would be of the brightest and most captivating nature'. S. refers to him in Letter 558.

387. To Richard Peake

Boston Public Library MS., Mass. *Address*: Farnham April seven 1800 | Mr. Peake | Charlotte-St. | Rathbone-Place | London *Fr.*: Free | R B Sheridan *Dock.*: Mr. Sheridan

7 April 1800
Monday on the road[1]

Dear Peake

I have written to Siddons and Kemble to suspend their Draughts to the middle of next week and you may rely on their doing it—so send Wright an account of his and Graham's Bills etc. I have written to put off the £100 they want.—If this is not done the moment you receive this I *know* that every thing in H. St. will be pull'd to Pieces[2]—*I rely on you* | yrs ever | R B S.

388. To Richard Peake

Harvard MS. *Address*: Lymington April tenth 1800 | Mr. Peake | Charlotte St. | Rathbone Place | London *Fr.*: Free | R B Sheridan *Dock.*: Mr. Sheridan

10 April 1800
Thursday
at H Scotts Esq
Lymington

Dear Peake

Beg borrow or steal and send me £30 and send it *by return of Post*. I shall then be in Town for the Lord Mayor's Monday without fail. I trust in nothing disappointing De Montfort[3] for monday— | Yours ever | R B S.

I have not had a Line here from a soul—

[1] To Lymington.

[2] On 20 Jan. 1800 John Graham (Wright's partner as Sheriff's officer) wrote to Peake to say (Dufferin MS.) that Wright was inexorable and that either Howlett or Postan must 'go to Hertford Street' (i.e. take possession there). D.L.Th. Salaries, 1799 to 1802 (Folger MS.), records on 19 Apr. 1800, 'Graham Money paid for House £25'.

[3] Joanna Baillie's *De Monfort* was acted at D.L.Th. on Tuesday, 29 Apr. 1800. S. said in the Commons that her 'admirable works were an honour to her and the country' (Hansard, 1st Ser., xix. 1146).

389. To Richard Peake

Egerton MS. 1975, ff. 63–64. *Address*: Mr. Peake *Dock.*: Mr. Sheridan

[*3 May 1800*]

Dear Peake

Without fail and immediately give the Bearer 5 Guineas to buy Hay and Corn for my Coach Horses[1]—they have not had a morsel of either since last Night | R B S.

I shall call on you presently

390. To William Adam

Adam MS. *Dock.*: Mr. Sheridan | 19th July 1800

Saturday
July 19th *1800*

My Dear Adam,

You shall positively have my Letter respecting Coutts on monday. I call'd on you yesterday to beg you in the interval to get . . .[2] to suspend Proceedings or I am told something will be done on Monday that will put me to great expence—I return to Town Monday. | Your's ever | R B Sheridan

391. To His Wife

Osborn MS. *Wm.*: 1800

[*23 July 1800*]
Wednesday

My Sweet Girl—You must not be angry at this Fif.[3] I am this moment getting into the chaise with Lord W. Russell[4] for Wobourn—I will write you an immense Letter tomorrow. When I got to the House of Commons Monday—I found

[1] D.L.Th. Nightly Accounts, 1799 to 1800 (Folger MS.), notes on 3 May 1800 payment of £5. 5*s.* 0*d.* to 'Tom Groom for Mr. S.'

[2] Illegible.

[3] A word meaning 'letter' frequently used by S.'s first wife.

[4] William Russell (1767–1840) was M.P. for Surrey, 1789–1807, and an old friend of S.

Burdett[1] had put off the Prison business to yesterday—not liking to go on without me—and accident made me five minutes too late. So I was compell'd to stew another Day in Town. However it has turn'd out luckily for yesterday's Debate turn'd out more to my satisfaction than almost anything I ever took a Part in since I have been in the House of Commons. I made the Speaker *bitter*[2]—and I really think smote Pitt's conscience In short we carried our Point—and have voted *nem con* an address to the King to institute an immediate Enquiry to the Conduct of this Prison etc. etc. I own I am extremely pleased[3] at this event tho' it does not seem of the importance of great political Questions. The Gallery was immensely full—and the result gives universal satisfaction. I don't send you the Papers—for there is not one of them that gives an idea of the Debate, which the Citizens who have been with me this morning are outrageous at. However the Good is done. Bless thy Heart I see you now as I left you in the Field looking kind sorrow at Dan's going.

O shame! 3 such pretty Wenches and no Tiger! | S

392. To His Wife

Price MS.

[*24 July 1800?*]
Wobourn
Thursday Night.

Well Ma'am here I arrived yesterday evening with Lord W. Russell and my own Horses—and now it comes into my Head that you may want the carriage[4] and I am as mad

[1] Sir Francis Burdett, 5th baronet (1770–1844), political reformer. He complained that the Middlesex magistrates were grossly negligent in supervising the Cold Bath Fields gaol, where a number of reformers and mutineers were detained. A select committee was appointed to investigate conditions, and reported on 19 Apr. 1799. Burdett and S. attacked the findings, but did not succeed in obtaining another inquiry into the management of the prison until 22 July 1800.

[2] Oddly written. Rae (ii. 228–9) prints 'blubber'.

[3] He seconded Burdett's motion for an inquiry. On 18 Feb. 1808 he referred with pride to their success on this occasion in making Pitt give way (Hansard, 1st Ser., x. 662).

[4] *The Oracle*, 1 Apr. 1799, reported that 'Mr. Sheridan launches an elegant carriage in a few days'.

as can be with myself for taking it—and now it is not worth while to send it back. We keep such good hours here that I may sit up a little in my room to write Letters. Tomorrow I confide in receiving one from you that shall make me hear and see you and know all about you and above all that you and the Varlet are well and that you have got a better appetite. I dare say you live almost in the wood like 3 Gypsies with two Bratts.

The Party here[1] consi[s]ts of

Duke of Bedford	Lord John Russell
Duke of Devonshire	Lord W. Russell
Fox	Francis
Fitzpatrick	Lord R. Spencer
Hare[2]	Richardson
Lord John Townshend	E. Faulkener
Grey	Adair
Sheridan	

Fox was very glad at my coming—and we have had a great deal to talk. Dinner is at four and a walk always after Dinner. —In Wine all moderation. I have made a rare Levy on all for my Library.[3] The Duke of Devonshire gives me the finest Edition of all Rousseau![4] There's for you Ma'am. Nothing can be more compleat than the Library[5] here, and the Favor is beyond anything I had conceived. My old companions are certainly superior men in point of Pleasantness especially the four Fox Fitzpatrick Hare and Jack Townshend—but by all that's true and sincere on earth I have no Delight in any society where I can no way turn and see you bounding or hear you Chirping. I think less of it when business separates us—but what [would] make [me] like two or three Days very well would be to have you in a sly

[1] Grey's list of people present or arriving included Dudley North, but (written a day earlier than S.'s) omitted the Duke of Devonshire, Lord John Russell, and E. Faulkener. See G. M. Trevelyan, *Lord Grey of the Reform Bill* (1920), pp. 107–8.

[2] James Hare (1749–1804), wit. M.P. for Knaresborough, 1781–1804. He once said he hated all Irishmen but Dickson and S.

[3] See Moore, ii. 313, and Moore, *Journal*, ii. 232–3, for S.'s plan 'of levying contributions on his friends for a library'.

[4] The five sentences from 'Fox' to 'Rousseau' are quoted by Rae, ii. 223.

[5] See *Leveson Gower Corr.* i. 178.

corner or in a hollow Tree, so that I could stroll on my short whites and see my roses and Emeralds, when I liked and bring you some of the nice things that abound here.

393. 'To Mr. Peake'

Add. MS. 35118, ff. 79–80. *Dock.*: Mr. Sheridan | Particular Authority

August 15th. 1800

The Trustees having decided to sell out Mr. Grubbs Stock to make up the Deficiency on the New Renters account I hereby authorise you to receive from Mr. Adam the first monies paid to him either by Mr. Kemble or Mr. Richardson on account of their respective Purchases[1] in Drury-Lane-Theatre and to apply the same in replacing the said Stock with Interest as it stood before— | R B Sheridan

394. To Richard Peake

Widener MS. *Address*: Southampton August twenty five 1800 | Mr. Peake | Charlotte-St. | Rathbone-Place | London *Fr.*: Free | R B Sheridan *Dock.*: Mr. Sheridan

25 Aug. 1800
Southampton—
Monday

By a d——d mistake my Letters were not put into the Post as we pass'd thro' Southampton on Friday and we did not get back from the Isle of Wight till 12 last Night—so I have not got a Line here from Town nor a shilling. Direct to me by return of Post to the Post-Office Salisbury— | yours ever | R B S.

[1] J. P. Kemble agreed on 1 Feb. 1800 to buy a quarter share in D.L.Th. for £25,000. Richardson decided to do so too, at the same figure. Eventually Kemble withdrew and invested his money in C.G.Th.; and Richardson's friends were able to raise only £13,500 of the agreed amount. See the 'Assignment of twelve Debentures . . . from Mrs. S. Richardson . . . 1 June 1813' (New York Public Library MS.).

395. To His Wife

Yale MS. *Address*: London September fifth 1800 | Mrs. Sheridan | Polesden | Leatherhead | Surry *Fr.*: Free | R B Sheridan

5 Sept. 1800
Friday

My own dear bit of Brown Holland.

We[1] got quickly to Town but in rain at last which made my bones ach[e] for my Harvest.[2] O ye Gods that my ricks had been thatch'd even with Fern and green boughs! This will be [an] in Doors day with you so you will write Dan a long Letter—and perhaps a Play or two with a prologue and Epilogue by Anne. When you cast it give the Tender Part to Charles—Anne—the imperious Heroine who stabs him at her Feet, poor dear Angel! Tom and I supp'd with Burgess on a tough cold Duck and stale warm Oysters. I went to bed very early, and am early up, and write my Wench a Line before I go out as I have so much to do. Old Wallis died on Wednesday Night—I am curious to learn how He has bestow'd his ill-gotten hoards.[3] If He had a living conscience in his Bosom when He made his will He will have restored me some thousands.[4]

I trust Henry[5] got the Cord and that my Heccate's mouse-Trap was compleated. Still Honor bright you are never to neglect the Ribband bless thy heart a guinea, and Anne fourpence halfpenny and the Chicks the same in due proportions.— | S.

[1] Rae, ii. 205 and 221, quotes four sentences from this letter.

[2] The *Morn. Her.*, 5 Jan. 1799, reported that S. 'd——d all cross-grained plots, political and theatrical, and having become a Surrey farmer, now prays "God speed the plough!"'.

[3] His death at the age of eighty-seven is reported in the *Morn. Her.*, 5 Sept. 1800. His will contains many bequests but has no reference to S. The bulk of his fortune went to Lady Bayly and then to her son, Lewis Bayly-Wallis (*c.* 1775–1848), M.P. for Ilchester, 1799–1802 (Judd).

[4] See S.'s statement (quoted in Rae, ii. 216): 'the detected villainy of two lawyers and one banker stole £30,000 from the fund . . .'; and the note in Sichel, ii. 275, 'we actually paid Messrs. Wallis and Troward above £27,000 for law expenses'.

[5] Mrs. S.'s brother, Henry Bertram Ogle (1774–1835). He was a Fellow of Christ's College, 1800–2.

Send me some commissions—I come Sunday without fail. I open my Letter to send the enclosed[1]—the ninth instance within this week and below is Hecca and the boy playing with our pretty little Norman.[2]

396. To Richard Peake

Egerton MS. 1975, ff. 41–42. *Address*: Mr. Peake *Dock.*: Sheridan

20 October [*1800*]
Monday Evening

Dear Peake

Newton has just left me and there is no remedy but your THIS NIGHT sending two Draughts to Bacon[3] for £50 each one dated *tomorrow* the other *tomorrow sennight*—

address them to him as follows

Sir By Desire of Sheridan I enclose you two Draughts for 50 each which you may rely on being punctually answer'd as well as Mr. Sheridan's further instructions on this subject.

I am Sir
Yours
R Peake.

Monday Oct 20th

Pray don't fail to be with me at 12 precisely tomorrow. Mr. Fox has applied to Mr R[4] to have the name of W. Manners junr. put on our free List so do it
Edwards will take the Draught to Bacon

397. To His Wife

Osborn MS. *Address*: London November twenty | two | Mrs. Sheridan | Holy-well | Bishops-Waltham[5] | Hants *Fr.*: Free | R B Sheridan

22 Nov. 1800
Saturday—

O my Hecca I am wearied to Death I have been the whole

[1] A sketch by S.

[2] A bull of this breed.

[3] D.L.Th. Receipts and Payments, 1800 to 1801 (Folger MS.), notes on 20 Oct. 1800 a payment of £100 to 'Mr. Bacon Attorney'. He was probably Henry Bacon of Southampton Street, Covent Garden. William and Benjamin Newton were notaries, of 17 Birchin Lane.

[4] Richardson.

[5] Harry Scott and his wife lived there.

morning shut up in the Corn-committee at the House of Commons and I write a Line that I may not miss the Post before I go home—and there I trust I shall find a nice Letter from thee. I joined Tal[l] after the House of Commons on thursday Night. My Speech is horridly given[1]—as no Debate was expected—but Pitt attack'd me, and Dan he trim him I assure you.[2] As for the effects of the Scarcity I do solemnly believe there will be a general Insurrection the moment Parliament rises. They are nearly in that State at this moment round Birmingham[3] and throughout Staffordshire—

I am plagued in the midst of all this sadly by the Lawyers Delay in the Theatre Business and obliged to break engagements made on the Faith of their assurance that everything should have been finish'd a fortnight ago[4]—and Kemble is in fact playing the rogue—that is he suffers their Procrastination while He is stocking the house Scenery and Dresses and building even new Scene rooms without sharing the expence[5]—I begin to think the World is not pure white Globe—

But bless thee ever my wench. Tall's account of you delights me—nothing but your health should allow this separation—kiss our little Vil[l]ain for me— | S.

They shall send more money still on monday.

[1] On 20 Nov. S. moved for the production of papers concerning affairs in Egypt and policy towards Austria. Pitt accused him of inconsistency, on the ground that S. had (in the debate on the Address on 11 Nov.) 'with a degree of candour which reflected the highest honour on his feelings, recommended unanimity and a cordial co-operation . . .'. S. replied, 'It was in the nature of the Minister not to accept with grace, any submission, either from a parliamentary opponent or from a public enemy. Every man who stood independent and aloof was, of course, to be considered as in a state of hostility' (*Morn. Her.*, 21 Nov. 1800). S. added that he spoke boldly because he felt consistently. Unlike Pitt, he had not at one time favoured parliamentary reform and afterwards abandoned its advocacy, nor had he deserted his associations of earlier years. He ended by declaring he did not think Ministers sincere in their desire for peace.

[2] Cf. Rae, ii. 229.

[3] A troop of light horse had been used to disperse corn rioters at Birmingham at the end of September (*Morn. Her.*, 3 Oct. 1800).

[4] The holders of D.L.Th. debentures met at the Crown and Anchor in the Strand on 4 Nov., to choose a trustee in Wallis's place. They elected Charles Butler to that office (Egerton MS. 1975, f. 11). I assume that S. refers to the settlement of Wallis's estate, but it may be that some allusion is also intended to the proposed purchase of shares in the theatre by Kemble and Richardson.

[5] See H. Baker, *John Philip Kemble* (Cambridge, Mass., 1942), pp. 239–40.

398. To Richard Peake

Egerton MS. 1975, ff. 14–15. *Address*: Mr. Peake *Dock.*: 1800 Mr. Sheridan

[*22 Nov. 1800*]
Saturday Evening

It is impossible to say the Shame and Distress you bring on me when after a few small Payments are *settled* positively between us, you totally disappoint me and make me a Liar to my own Servants.—If what Harry tells me is not true I shall turn him away directly—but He avers after He sent the Note that Dunn[1] said you would not come out of the Boxes or give any order on the Treasury. The Infamy I have suffer'd on account of Mr. R.['s] disappointment[2] is not to be conceived, and Here is Wood[3] kept 4 days in Town on account of the £15 Draughts as expences when a call of two minutes in Hertford St. would have settled all. He must have two guineas for his expences and the £15 to Night | R B S

399. To Charles Grey

Grey MS. *Dock.*: Mr. Sheridan | 1800 *Wm.*: 1799

[*23 Nov. 1800?*]
Hertford-St.
Sunday Evening

Dear Grey

Having an idle Servant and Horse I answer your's tho' I shall see you tomorrow to say that I will be with you without fail in Stanhope St. a little before three—and if Tierney[4] were to be there at the same time I think it would be best. I agree with you that any appearance of disagreement between us is only matter of Triumph to our Enemies and you cannot,

[1] William Dunn was Peake's assistant in the Treasury of D.L.Th.

[2] His inability to find the money immediately to buy a quarter-share in D.L.Th.

[3] Egerton MS. 1975, f. 213, is a note from S. to Dunn dated 22 Nov. and ordering him to 'Pay immediately Mr. Wood 15 and two Guineas'.

[4] George Tierney (1761–1830).

believe me, more sincerely wish to avoid the possibility of it than I do. And now one frank word respecting the first Day of the Session[1] which I assure you did not leave a minute's unkind feeling on my mind tho' I thought my self the ag[g]rieved Person. Tierney undoubtedly in answer to a question from me said[2] that he saw not one word to be objected to in the address and as I understood him agreed with me in regretting that Burdett had opposed it. I afterwards turn'd to you and you said you should not speak at all. Now I have only to say that if you had said in one word that you could not agree to the address I should not have said what I did when I spoke, or if you had spoken in the Line I did I protest nothing would have induced me *on that Day* to have taken any other. I thought Your words 'such unanimity is treason' tho not intentionally pointed at me yet unfriendly and careless as liable to that construction yet if I said anything afterwards that seem'd peevish and retorting[3] I declare to you I am very sorry for it. Now one word on the business with Tierney[4] and this again turns on Questions of Fact. I neither meant nor expected the least Debate on thursday,[5] but was entrapp'd into it by Pitt's arrogance and others going into the Papers. I think it was extreme ill-judgement in me to follow them at all, but so I

[1] Parliament met on 11 Nov., and the King's speech referred to the high price of provisions and to the difficulties of the poor, and also to the decision to lay before Parliament papers concerned with the negotiations for peace with France. In the subsequent debate in the Commons, Sir Francis Burdett argued forcibly that the war was the real cause of distress in the country, but Pitt denied this, seeking to prove that the seasons and not the war had raised the price of grain. S. disagreed with Pitt on this point, but said that he approved of the Address and could conscientiously vote for it. Grey then stated that unanimity was impossible while Pitt's government remained in office, referred to the failure of the expeditions to France and Spain, and moved an amendment (later negatived) to omit the last paragraph of the Address.

[2] Privately. He did not speak on the first day (11 Nov.: see *Colchester Corr.* i. 210). Writing to O'Bryen on 20 Nov. Fox stated: 'I have said all I could to soften Grey in regard to Sheridan and know him enough to think that if occasions call for their acting together, it will not be his fault if they do not. I am afraid S. has an incurable jealousy of Tierney . . .' (Grey MS.).

[3] ' "While our mouths", said he [S.], turning pointedly to Mr. Grey, "are full of high-swelling words, our Constituents are looking to us to fill theirs with food" ' (*The Sun*, 13 Nov. 1800).

[4] In the debate on 12 Nov. Tierney had given notice that on Friday fortnight he would move that the House should resolve itself into a Committee to consider the State of the Nation. He did so on Thursday, 27 Nov.

did and really the future discussion of the subject is only an adjourned Debate tho' no account was given of the argument on the Papers in the Public Prints. It was still more foolish in me to put off my motion,[1] which I did not however on my Legs, but merely scratch the notice out of the order-book fretfully after the Question was over. I might at the time have fix'd it for tuesday as they talk'd of bringing the report from the Corn-Committee on monday—but I did not. On very little reconsideration I determined not to postpone it—tho' to bring it [in] on monday was out of the Question as I had told several on the other side and some who said they should go out of Town that it certainly should not be on that Day—Friday evening I call'd on Tierney and told him my intentions and ask'd him to give me Wednesday which he declined solely on the ground that he refused Dundass I then told him that I would take the Tuesday to which he said 'there was no *manner of objection but one which was entirely my own affair*' (and this he repeated more than once) namely the aukwardness of changing my mind so suddenly and the appearance of taking the House by surprise—but upon my honor he never utter'd one word that could lead me to think it made the least difference or was the least embarrassment to him, which if he had I have no doubt I should have given the matter up tho' it is extremely distressing to me to stay in Town after wednesday. When I saw him yesterday evening and told him I had seen Pitt and a House-full at the Corn committee and settled it all without the least aukwardness I sincerely conceived I was communicating something satisfactory to him, when to my no small surprise I learn'd that He should think himself very ill-used and that he should declare so on my Notice tomorrow and that He would not attend on tuesday. Of course I took my leave only saying that I should equally attend his motion on wednesday. I am sure Tierney will himself admit the accuracy of all I have stated.—I am surprised and ashamed almost to perceive that I have written so much on so slight a matter—and now to bring it to a conclusion—the Desire you express on the subject has in one word decided me to put my motion off,

[1] 17 Nov. 'Sheridan's motion on the Negotiation postponed' (*Colchester Corr.* i. 211).

only let us concert some decent mode of my doing it. And surely Jones[1] properly applied to cannot be unaccommodating.

If I had not scribbled so much almost about nothing I should say more upon general and more important matters, but on these I will talk or write to you another time. I will only say at the present that I am sincerely glad you are returned to Parliament[2] as well on Public grounds as because I truly think that activity of exertion in a sphere your Talents are peculiarly calculated for, and the interest that application of them creates in your mind are as essential to your own happiness as to the character and lead you ought to hold in the country. I will not deal in Professions but whether I shall be diligent or idle you will always find me fair and sincere in supporting the cause and Principles which I am sure are your objects as a public Man. | Your's Dear Grey | ever truly | R B Sheridan

400. To William Adam

Adam MS. *Dock.*: Mr. Sheridan | Jany. 1801.

Holywell
Bishop's Waltham
Sunday one o'clock *Jan. 1801*

Private

My Dear Adam,

It was my intention in the course of to Day to have written to you to express the strong and lasting Gratitude I feel for the zealous and successful exertions of Friendship I have experienced from you, it will be hard indeed if the enclosed just received from Burgess shall defeat the success gain'd by your kindness and crush me in disappointment after all.—I cannot explain now the reasons of a domestic Nature and very Peculiar, which make it *impossible* for me to leave my Wife at this moment, and come up as I otherwise would do instantly and she cannot come with me nor can I explain to

[1] Thomas Tyrwhitt Jones (1765–1811) had supported Grey in his opposition to the Address, on 11 Nov.

[2] He had seceded with Fox in 1797.

her the cause. I cannot but think that Coombe would if kindly applied to advance £500 on account of Richardson—or if He or Two or Three more of the Subscribers would advance £200 or even £300 each, and were ask'd for that as a particular accommodation to me, that the sum wanted might assuredly be made up.[1] I would stake my existence on replacing any Part of the money in the course of next week that should be borrow'd on that condition. I send my servant with this and I send to Burges[s] a List of resources that may be applied to—I send also *£100* (my Quaker's[2] Legacy)—last Night's receipt may spare *£200*. Cocker has a Draught of Peakes for *£150* which I am confident He would lend if not more. Wilson has advanced at my request thro' Richardson *£200* on account of his subscription I think He would advance the remaining *£300* or part of it if spoken to by you and assured of the urgency of the case.[3] Peake certainly could not hesitate to raise 2, or £300 on his own credit,[4] or rather to lend it to me from his own Money—and another *£100* might be yielded from monday Nights Receipt. The whole sum wanted if they are ever so flinty is but £1000—and trying for it only by small assistances I could assuredly raise it were I in Town—but believe me it is not Idleness, but a very different Feeling that prevents me. I write to Peake Burgess Cocker and Richardson—and have requested their exertions, and that They will attend your counsel at 9 tomorrow morning. I am ashamed to give you such trouble, and trouble of such a Nature but I should be more ashamed to pester you with apologies after what I have seen.

1 Many demands were now made on S. John Smith and John Henry Bateman wrote to Peake on 22 Jan. requesting him to pay S.'s share of D.L.Th. profits to them (Winston, 1798–1801). Arrears were claimed by Thomas Church (see p. 151). D.L.Th. Receipts and Payments, 1800–1 (Folger MS.), notes payments to 'Mr. Moody by Burgess to complete 100', on 28 Jan.; to 'Jennings for Campbell and White £100', on 31 Jan.; to Bacon £200, on 5 Feb.; to Augustus Strict £125, on 7 Feb. But the above references may be to the great pressure exerted by the trustees, Ford and Hammersley, for money due to the trust. The Court of Chancery made an order on 6 Mar. 1801 'authorizing them to receive certain sums from the pit receipts of' D.L.Th. until their arrears were satisfied: see the *Monthly Mirror*, xii (1801), 347.

2 Cf. iii. 281, no. 147.

3 Ll. Reed lent R. Wilson £1,000 in 1801 to buy Richardson a share: see Winston, 1798–1801.

4 D.L.Th. Salaries, 1799 to 1802 (Folger MS.), notes, under 17 Jan. 1801, 'Peake on account of 280 lent Mr. Sheridan 35'. See the next letter.

I shall infallibly be in Town on wednesday or Thursday at latest. In speaking to Geary[1] it is always to be remember'd that I did not purchase the Estates without means of compleating the Purchase for independent of my resources from the sale of the Theatre my Trustees possess'd ample means of fulfilling the Contracts. You are the only Person of whom Cocker[2] has any awe. I hope He will not be playing Tricks with the Deeds. I came here to Mrs. S. after a protracted Absence that has tired her much and after much worry of my own mind in hopes of 3 Days quiet but, this d——d intelligence has ruin'd all—it was Cocker's assurance I took that after the 70,000[3] [was] paid I might leave Town without fear. | yours Dear Adam ever | R B Sheridan

I hope my Servant may return tomorrow Night with your News. If *indispensable* order me up tuesday—

401. To Richard Peake

Widener MS. *Dock.*: Mr. Sheridan | Particular

[*Jan. 1801*]
Holywell
Sunday past one

Dear Peake

I cannot wait to explain why but tho' I am as eager as for

[1] Richard Smith, clerk to Jenkins and James, deposed on 12 Nov. 1800 that when a search was made among the title deeds of Sir W. Geary for the abstracts relating to the estates purchased by S., he could not find those belonging to Lot 1, but only those of Lots 2 and 5. From an abstract of a bill of law charges, he found that the abstract of Lot 1 had been delivered to the Rev. Julius Hutchinson who had purchased the Estates comprised in Lot 1 on behalf of Mr. Sheridan, but who was at that time considered by Jenkins and James and Sir W. Geary, as the purchaser of Lot 1 on his own account. Smith suggested that Burgess apply to Hutchinson's solicitor, Carpenter, or to Dunn, solicitor to the marriage settlement, for them, but Burgess refused to do so. The loss of the abstract was given as the reason for delay in completing the purchase. See P.R.O., Chancery Procs., C 31/298 / Geary *v.* Sheridan.

[2] On 11 Dec. 1800 Geary granted to Cocker twenty-one acres in Great Bookham occupied by William Willeter, and excepted out of the estates sold to Whitbread and Grey (as trustees for S.'s marriage settlement) in 1797.

[3] Mansfield, as leading counsel for the trustees of D.L.Th., declared in the Court of Chancery on 10 Nov. 1801, that Henry Holland had agreed to finish the new building for £75,000, but had left it in an unfinished state and with a debt of £70,000 over the estimate. 'This debt the Proprietors had agreed voluntarily to liquidate, and a great part of it had been discharged' (*Morn. Chron.*, 11 Nov. 1801).

Life not to be beat and disgraced in this business I *cannot* leave Mrs. S. to Day nor explain to her my situation. I have written to all Friends to assist. £*200* or £*300* out of last Nights Receipt must *positively* be applied to this object. Now Peake I know that on such a Pinch you can assist me if you have the Friendship to do it—I request of you earnestly as you profess to have that Friendship to advance in this exigency 300. Your Friends will assist and if you give them cheques dated forward I protest by all thats sacred I will sell all the Private Boxes left for a third of their value sooner than you shall be in any risk—you have also the whole command of the Treasury and I authorize that every thing else shall give way to indemnifying yourself or Friends—in one word I rely on your *Friendship* in this difficulty, and you shall not be ask'd a similar thing | yours ever | R B S.

I return with Mrs. S. wednesday or Thursday at latest Burgess has only the nest egg of my Quakers £100

402. To Richard Peake

Victoria and Albert Museum MS. *Wm.*: 18/

[*1801?*]

My Dear Peake,

I am most sorry to annoy you to night—but by all thats good you must send me two pounds[1] by the Bearer or I shall be in the most disgraceful scrape I ever was in in my whole Life.

As I must acquire a sum of money in the course of next week these little scraps shall be returned to you, but I cannot describe the exigency of to Night. | Yrs | R B S

403. To William Adam

Adam MS. *Address*: Wm. Adam Esqr. *Dock.*: Mr. Sheridan | Jany. 31st 1801

Hertford-St.
January 31st *1801*

My Dear Adam,

I have long been anxious once for all to make a thorough

[1] D.L.Th. Salaries, 1799 to 1802 (Folger MS.), notes a payment on 24 Jan. 1801 to 'Mr. Sheridan £2.0.0'.

and final settlement of my affairs and never did I hear anything with more satisfaction than Richardson's communication to me that you were consenting to act as my Trustee in them (which I can only request or accept as far as it can be effected with no particular inconvenience to you) in the manner and on the Plan by which I know you have so effectually and honourably rescued the Duke of York from his Embarrassments. Burgess tells me that you have proposed that He should see the Draught of the Duke of York's Deed of Trust. Allow me to request that you will put him in the way of doing this as soon as possible. There are *various causes* that make every hour's Delay on this subject of peculiar import to me, of which more another Time.

The outline of my Proposition in one word is to assign to a Trustee for the Payment of certain *specified* and *subscribing* Creditors the *whole* of my Profits from the Theatre after reserving to myself for subsistence etc. £2,000 per ann. and £500 per ann. for my son and to make over to the same Trustee 14 private Boxes my own reserved and exclusive Property in Lease for 21 years from the Day the Trustee shall be entitled and bound to sell them—i.e. after the close of the two next ensuing Seasons—in order to discharge any part of the Debts which shall then remain unliquidated.[1] On the most moderate estimation These Securities would be in

[1] To meet the arrears of £40,000 owing to performers and tradesmen, S. decided to make over two private boxes to Cocker, and twelve to Adam as trustee, for 31 years. S. also intended to assign to Adam the clear profits of a moiety of the nightly receipts of D.L.Th. From the produce of the boxes and nightly receipts, Adam was to pay S. £2,000 and Tom S. £500 a year. He was also to pay the expenses of the Trust, and then to make over five shillings in the pound (with interest) each year to the creditors. S. had no authority from the D.L.Th. trustees for this plan, and when they objected, he broached the subject during the Court of Chancery proceedings. When the Lord Chancellor asked him on 23 Dec. how he proposed to pay the performers what was owing to them, S. replied that he had 'prepared a trust deed making over the whole of my interest in the theatre, except £2,000 a year, to William Adam Esq., a Gentleman of the nicest honour and the most unremitting punctuality. I suspended this deed that I might throw no obstacle in the way of the applicants, and that they might not say I attempted to weaken their case. The deed will now be executed without delay. . . .' (*Morn. Chron.*, 24 Dec. 1801.) It was executed on 7 Jan. 1802: see Add. MS. 42720, f. 23; Winston, 1801–4. An abstract (Folger MS. T. a. 67) is docketed by J. Brand, 'This I believe never took effect.' It also contains the sentence, 'The Treasurer is to give security for £5,000 that he will not permit Mr. Sheridan to take more from the receipts than is mentioned in the Deed.'

value nearly double the amount of the Debt I propose to charge on them—to be paid with interest etc. etc. I have proposed the matter to no creditor who seems to hesitate in consenting to accept the Terms—but I must no longer trust my dilatory and procrastinating manner in carrying into effect anything to the advantage of my own affairs, tho' incalculable has been my Loss by inattention and Delay. I am sure I need say no more to win you to speed on the preliminary step. The difficulties I have been engaged in, and above all those produced by the enormous Debt the new Theatre-building left me in have worried my mind and misoccupied my Time beyond measure. It will be the happiest Day of my Life to feel that I am in Debt to no one, or at least that I have no debt for which there is not an adequate and accepted Security—and all I can say is that your thus aiding me to gain that situation is in you a consistent *Roman* proceeding—tho' it should create in my mind the only Debt I cannot sufficiently repay. | your's ever sincerely | R B Sheridan

404. To His Wife

Osborn MS. *Address*: London February ninth | Mrs. Sheridan | H. Streatfeild Esr. | Chiddingstone | Seven-Oaks | Kent *Fr.*: Free | R B Sheridan *Pm.* 10 FEB *Wm.*: 1795.

[*10*] *Feb.* [*1801*]
Tuesday

My own Hecca,

It is very provoking to find that I might without neglecting the House of Commons have remain'd with you at Chid both yesterday and to Day for on my arrival I found no House sitting and all the principal Ministers OUT. It was comical enough that I overlook'd yesterday morning the Letter giving me an account of this Change and which occasion'd Tom Groom being sent to me and thought his coming owing only to [a] private Paper Burgess sent me to sign. However They wanted me in Town to plan what we are to do. Pitt,[1] Grenville, Wyndham Dundass and Lord

[1] After the King's refusal to consider Catholic emancipation, Pitt virtually resigned on 3 Feb., but agreed to remain in office until the new administration was appointed. The King persuaded Addington (5 Feb.) to form a ministry,

Spencer[1] are gone out. The D. Portland remains, and Addington the late Speaker, (for He resign'd the chair to Day) is First Lord of the Treasury, and Chancellor of the Exchequer. This is very ridiculous, and no one thinks it can last. Tho' I think Fox has contrived to put us out the Question at present.[2] However while Hecca likes better that it should be so I am happy in our exclusion.—There is a great Ferment—great caballing, and great speculation—my own surmise is that it will end in their calling in Lord Lansdown to their aid[3]—and his introducing Tierney, and (but say this to no one) *Grey* on the Pretence of making Peace,[4] with a sort of approbation from Fox.—But Hecate does not care for Politics—and I must go and attend a meeting at Lord Fitzwilliams—so Hea*venn* bless thy Heart—This is the first Winter Day there has been—wrap yourself up in wool like a Dormouse if it continues—above all the Net the Net. I enclose two Letters

405. [To Willoughby Lacy]

Shuttleworth MS.

[*12 Feb. 1801?*]

Dear Sir

I cannot describe to you the Shifts I have been put to to get you the enclosed two Pounds[5] | Yours truly | R B S

and he resigned as Speaker on 10 Feb. Portland remained in office as Home Secretary.

[1] First Lord of the Admiralty from 1794 to 1801.

[2] By the Foxite secession from Parliament.

[3] Fox refers to this rumour in a letter to O'Bryen of 2 Feb., and dismisses it as nonsense in a further letter of 19 Feb. (Add. MS. 47566, ff. 70, 74v).

[4] In a letter to Fitzpatrick of 9 Feb., Hare states that Addington had met with many refusals in his attempt to form a Cabinet. He adds that Fox alone of the Opposition leaders could 'act and speak with propriety . . . Grey is too wavering, Sheridan too absurd: that higler Tierney will be open mouthed at the loaves and fishes' (Add. MS. 47582, f. 221). Neither Grey nor S. took office, but Tierney became Treasurer of the Navy later in the year.

[5] The D.L.Th. account book (Add. MS. 29710, f. 167) notes, under 12 Feb. 1801, 'Lacy 2'.

406. To Richard Peake

Egerton MS. 1975, ff. 75–76. *Address*: Mr. Peake *Dock.*: Mr. Sheridan's Letter about the Doyles. *Wm.*: 1794.

[*Mar. 1801?*]
Sunday Night

Dear Peake,

By no means put the Doyles[1] on the list. vid: a Letter I have sent to Kemble.

Give Johnston a little money to go on. Keep as punctual with Kemble[2] as you can.

borrow and fear not.—

We have settled the Sequestration business[3] should the last push come with Burchell there will be no remedy but accepting the £100. God help you 'till I see you again when I will make a success of all difficulties. | Yrs ever | R B S.

407. To William Adam

Adam MS. *Dock.*: Mr. Sheridan | April 1801.

Apr. 1801

My Dear Adam,

I call'd yesterday with full Powers of sale etc. from Cocker. I could not get to Lincoln's Inn to Day but will track you out tomorrow—

Have you changed Saturday for Sunday with Erskine?—and engaged my young Friends? | yours ever | R B Sheridan

Tuesday Evening

[1] Margaret and Anne Doyle, daughters of Alice Doyle of Lambeth, were apprenticed at D.L.Th. for seven years from 13 Oct. 1797 (Dufferin MSS.). The D.L.Th. account book (Add. MS. 29710, f. 168) notes on 28 Feb. 1801 'Mrs. Doyle on ac. 10'.

[2] See his complaints, in this season, in J. Boaden, *Life of . . . Kemble* (1825), ii. 289–91. One of them refers to a Sunday when he had asked Peake for sixty pounds.

[3] On 27 Feb. 1801 Thomas Church exhibited a bill of complaint in the Court of Exchequer, and a writ was issued to sequester S.'s property until he appeared at the Court. See Winston, 1798–1801.

408. To William Adam

Adam MS. *Dock.*: Mr. Sheridan | May 1801

May 1801

My Dear Adam,

I have pledged myself so in confidence of Richardson['s] business being settled before this and our Treasury so drain'd by the Failure of this Monk Lewis's damn'd Play[1] that I know not where to turn for a small sum immediately necessary. Pray cause me the enclos'd to be discounted and stop it from Richardson's money.

I enclose my answer to Ritson[2]—I think no difficulty can remain with Wilson for Kemble—with Richardson more does[?].—I have had the enclosed every Day in my Pocket from Cocker—and now I find his money is nearly ready. I enclose also Papers for Gotobed. | Yours ever | R B S

Shall meet at 9.

409. To Richard Peake

Adam MS. *Dock.*: [By Peake] I undertake to pay the said Profits to Mr. Adam instead of Mr. Sheridan if the above mentioned agreement between Mr. Sheridan and Mr. Richardson is not completed (to the amount of £1000) R Peake. [By Adam] R. B. Sheridan | 22d May | 1801 | Redg. the | Trust

May 22d. 1801

Sir,

I authorize you to keep back all profits which otherwise would be coming to me from Drury Lane Theatre under the Trust Deed undertaken by Mr. Adam and to pay the same to Mr. Adam for the repayment of the sum of £1000 this Day advanced to me by him in the case of any circumstance

[1] M. G. Lewis's *Adelmorn, the Outlaw*, produced at D.L.Th. on 4 May 1801.

[2] Joseph Ritson, the antiquary (1752–1803), who worked as a conveyancer at 8 Holborn Court, Gray's Inn: see J. Hughes, *The New Law List* (5th ed., 1801), p. 33.

breaking off or retarding Mr. Richardson['s] Purchase of a Quarter Share of the said Theatre | R B Sheridan

To Mr. Peake Treasury
Theatre Royal Drury Lane

410. To His Wife

Osborn MS. Wm.: 1794

[*2–3 June 1801?*][1]

My own Dearest Hecca,

If I had left Town on Sunday I should have lost Billington and now I have *secured* her which I am truly delighted at

Tuesday Evening

My Dearest Girl—I sat down to write to you in very Good Spirits this morning, but I was interrupted and obliged to go out—and now poor Dan is not in very good Spirits. The case is I was again taken with that Giddiness in the Street and obliged to take Shelter—I own I am a good deal frighten'd about it nor have I felt right ever since. I went however after to the House of Commons, but not being well enough to speak and the Question very particular I got Grey to put off the Debate. We are now all come to Brook's to Dinner at ten o'clock—and I write this that I may send it off early in the morning. I shall touch no wine. I think of being cupp'd before I go home which Grey and Whitbread advise me to very strongly—On second thoughts I will not send this till the morning that I may know how I am.

[1] Sichel docketed the MS. 'c. 1799?'. Rae, ii. 229, dates it 1802. The singer Elizabeth Billington (1768–1818) was reported (in *Morn. Chron.*, 14 Aug. 1801) as having agreed to sing at both theatres, and it seems likely that negotiations had begun soon after her return to England in May 1801. If this period is accepted as correct, then the letter must have been written before 2 July, when the parliamentary session ended. The most probable date of writing is the two days before 4 June, when S. appeared at Court for the King's birthday: see *Morn. Chron.*, 5 June 1801. This idea is supported by the references to cupping in S.'s letter of 8 June, and to Nield in the letter of 12 June. Grey took part in the debate on the evacuation of Egypt, in the Commons on 2 June (*Parliamentary History of England*, xxxv (1819), 1443), but I can find no allusion to his withdrawing a motion then.

Wednesday morning

I was obliged to be up and out at eight on business this morning—my diz[z]iness is better—but I will see both Turton[1] and Birch.[2] I ought to go to St. James's tomorrow—but if I dont find myself quite well throughout this Day I will certainly come to Polesden instead—should I stop I will see thee my Beloved on Friday. I die for Quiet and the air of Polesden if it be only for 12 hours—Then we will go to Hampshire and I shall be well. My sweet Hecca dont think it negligent or unkind my not having written—no the reverse has been the cause. Let me have a kind Letter from you my Hecca by the Bearer. At no Time has your kindness been more necessary to me. Do not fail me my Dearest and let the man come back immediately.

I have not been cupp'd but will if I have the least return.

I will write again by Post and decide for Thursday or Friday. Heaven for ever bless and guard you and my Boy. Love to Kate.

411. To William Adam

Adam MS. *Dock.*: Mr. Sheridan | 8th June 1801

8 June 1801
Lincoln's Inn

My Dear Adam,

You did me as usual service beyond measure the other Night. A little ready money is only wanted to smooth the w[h]eels and get[?] everything going right—Cocker has no objection to £500 (and with a word from you I think would make it £1000) being borrow'd for my accommodation on his Debentures, with a Punctilio which He will explain to you if you will have the goodness to see him this evening—Since you wrote Ritson Wilson and Richardson have made [haste?] and they now proceed with every possible expedition. | Yours ever | R B Sheridan

[1] John Turton (1735–1806), physician.

[2] John Birch (1745?–1815), surgeon to the Prince of Wales.

I was cupp'd on saturday etc. and have now got perfectly well—and am making the most punctual exertions for settling everything and for a little Quiet

412. To William Adam

Adam MS. *Address*: *Private* | W. Adam Esqr. | Lincoln's-Inn-Fields. *Dock.*: Mr. Sheridan | 8th June 1801.

8 June 1801
Monday Night

Private
My Dear Adam,

Butler means to call on you early in the morning—having gone while I was at *his* chambers to *your's* to Night—but too late—the object is to know if Mansfield[1] really dealt out those hostile threats against me—as I assured him He would have the more exact Truth from you—I am willing to fulfil everything I am engaged to—even in their Terms—but I must know whether they propose hostility or not without the excellent pretence given on my Part—. Mr. Butler knows the last Delay has been owing for nine Days to Mr. Wear as Nowell alleges | yours ever | R B Sheridan

413. To William Adam

Adam MS. *Dock.*: Mr. Sheridan | 12th June 1801

June 12th 1801

Dear Sir

Please to pay to Mr. Nield[2] on account of Mr. Jeffrice's assignees the sum of two hundred and fifty Pounds from the first disposeable money received by you on account of Mr. Richardson's Purchase of a Quarter of Drury-Lane-Theatre —Your obedient Servant | R B Sheridan

To Wm. Adam Esq.
Lincoln's-Inn-Fields.

[1] Counsel with Richards, Romilly, and Wear, for the bankers, Hugh Hammersley, Montolieu, Brooksbank, Greenwood, and Drewe, in their suit against S., Ford, and Thomas Hammersley. See Add. MS. 42723, f. 9.

[2] Mrs. Billington's solicitor.

414. To William Adam

Adam MS. *Dock.*: Mr. Sheridan | 13th June 1801

June 13th 1801

Dear Sir

Please to pay to Mr. Wilson the sum of two hundred Pounds from the money to be paid into your Hands on account of Mr. Richardson's Purchase of a Quarter Share of Drury-Lane-Theatre— | I have the Honor | to be your obedient Servant | R B Sheridan

To W. Adam Esq.
Lincolns-Inn-Fields.

415. To William Adam

Adam MS. *Address*: Wm. Adam Esq. *Dock.*: Mr. Sheridan | July 1801

Saturday June 20th *1801*

My Dear Adam,

I return you the Paper[1] which is everything right. I have made only a slight alteration which of course I submit to your Decision.

I am willing that every shilling of R's money should go to the immediate payment ever of Debt so I could be once free and then never Debt of one Pound will I incur again—but the expence and worry of the present Pressure is dreadful.

[1] Adam wrote to S. on 19 June 1801 (Adam MS.), and suggested that a candid application to subscribers would produce an advance, and that S. or Richardson should see Combe about it. He enclosed a draft paper, which (if Combe approved) he would send out on Monday. This stated that the 'Transaction between Mr. Sheridan and Mr. Richardson to which you have been so good as to subscribe is now nearly completed. The Subscription of 50 Shares, The Number required is now certain . . . requires only a little time to obtain the Names of the remaining Number, all of whom have promised.' It added that 'in the meantime it would be a very great accommodation to Mr. Sheridan to have a small advance made now'. S. inserted the words, 'as He is bound to settle all the Debts of the Theatre previous to your accepting his conveyance on the Part of Mr. Richardson and the doing so will avoid many [then comes Adam's phrase] expensive and vexatious proceedings at Law'.

I mean principally where the Sheriff[1] is concerned for nearly all the rest sign the Trust Deed very willingly—

Necessity to avoid immediate extremities has compell'd me to give more of these immediate Drafts on you—at the same time I am vex'd to the Heart and asham'd to trouble you with such references. If I do not find you this evening I understand we meet at Dinner tomorrow— | yours ever | R B Sheridan

416. To William Adam

Adam MS. *Dock.*: Mr. Sheridan | 28th June 1801

28 June 1801

My Dear Adam,

One Line only to Ward[2] White or Humphreys to stay proceedings only for a few Days. Forgive my repeated intrusions—but all these Things press tomorrow. | Your ever obliged | R B Sheridan | Sunday June 28

417. To His Wife

Osborn MS. *Address*: London July eight 1801 | Mrs. Sheridan | R. Streatfeild's Esq. | The Rocks | Uckfield | Sussex *Fr.*: Free | R B Sheridan | to be delivered early

8 July 1801
Wednesday

Indeed my Dearest Hecca I had not nor ever have an unkind Thought towards you. I did not receive a Line from you till yesterday which I thought unkind on your Part. I have no

[1] See the footnote to the next letter.

[2] A subpoena (dated 27 June and signed by J. Ward, 15 Newman Street) is enclosed, summoning S. to attend at the Court of King's Bench on Monday, in the cause of John White against 'Perring Esq. and Cadell Esq.' This appears to be connected with a debt incurred (presumably on behalf of D.L.Th.) by Westley: in a letter from Pall Mall on 7 Dec. 1797 (Harvard MS.) W. B. Cabbell stated that his firm had presented Westley's draft to Peake who could not pay for it, so Cabbell advised Westley to go to White of Storey's Gate and arrange matters with him. On 3 June 1801 Samuel Goodenough reported (Brinsley Ford MS.) to Richard Ford that the bailiffs sought Westley.

anxiety or real care but for your Health and Safety—Scott is returning to Polesden this evening—but as you are not there I defer going till tomorrow—which will enable me to stay the longer. I write this line to catch you at the Rocks, that your Green eyes may not look grave when we meet. I have been better in feel of Health these two Days than I have been for two months | S

418. To His Wife

Harvard MS. *Address*: London July seventeen 1801 | Mrs. Sheridan | Polesden | Leatherhead | Surry *Fr.*: Free | R B Sheridan

17 July 1801
Curzon St
at Burgess['s]

Altho' it is but an hour since I wrote to you I feel so indisposed to everything but to turn and think of you that I must add a Line for fear I may have express'd myself just now in so desponding a way as to make you unhappy. No my Hecca you can make me amends for everything, and I live for nothing else—and your slightest wish shall be my Law and Rule | bless thee my Heart and think kindly of poor Dan. | S

419. To Henry Bate Dudley[1]

Cornell University Library MS. Copy. [Ph.]

July 20. 1801

Dear Dudley

I received a Note from Harris dated Saturday which was intended to apprize me that you were in Town but it did not come to my hands 'till two at Night and early the next morning I found you were fled—otherwise you might have been saved the trouble of my intruding on you in the Country and sending a messenger to follow you to the assizes.

[1] 1745–1824; became first baronet, 1813. He was a clergyman, journalist, dramatist, and land-improver.

In one word I may assume that you are acquainted with the Dilemma which has arisen between the two Theatres[1] on the subject of Mrs. Billington and confident I am that your good wishes to them both would lead you to exert your friendly offices to remove misunderstanding on either side and to preserve between Harris and me that confidence and mutual good-will in which we have so long lived.

At present I think I ought to say no more than that we have both readily agreed to leave the matter to your arbitration, Both equally convinced of your Friendship Honor and Impartiality.

I should hold it improper to offer any statement of circumstances to you 'till it had been shewn to and approved of by Mr. Harris. Therefore all I have to add is to express my earnest hope that you will not decline the mediation we request, and that you will favor us with seeing you in Town as speedily as may be consistent with your convenience. | I am, my Dear Sir | Ever yours sincerely | R B Sheridan

The Revd. Mr. Dudley

420. To Richard Peake

Egerton MS. 1975, ff. 38–39. *Address*: Mr. Peake | to be given | immediately *Fr.*: R B Sheridan

[*1801?*]
Monday

Dear Peake,

Mr. Scott's coming to Day keeps me 'till tomorrow morning, when I *will* be *early* in Town. Pray hasten the Wine[2] and add Sherry to it or we are all aground— | Yours ever | R B S.

[1] Both theatres claimed the services of Elizabeth Billington, and asked Dudley to act as arbitrator. In a letter to S. and Richardson of 19 Mar. 1802 (printed in *The Times*, 22 Mar. 1802), he stated: 'The agreement . . . plainly stipulated that the Vocal Performances of that Lady should be equally apportioned between them for the interest of both Theatres, in Oratorios, as well as Dramatic Entertainments.'

[2] D.L.Th. Salaries, 1799 to 1802 (Folger MS.), records under 22 July 1801: 'Pd. for Wine Cash Pr. Peake £4.4.0'.

421. To William Adam

Adam MS. *Address*: Wm. Adam Esqr. | Kings Counsel | Chelmsford *Dock.*: Mr. Sheridan | 23d. July 1801

23 July 1801
Thursday Evening
Hertford-St.

My Dear Adam,

Believe me I will sacrifice everything sooner than you should be push'd to discredit on my account—but I trust there cannot be a difficulty with Cocker. I have been so occupied and worried in Billington's business that I may have appear'd neglectful in what you are principally interested in—but indeed I am not so—pray a Line by the Bearer whom I send to Dudley to tell me your motions.| Yours ever | R B Sheridan

422. To William Adam

Adam MS. *Address*: W. Adam Esq. *Dock.*: R B Sheridan | 7 Aug. 1801 | Inclosing one of B. Dudley's[1]

Friday Night *7 Aug. 1801*

My Dear Adam

It is very foolish not to speak frankly to a Friend when you are with him—but such is my Nature that sometimes I cannot. I wanted a Receipt from you to Coombe for £500 which I am sure he will advance and without which I personally and the Theatre shall be in the greatest Distress. I have appointed to see him at ½ past 3 tomorrow. A Line from you stating the real ground on which this advance may be made as by others I am sure will succeed.

I enclose a warrant to your Destination of all the rest of the money—but words cannot tell you what the denial of this accommodation would be to me | yours ever truly | R B Sheridan

[1] Dudley wrote to S. from Bradwell Lodge on 6 Aug. 1801, saying that he hoped 'all proceeds well with Billington and Co.' (Adam MS.).

423. To William Adam

Adam MS. *Dock.*: R B Sheridan

Friday Night [*7 Aug. 1801?*][1]

My dear Adam

I am destined to torment you as well for others as myself —I did not open the envelope which convey'd this[2] till I had finish'd my own Note to you. Dudley sent it open for me to read. His hastiness is folly—and I will check it—his disposition to assail the Duke of York[3] absurd—. A hint from you will direct my answer— | yours | R B S

I suppose Dudely does not mean you should see her[4] Letter to me but I must confide in you everything. I will try hard to catch five minutes of you in the morning—

424. [To Henry Burgess?]

N.L.I. MS. 3901, ff. 4–5. *Dock.*: Augt. 1801 | Mr. Sheridans Letter | Respectg Deed

Aug. 1801
Monday Evening

My Dear Sir,

I have been lately and particularly to Day worried to Death with a variety of business—therefore you must not

[1] Mr. D. E. Ginter notes that the letter was part of a bundle docketed 'Aug. 1801'.

[2] Dudley's note of 6 Aug. 1801?

[3] In his note Dudley had asked S. to send to Adam 'to press the necessity of the Duke of York's prompt interference, or fairly declining it'. The reference is to the proposed presentation by the Crown of the Duke's chaplain, the Rev. J. Gamble, to the living of Bradwell. Dudley had bought the advowson (with the alternate right of presentation with the Crown) in 1781, and had unsuccessfully tried to present himself to it in 1797. Feeling in Essex in 1801 was strongly in his favour because he had spent some £28,000 on the living's buildings and land. On 12 June William Adam approached the Prime Minister, complained of 'the extreme hardship' of Dudley's case, and presented a testimonial (signed by the magistrates of Essex) to his work as magistrate and landowner. In the debate on the Clergy Non-residence Bill on 19 June, S. contrasted Dudley with Parson Trulliber and asserted that he was a public benefactor. However, Gamble successfully ejected Dudley from the living in the spring of 1802. See *Gent. Mag.* xciv (1824), pt. 1, 274; and *Parliamentary History of England*, xxv. 1553.

[4] Mrs. Billington's?

mistake any impatience of mine this morning. On the subject of the Trust-Deed[1] mould it as you please and I shall be content. But let us always remember that some Degree of confidence is necessary on both sides and that in 9 cases out of 10 I give a good security in lieu of none and in many of those case[s] upon most extravagant and unexamined charges. In short my wish is that *you* should act as the *sole Solicitor* for *my Trustee Mr. Adam*, and in that Character I am confident you may do me much service and I shall feel much obliged— | yours truly | R B Sheridan

425. To George Edwards

Harvard MS.

Kirkley[2]
August 28th: 1801.

G. Edwards

Mr. Peake and Party to shoot at Polesden—and I am sure you will provide for them the best you can as well as Lilly[3] | R B Sheridan

426. To William Adam

Adam MS.

23 Sept. 1801

Dear Sir,

Please to pay Mr. Siddons the sum of four hundred Pounds from Mr. Richardson's Purchase money previous to any further money being paid to me on my account— | R B Sheridan

To Wm. Adam Esq.
Lincoln's-Inn-Fields
September 23d. 1801.

[1] With Adam as trustee. See p. 148, n. 1.

[2] Kirkley Hall, the home of the Ogles in Northumberland. See Ogle, pp. 310–11.

[3] One of S.'s servants.

427. To Richard Peake

Egerton MS. 1975, ff. 93–94. *Address*: Mr. Peake.

[*Oct. 1801?*][1]
Stamford

My Dear Peake,

I am so uneasy I send Edwards back. I am sure you will do every thing possible to keep things right for a Fortnight. I am without a shilling for Tom and Mrs. S. Try a few small lairs as a personal favor to me. I never ask'd anyone but Mitchell.[2] Don't write me a croaking Letter and you shall see what a lasting settlement I will make on my return so that you shall have no more of these anxieties. God bless you | Yrs ever | R B S

I owe £40 at Newcastle

428. To Richard Peake

N.L.I. MS. 3901, ff. 17–18. *Address*: Mr. Peake | Treasury | Drury-Lane-Theatre | if absent | Mr. Dunn *Fr.*: R B Sheridan *Dock.*: Mr. Sheridan *Wm.*: 1798

[*Oct. 1801?*[3]]
Tuesday Evening

Dear Peake,

I find it better to finish my Paper to Butler than to come to the Theatre—but now mind what I say—send the whole of this Night's receipt to the Bankers by 9 in the morning and let Dunn only take this line from you '*Mr. Peake sends*

[1] The D.L.Th. account book (Add. MS. 29710, f. 181v) has the following entry under 12 Oct. 1801: 'Sheridan sent to him at Durham 20'. He was reported on the same date 'on an electioneering visit to the Burgesses of Newcastle' (Egerton MS. 1975, f. 160).

[2] At the end of the season of 1801–2, D.L.Th. owed Mitchell, coal merchant, £244: see Winston, 1798–1801, 'Arrears to tradesmen'. Cf. A. Bunn, *The Stage* (1840), iii. 154 n.

[3] D.L.Th. Receipts and Payments, 1801 to 1802 (Folger MS.), notes payments to Bland (a member of D.L.Th. company) of five pounds on 26 Sept. and 3 Oct. 1801, and of £6. 13*s.* 4*d.* on 10 Oct. 1801. It also contains entries reading 'Mr. Fosbrook towards paying Mrs. Billington's Bill', on 8 and 10 Oct. 1801, when the sums involved were £100 and £110.

£3 to be placed to his private account.' Then give Fosbrook a Draught for his money and tell him not to take it 'till between 3 and 4—and so with any other Draughts you are obliged to give pay Bland what you can. I will be with you early in the morning— | R B S.

If Burgess is at the Theatre I want to see him much.

429. To Richard Ford and Thomas Hammersley

Osborn MS.

Friday Evening
November 13th: 1801

Gentlemen

We understand it to be the opinion of Counsel on both sides that we should ill obey the suggestion of the Lord Chancellor[1] if we did not among ourselves endeavour in the first assistance to prepare the outline of an amicable settlement—. The result to be submitted to legal consideration.

We propose therefore to meet you tomorrow evening at eight o'clock at Mr. Hammersley's should that Hour be convenient.

We have the Honor to be | Your obedient Servants | R B Sheridan | J Richardson[2]

To Messrs. Ford and Hammersley.

[1] On 10 Nov. 1801 the Court of Chancery was asked to consider the order of 6 Mar. authorizing Ford and Hammersley to take the whole of the receipts of the pit at D.L.Th., and the order of 11 June, authorizing Hammersley to receive the takings of the boxes. The trustees moved that a receiver be appointed under their authority. S. claimed that both orders should be discharged, and argued that if the trustees took more from the pit than £45 a night the performers could not be paid. On 11 Nov. the counsel for Ford and Hammersley admitted that the performers must be the first to be paid and said that his clients would not now press for the execution of the letter of the order, but that they still demanded the appointment of a receiver to take all the money at the pit doors. The Lord Chancellor then urged the parties to agree among themselves 'because the court could . . . not do that ample justice to all parties . . . which equity required' (*The Monthly Mirror*, xii (1801), 347–53).

[2] The signature is in Richardson's hand; the rest of the letter in S.'s.

430. To Richard Peake

Egerton MS. 1975, f. 85. *Address*: Mr. Peake

[*11 Dec. 1801?*][1]

Dear Peake

Pray be very precise with Dunn, to be only enough with the £32, at the Bankers.

and send Billingtons 50 Guineas with a civil Note to Neild in the morning | Yrs ever | R B S

I am writing for a few Guineas.

431. To Richard Peake

Add. MS. 35118, ff. 133–4. *Address*: Mr. Peake *Dock.*: Mr. Sheridan *Wm.*: 1801

[*1801?*]
Wednesday

Dear P.

Do for God's sake give G. Edwards money for the enclosed. Any Tinker in the Neighbourhood will discount it for you—I have not time myself to apply—| Yours | R B S

it must be to Day or it will be no use to me

432. To Richard Peake

Widener MS. *Dock.*: Mr. Sheridan about Watkins *Wm.*: 1799

[*1801–2*]
Monday Evening

Dear Peake

you know that I am sincerely reluctant ever to involve you personally in any Theatrical Debt—But Watkins's is become a case of the last Necessity—I enclose what I conceive a perfect indemnification to you for anything you engage

[1] Dated from entries in the D.L.Th. account book (Add. MS. 29710, f. 191v): 12 December 1801, Sheridan £2. 2*s*. 0*d*.; Billington £52. 10*s*. 0*d*.

in.—N.B. Mr. Adam has actually 20 Names *down* for Richardson[1]—and ten more promised whose subscriptions he will now collect. I can't call on you tomorrow—a House of Commons Day—and this business presses to an hour unless J. Watkins whom I saw to Day has got a weeks reprieve | yrs ever | R B Sheridan

433. To Richard Peake

Saltikova-Schredin Library MS., Leningrad. [Ph.] *Address*: Mr. Peake | Charlotte-St. | Rathbone-Place.

[*1801–2?*]

House of
Commons—
Saltash Committee-room
or Alice's Coffee house[2]
Friday morn past ten—

Dear Peake—

you must come to me here and not mind Trustees or anything else— | Yours ever | R B S.

434. To Richard Peake

Pub.: S.C., 8 July 1878, lot 274. *Address*: To Mr. Peake

[*1801–2*]

Observe to obey what is written here—I have made up my mind—and my letter to Grubb will convince him that *we must part*.[3]

[1] The subscribers to the fund to buy a quarter share for Richardson included the Dukes of Bedford, Northumberland, and Devonshire; Lords Fitzwilliam, Thanet, and Moira; H. C. Combe, Alexander Davison, Francis Baring, James Ramsay, George Shum, and Richard Wilson.

[2] D. G. Macdonnel, editor of the *Morning Herald*, met S. 'in the coffee-room over the House of Commons' on 27 Dec. 1799. See J. O'Keeffe, *Recollections* . . . (1826), ii. 372–3.

[3] On 16 Nov. 1801 Grubb empowered Troward to recover his shares in D.L.Th. (Harvard MS.). S.'s notice of dissolution of partnership is dated 15 Sept. 1802 (Harvard MS.).

435. To Dudley

Clements MS. [Ph.] Cf. S.C., 17 Mar. 1930, lot 576. *Dock.*: Sheridan

[1801–2?]

My Dear Dudley

Nothing would give me more Pleasure than the Party you propose, and I should be particularly glad of the opportunity of paying my respects to Col. Burgoyne[1] but they are the very days in the House of Commons I must not miss on any account.

I will come to you or expect you any hour you please tomorrow | Your's ever | R B Sheridan

436. To the Editor of *The Courier*

Yale MS. Draft. *Pub.*: *The Courier*, 14 Jan. 1802.

Jan. 1802

Sir,

As by your insertion of certain French Epigrams you have commenced what I conceive to be a very scurrilous attack on the French National institute for electing Mr. Haydn,[2] the celebrated musician, as the representative of the Literature of Europe in Preference to one Sheridan, who, whatever may be said of his Writings Wit or Eloquence, I am credibly informed cannot support a Part in a Glee even at the Prince's Table, I beg you will follow that sound[3] rule of Equity—audi alteram Partem. I therefore transmit to

[1] Probably Sir Montague Roger Burgoyne, 8th baronet (1773–1817). He became a lieutenant-colonel in 1795.

[2] 'The Primary Electors of the National Institute of France having proposed Haydn, the great composer, and Mr. Sheridan, as candidates for the class of Literature and the Fine Arts, the Institute, with a choice not altogether indefensible, elected Haydn. Some French epigrams on this occurrence, which appeared in the Courier, seem to have suggested to Sheridan the idea of writing a few English *jeux-d'esprit* on the same subject, which were intended for the newspapers, but, I rather think, never appeared' (Moore, ii. 303). Moore is wrong: the verses appeared in *The Courier* with the above letter, and are continued in the issue of 18 Jan. The two French epigrams that inspired them, were printed in *The Courier*, 12 Jan. 1802, over the name of 'Le Cte. J. De Mac Carthy'.

[3] Carelessly written. This may be 'sacred', as in *The Courier* version.

you these Counter-Epigrams if I may so call them, which, I am assured do full justice to Mr. Haydn, tho' from my Ignorance of the English Language I cannot judge of them, and am even obliged to trust this communication to a Translator. | Yours with great consideration | Jan Caspe Spreinck

Titchfield St.

Epigrams

For the Morning Chronicle

National Institute of France

Haydn versus Sheridan

The two Candidates proposed by the Primary Electors for
The Class of Literature and the Fine Arts

Haydn successful!

The wise decision all admire
Twas just beyond dispute[1]
Sound Taste! which to Apollo's Lyre
Preferr'd—a German Flute!

another

Haydn Loquitur

N.B. as Mr. Haydn, the foreign Representative of Literature and the fine Arts of Europe in the national institute of France supposes[?] himself to be only a very eminent *composer* of Musick it would be extremely unjust in any of our readers to be hypercritical with respect to a few trifling errors which may occur in the metre or rhythm of this his first attempt at *Literary* composition indeed we have ourselves taken the Liberty of correcting in many Places the Grammar and Spelling of this little practical jeu d'esprit both in the original German of Mr. Haydn and in the Translation which his English Correspondent Mr. Florio has so obligingly furnish'd us with.

Haydn to Florio a distinguish'd Performer
on the German Flute

The wond'ring World has heard with admiration
my Fine English Oratorio call'd Creation Indeed
it succeeded greatly beyond my expectation.

[1] S. adds an alternative line: 'And worthy of the Institute.'

And since the Days of Handel
I may say it without Scandal
No such Piece of Messiah has been heard in this their Nation
But now the *national institute* of France
have thought proper this humble Servant to advance
And member of that Institute *created* me
in spite of Sheridan's presumptuous Claim
To all that Genious can derive from Fame
For Wit and Eloquence and Poetry.
I be only fearful in my new Station,
that this the Institutes *Creation*
if it be not in truth a Blunder
may cause more admiration
And create more wonder
Than did my said delightful Oratorio.
—Pray tell me what you hear dear Florio
yours Haydn

Foreign Representative of the Literature and fine arts of Europe—

Another

Pass by Wit Eloquence and Poetry
Give way to Claims of higher Place
Give way to—Tweedledum and Tweedledee
Make room make Room, for Thorough Bass

Another

Time was when Pindars sacred Fire
And bold Alcaeus' Song
And gay Anacreon's festive Lyre
Assumed the homage of the human heart.
Yet gave to 'concord Sweet' its praise and Part
Time was when Music was the Poets Tongue.

Then modest melody, thy Task and Praise
Follow'd the Bard and his inspiring Lays
A gentle helpmate by his side you stood
Watch'd his commanding Eye and own'd the Muses God.

[Poet!] that time is past—subdue thy pride—[1]

[1] Continued, with other verses in different order, in *The Courier*. There are twelve further lines in Mrs. S.'s hand (and cancelled) in the manuscript.

437. To Arthur Palmer[1]

Harvard MS. *Address*: Arthur Palmer Esqr. | Sergeant at Law | etc. etc. etc. *Dock.*: Letter of 2 Feb. 1802 from | Messrs. Sheridan and Richardson inclosing the | Agreement signed by | them

Tuesday Evening Feb. 2d: *1802*

Sir,

We have the Honor to return to you the enclosed Memorandum to which we perfectly agree and which we have sign'd.

We are your obedient Servants, | R B Sheridan | J Richardson[2]

438. To Henry Greville[3]

Osborn MS. *Wm.*: 1799

17 Feb. 1802

Dear Sir,

My Son has mention'd to me that you were desirous of seeing the '*Final arrangement*' respecting the establish'd Theatres which received the Sanction of his Majesty signified by the Lord Chamberlain's Name to the Deed as well as that of his Royal Highness the Prince of Wales and of his Grace the Duke of Bedford. As I owe you in respect to old acquaintance every attention and civility I shall direct a copy of the material Passage to be sent to you as well as any other information you may wish to have. You will see at once that any attempt to open another Theatre on however reduced a scale or on whatever pretence money is to be paid for being

[1] By the Lord Chancellor's order of 20 Jan. 1802 Palmer became the arbitrator in the dispute between S. and Grubb. On 5 Feb. 1802 Palmer made his award, outlined in the draft indenture (Grubbe MS.) of Dec. 1803.

[2] In Richardson's hand. The remainder of the letter is in that of S.

[3] Henry Francis Greville (1760–1816) was one of the organizers of the Pic-Nic Society, a band of aristocratic amateurs who had

> Agreed ten times a year to meet
> To Act, to Dance, to Chat, to Eat.

Their rules were printed in *The Times*, 23 Feb. 1802. Their desire to present plays at their rooms in Tottenham Court Road was opposed by the managers of the patent theatres, who were afraid they would lose their chief patrons.

present at the Performances is directly contrary to the Pledge contain'd in that settlement, upon the Faith of which the immense sum expended on Drury-Lane-Theatre has been raised, and consequently that the Proprietors of the establish'd Theatres are, on the first endeavour at in[n]ovation, bound to appeal to the Protection of the exalted Persons I have stated to have guaranteed their Property and from whose Justice They are confident of Support.[1]

I think . . .[2] to apprize yo . . . such an appea . . . however I hav . . . myself to be bou . . . consideration, to . . . legal means and fair . . . scheme which tho certainly not so intended leads in my firm opinion to the utter Destruction of the Property of the establish'd Theatres. | I have the Honor to be | Dear Sir | Your sincere and obedient | Servant | R B Sheridan

Feb 17th 1802
H. Greville Esqr.

439. [To the Editor of *The Oracle*]

Pub.: *The Spirit of the Public Journals for 1802* (1803), pp. 181–3.[3]

18 Feb. 1802

Mr. Editor,

I understand the following is to be the *arrangement* of the *volunteer theatre*, which I therefore beg leave to lay before you:—

Its name is to be that of '*Le Theatre des Enfans Gâtés*; or, *The Theatre of spoilt Children!*' Over the door is to be a bass-relief representing *Momus* mounted upon an *ass*, with the attributes of *Apollo*, attended by *nine ladies* of *easy virtue*, in the characters of the *nine Muses*.

The *curtain* will be painted with an historical piece taken from Homer, where *Thersites* makes mouths at *Ulysses*;[4] but, that *unity of action* may be observed, the drubbing he afterwards received will not appear.

[1] For Greville's view, see *The Pic Nic* (1803), I. ii–xxii.

[2] Torn.

[3] I have not been able to find a copy of *The Oracle* in which this letter originally appeared.

[4] *The Iliad*, Bk. II, ll. 211–41.

Some of the *scenery* will consist of the fine German *cobweb* painting,[1] as it is presumed that ordinary scenes would be too *heavy* for their *drama*. The rest will be of *gauze*, or *calico*; so that if two plots are going on, the audience will be able to *see* them *both at once*.

Instead of benches, the audience will be seated on *easy chairs*, in each of which a *nightcap* will be placed, that such as are fatigued with clapping, or feel the happy effects of the performance, *may take a nap in comfort*.

The *rules* of *admission* are not quite agreed upon; but it is said that a blush proved upon any candidate operates to a positive exclusion,[2] and that this statute is not limited by time.

The *theatre* is to open with a *new tragedy* by Mr. Monk Lewis,[3] founded upon the story of Dr. Faustus. This will give ample scope for the display of *ghosts*, *devils*, *machinery*, etc.

THE FABLE

I am informed, is to be as follows:—*Faustus* having sold himself to the *Devil*, takes a fancy to *Donna Angelina*, who has a Sylph for her guardian. As he is determined to have her upon any terms, he employs *Cacophon*, his attendant evil spirit, to entice her. This introduces a most spirited dialogue between the two spirits, which is overheard by *Faustus*, who had hid himself in a large broom. The first act concludes with an objurgatory remonstrance from the *Doctor* to *Cacophon*.

The *second Act* presents *Donna Angelina* in a garden plucking grapes, which, by *Faustus's* power, become diamonds and rubies the moment she touches them; in the mean time two owls, which he had endowed with human voices, sing a charming duetto in praise of the *Doctor* and magic. Towards the end he enters all bloody, having killed an old woman, nobody knows why. As he hears the noise

[1] Only six examples of paintings on cobwebs are said to be in existence. See *Notes and Queries*, clxxvi (1929), pp. 261, 338, 376.

[2] 'A Husband and a Father' criticized the Pic-nic theatre as 'a hot-bed of vice and temptation' in *The Times*, 23 Feb. 1802.

[3] In the Court of Chancery S. referred to him as 'having rescued from Oblivion certain Tales of Wonder written by some insignificant scribblers such as Parnell Dryden and Chaucer' (Osborn MS.): see *Morn. Chron.*, 24 Dec. 1801.

of persons pursuing him, a pair of bat's wings start out of his shoulders at his command, and he flies away.

In the *third Act* the *Devil* appears, and *Faustus* expostulates with him for having broken his word; but the Fiend replies, that though he promised him to do *what* he would, he could not promise him to do it *when* he would. The *Devil* then binds himself by a solemn imprecation, that he should have *Angelina*. The next scene displays *Angelina's* bedchamber, with a great number of celestial *Spirits* in waiting, whose moral and sentimental dialogue cannot but interest and amend every heart. This is interrupted by a lustful *Monk*, who peeps in, and throws all into confusion. He is, however, driven out by the *Spirits*; and *Angelina* awakes with the uproar, and sings a bravura song.

The *fourth Act* opens with a *grand council* of *Magicians*, whom *Faustus* has called together. A *solemn incantation* is performed; after which they agree to call up the *Ghosts* of the most celebrated *Lovers* of *Antiquity*. The first that appears is *Sappho*, who sings a plaintive *Greek ode*, and then advises *Faustus* to take the lover's leap. *Anacreon* comes next, and, after a Greek ode of a cheerful sort, advises him to get drunk. *Horace* recommends him to go to court, where, though there were many *jugglers*, there were few *conjurers*.—Lastly, *Ovid* makes his appearance, and advises him to run away. Not satisfied with the advice of these pacific lovers, he calls for *Hercules*, *Alexander*, *Tarquin*, etc. etc. who sing a chorus, in which they direct him to ravish her. To this the *Devils* object, and tell him that he had best inveigle her into marriage, which they would promise him should be brought about that very evening.

The *fifth Act* introduces the *Doctor*, dressed in the most fashionable Parisian *costume*, and as the Sylph which guards *Angelina* knows that his contract with the *Devil* expires that night at twelve, permits his charge to promise him her hand.

Then follows a *grand procession* in honour of the *marriage*, which is no sooner ended than the *Devil* calls *Faustus* aside, shews him his bond, and flies away with him in a sheet of fire! | Yours, etc. | R. B. S.

Piazza Coffee-house, Feb. 18.

440. To Henry F. Greville

Pub.: *The Times*, 17 March 1802.

[*Mar. 1802*]

The Proprietors of the Regular Theatres, compelled by a principle of duty to the extensive interest embarked in their Establishment, have been obliged to oppose the above project.[1]

But being very desirous not to have recourse to the strict remedies of the law (which they are well persuaded would afford them sufficient protection) *as to thwart* the amusements proposed, it is agreed, as far as depends on them, that all opposition shall be withdrawn on the following terms, namely,

That the number of Dramatic Performances of any sort, Plays, Proverbs,[2] etc., shall not altogether exceed ten in the course of a season, and that no paid Performer, nor any person in any way receiving, or expecting to receive, remuneration, or which is a paid Performer of any of the existing Theatres, shall take a part in the same: The Dramatic Amusements in Tottenham-street, either in French or English, shall be *bona fide* carried on by Ladies and Gentlemen. For the fair and true performance of those conditions,[3] the Proprietors implicitly trust to the honour of the contracting Subscribers of the Society above mentioned. The Proprietors further expect, that on the evenings when there

[1] The heading was 'Private Theatrical Performances by a Society of Ladies and Gentlemen, in Tottenham-street'.

[2] *The Times*, 17 Mar. 1802, reported the performance at the Pic-Nic (or Dilettanti) Theatre of 'French proverbs, called *Zing Zing* and *Les Foux*'.

[3] Greville wrote to Richardson on 15 Mar. to say 'Had it been the Wish of the Managers to suffer our performances to proceed without fear of interruption, you certainly would not have delayed sending for my signature till ten o'clock last night to an agreement calculated to answer the end proposed . . .'. He complained that he had no time to consult his friends and that it was clear that S. did not intend to be accommodating. In a more formal letter to the Managers, of the same date, he disclaimed any intention of injuring the interests of the patent theatres, but added 'we are well assured, from the very first legal Authority, you have not the slightest right to assume' any capacity to prevent the Pic-Nic Society from opening its theatre (*The Times*, 17 Mar. 1802).

are any Theatrical Representations, the Conductors of those Amusements will announce in their Cards words to the following effect:

That such or such Dramatic Entertainment will be performed with the consent of the Proprietors of the Established Winter Theatres.

441. To William Adam

Adam MS. *Address*: W. Adam Esqr. | Lincoln's-Inn-Fields *Dock.*: Mr. Sheridan

[*Apr. 1802*][1]
Sunday morning

My Dear Adam

If Sutton moves as it is supposed he will certainly The Situation will be offer'd to your Roman Honor in the most becoming manner.[2]

I will come to you in the course of the morning. He makes Erskine is Chief-Justice[3] | yours ever | R B Sheridan

442. To William Adam

Adam MS. *Address*: W Adam Esq. *Dock.*: Mr. Sheridan | 16th April | 1802 *Wm.*: 1797

16 Apr. 1802

My Dear Adam

My not writing as I promised to Mr. Coutts has been owing to my not having been able to find the Paper of which I rely on and which I am sure when shewn to him will induce him to suspend the present Proceeding, which must be equally injurious to him and to me. I am confident I shall find it at Polesden and all I desire is the Delay of next week | yours ever | R B Sheridan | Friday | April 16th

[1] Mr. D. E. Ginter notes that the letter was one of a bundle docketed 'Apr. 1802'.

[2] *Aris's Birmingham Gazette*, 3 May 1802, reported that 'Mr. Manners Sutton has accepted the office of solicitor general to the Crown; and Mr. Adam will succeed to that of the Prince of Wales'. Thomas Manners-Sutton, afterwards 1st Lord Manners (1756–1842), was Solicitor-General to the Prince of Wales, 1800–2.

[3] Not so.

443. To Jennings[1]

N.L.I. MS. 3901, f. 6. *Address*: Mr. Jennings.

May 4th 1802

Dear Sir

I give you my word that before I receive another Shilling from Mr. Adam you shall have authority to receive from the first money of mine that comes to his hands the sum of £208-3-6 for which Mr. Wright is engaged for me to Mr. Gatty—but I cannot give Mr. Adam additional trouble or ask him to make any engagement—but this Note will be sufficient | Yours truly | R B Sheridan

444. To Richard Peake

McAdam MS. *Address*: Mr. Peake *Dock.*: Mr. Sheridan *Wm.*: 180/

[*5 May 1802?*][2]

Private

My Dear P.

Words cannot tell you the situation of this House there is not even a candle in it—or a little tea for Mrs. S.! I trust there will be no difficulty about the acceptance as I give up everything for it. But if I am not assisted with £20 to night Mrs. S. will be distracted. I can get the acceptance discounted tomorrow—I most anxiously wait your answer by the bearer | R B S

445. To Richard Peake

Salt MS. *Address*: Mr. Peake *Fr.*: R B Sheridan *Dock.*: Mr. Sheridan

[*1 June 1802?*]
Polesden
Tuesday Evening.

My Dear Peake,

I am here in a state of unhappiness not to be told. My

[1] Presumably Richard or Francis T. Jennings, attorneys, of 26 Great Shire Lane, Carey Street. See *Browne's General Law List for . . . 1797*, p. 77.

[2] Dated from entries in the D.L.Th. account book (Add. MS. 29710, f. 203v); '5 May 1802 Sher £20; Bill £105'.

sweet Child I despair of.[1] He is in a scarlet-Fever—I have Dr. Fraser[2] here and keep him all Night. He returns in the morning but comes back in my chaise in the evening—*the crisis*. I send Peter with him. I hope I need not say *put aside every other consideration*—and in the first place inclose a *£50 Note* in a cover *address'd to Dr. Fraser* with these words from you.—'Mr. Peake by direction of Mr. Sheridan respectfully sends the enclosed to Dr. Fraser.'

And then give Peter £50 for me—I must have it enter it at once in our book *£100* advanced to *me* on my son's sickness.[3] I will answer it to the Chancellor[4]—but *disappoint me on no account*.

Fraser and Ansell think he will recover—but I am out of all heart | R B S

446. To Richard Peake

Salt MS. *Address*: Mr. Peake *Dock.*: Mr. Sheridan

[*6 June 1802*]
Polesden
Sunday Night

My Dear Peake,

Tom will call you out of Bed with these—put a Person you can rely on in my House in George-St.

I am confident you will give Tom all the assistance requisite for the commissions He will shew you—There are hopes of our Child—and that is all—for a very short time must decide[5]—I myself scarc[e]ly hope—

[1] *The Courier*, 3 June 1802, reported that S. 'was sent for express yesterday to his residence near Dorking, in Surrey, in consequence of the sudden and alarming illness of his young son Charles'.

[2] William Mackinen Fraser, M.D. (d. 1807), practised at Bath and Southampton before removing to London in 1799. He became Physician Extraordinary to the Prince of Wales. See W. Munk, *The Roll of the Royal College of Physicians* (2nd ed., 1878), ii. 358.

[3] The D.L.Th. Receipts and Payments, 1801 to 1802 (Folger MS.), notes a payment of £80 to S. on 1 June.

[4] The affairs of D.L.Th. were discussed in the Court of Chancery on a number of occasions between March 1801 and Sept. 1802, and at least three orders were made by the Lord Chancellor. His first object was to ensure that the performers were paid. For a printed version of the order of 7 Apr. 1802, see the *Theatrical Inquisitor*, ii (1813), 268–70.

[5] *The Courier*, 9 June 1802, stated

Mrs. S. has been attack'd but I trust by the Physicians timely effort the disease is stopt.—She keeps her bed—Nancy and Lawson her own maid are gone to bed with the Fever this Evening.

The horrid stupidity that brought us here makes me mad | Yrs ever | R B S

every soul almost in the House is knock'd up, and I know not who may fall ill next—

447. To Richard Peake

Salt MS. *Address*: Mr. Peake. *Dock.*: Mr. Sheridan.

[*8 June 1802*]
Polesden
Tuesday 4 o'clock

My Dear Friend,

I should be very ungrateful if I did not satisfy the kind interest I know you feel about us if I omitted to give you a Line to say how matters are—Mrs. S. quite recover'd, Charles improving tho' slowly and cannot yet be pronounced out of Danger but If He goes on thus I trust may tomorrow evening—at least from the immediate effect of the Damn'd Disease. The two Girls extremely bad. Lawson in great Danger—I have sent for her Brother a respectable Person in Town. I myself but poorly constant irritation on my bladder but in good Spirits. Fraser and Bean[1] both left us this morning but have left an assistant here and Bean returns at Night. No words can do justice to their attention. I thought Lilly[2] was seized last Night—but hope it was only Fatigue | God bless you | R B S

that 'Drs. Frazer and Bain yesterday left Master C. Sheridan with fair hopes of recovery; a surprising change took place on Saturday night, his life having been despaired of in the morning. The disorder is of a most malignant nature, two of the maidservants lie dangerously ill; the labourer who brought it into the house is recovered'.

[1] Bain.

[2] One of S.'s servants. D.L.Th. Salaries, 1799 to 1802 (Folger MS.), records on 19 Sept. 1801, 'Mr. Sheridan by Mrs. Lilley £10'.

448. To Richard Peake

Salt MS. *Address*: Mr. Peake *Dock.*: Mr. Sheridan *Wm.*: 1800

[*9 June 1802*]
Wednesday morning

My Dear Peake,

Writing the enclosed yesterday in great haste with other Letters which I sent to Town I contrived to leave it open on the Table, which vex'd me much. However you will be pleased to hear our Dear Boy is still mended this morning. Dr. Bain takes this.[1] He thinks better too of the two Girls this morning—his assistance on the Spot at the moment has been everything to them. Look at the enclosed. I never saw his Letter 'till Tom told me what you said, that He would accept for £250. For God's sake my Dear Peake manage this *this Day* I am more press'd than ever. I have no Stamp—but it is no matter who draws. J. Edwards will give you this—my chaise comes back with Dr. Fraser at Night—for we must not hollow 'till we are out of the wood if matters continue improving I will be in Town on Saturday morn for a few hours but you shall hear tomorrow | God bless you | R B S.

The Husband of the Poor woman who washes for this house and lives in a cottage of mine is just come, and says all his children are taken ill—it is fortunate that I can send him assistance

449. To Richard Peake

Salt MS. *Address*: Mr. Peake *Dock.*: Mr. Sheridan *Wm.*: 1798

[*10 June 1802*]
Polesden
Thursday Night

My Dear Peake

Would to heaven Tom's report of *£250* had been true. I enclose the Draft. I entreat you not to fail to return the amount immediately address it for me at Dr. Bains Bruton-

[1] *The Oracle*, 10 June 1802, stated that 'Master C. Sheridan . . . was by the last accounts out of danger. He was attended by Drs. Frazer and Bain'.

St. care of Mr. Scott. They return together to Polesden at *3* tomorrow Friday—

The Boy goes on well—but as much skill and caution as have saved him from the Fever are still necessary to preserve him from its consequences—

I will write again tomorrow on *business* and fix the hour of a rendezvous in Town. | Your's ever most truly | R B Sheridan

the three Girls thro' *early* and skilful assistance, which our Child had not for four Days, are likely to do well. I am myself better.[1]

450. To William Adam

Adam MS. *Address*: W. Adam Esq. | Lincolns Inn Fields. *Dock.*: Mr. Sheridan | for a Meeting on Monday after 3 o'clock

[*June 1802*][2]
Polesden Saturday

My Dear Adam,

I shall be in Town, tho' with much domestic risk[3] on monday for a few hours. Pray let me know by a Line when I can attend you after 3 o'clock | your's ever | R B Sheridan

451. To Richard Peake

Salt MS. *Address*: Mr. Peake | Charlotte-St. | Rathbone-Place | To be deliver'd immediately *Dock.*: Mr. Sheridan *Wm.*: 1798

[*16 June 1802?*]
Polesden
Wednesday morning

My Dear Peake,

I shall be in St. James's Place tomorrow at three. The

[1] *The Courier*, 22 June 1802, stated: 'Mr. Sheridan has been indisposed with an intermittent fever. . . .'

[2] Mr. D. E. Ginter notes that this letter is from a bundle docketed 'June 1802'.

[3] In a letter to Adam (Adam MS.), Tom S. writes, 'My Father wished me to see you this evening. . . . He will be in Town Sunday or Monday at Farthest and begs me to assure you, that nothing but the Pain my little Brother has been in and his own present indisposition would have detained him so long from business'. His postscript adds, 'My Brother is out of Danger and I trust will do well. Mrs. S. is at present quite recovered'.

more I think of Stafford and my situation[1] on the whole the more I am determined to move *Heaven and* Earth to re-seat myself at the Old Borough. See Glossop and smooth the way—the mode of doing it must be by lodging one or two Shares in Trust as security. Grubb offers one for that Purpose. Sound Graham, your justice,[2] | Yours ever | R B Sheridan

all going on well here—except Mary Edwards—myself better.[3]

452. To William Adam

Adam MS. *Address*: [not by S.] Wm. Adam Esq. | Lincolns Inn fields | New Square *Dock.*: Mr. Sheridan

[*17 June 1802*][4]
St. James Place No. 37
Thursday Night

My Dear Adam,

In my short snatches of getting to Town pray tell me what hour it will be most convenient to you for me to call on you tomorrow after one till when I must wast[e] time | yours most | truly | R B Sheridan

[1] S. had hoped to succeed Fox as M.P. for Westminster, and Lord Holland accuses him of intriguing towards that end (*Memoirs of the Whig Party* (1852), ii. 63). Fox put the matter more charitably in a letter to O'Bryen of 24 June 1802: '. . . what I should on every account like best would be that he [S.] should have my Seat, and that I would do any thing I could to forward such an object, but that some Persons to whom I had suggested the idea, thought it impracticable; or at least they thought it would lead to enormous expences' (Add. MS. 47566, f. 118). O'Bryen 'won Mr. Fox from his purpose' at the end of June 1802 (ibid., f. 67). Fox, however, refused to believe that John Graham's candidature at Westminster in 1802 was sponsored by S. out of 'pure hatred' for Fox.

[2] Aaron Graham (1753–1818), the magistrate, became head of the Board of Management at D.L.Th. in Sept. 1802. He was 'formerly chief magistrate in Newfoundland. . . . Having a great personal regard for Mr. Sheridan, he gratuitously dedicated his time to the adjustment of [D.L.Th.] accounts' (*Annual Biography . . . 1820*, 402–21).

[3] *The Courier*, 22 June 1802, stated that S. was 'so much better as to be able to resume his parliamentary duties'.

[4] Mr. D. E. Ginter notes that this letter was part of a bundle dated 'June 1802'.

453. 'To the Worthy and Independent Electors of the Borough of Stafford'

Pub.: *Staff. Adv.*, 26 June 1802.

22 June 1802

Gentlemen,

Having had the Honor, in conjunction with my worthy Colleague Mr. MONCKTON, of representing your ancient and independent Borough through four successive Parliaments, I take the Liberty of again soliciting your Support on the approaching Dissolution, persuaded that the Friendship and Attachment which I have uniformly experienced from so great a Majority of the Electors remain as unimpaired in their Minds as the Sentiment of Gratitude is in mine.

The precarious State of Health of Part of my Family, as will be explained to you by the Friends[1] who do me the Favour to canvass for me, prevents me at the Moment from paying my personal Respects to you, but a very few Days will enable me to have that Pleasure, and to assure you on the Spot where I was first honored by your Suffrages, of the sincere and unalterable Regard with which I remain, | Your faithful and obliged | Friend and Servant, | R. B. Sheridan

Polesdon, June 22nd 1802

454. To Richard Peake

Add. MS. 35118, f. 78. *Address*: Mr. Peake | Charlotte-St. | Rathbone-Place *Dock.*: Mr. Sheridan *Wm.*: 1799

[*27 June 1802?*]
Polesden
Sunday

My Dear Peake

The Dissolution[2] will not be 'till Tuesday or Wednesday

[1] *Aris's Birmingham Gazette*, 28 June 1802, reported that 'On Friday Mr. Monkton and Mr. Sheridan jun. (in the absence of his father, who is attending his duty in parliament) . . . began their canvass . . . and experienced (almost invariably) the most gratifying reception'.

[2] S. has struck out 'Election' and substituted 'Dissolution'. The dissolution actually took place on Monday, 28 June.

—It is of vital importance to me that you send off the enclosed by a *special messenger* tomorrow (*Monday*) morn at *4 o'clock*—wait answer I shall be in Town by 4 afterwards—

G. Edwards came up to me yesterday to inform me Mrs S was ill in bed. She is so now a shocking cold and rheumatism —but not the Fever. This is all sadly worrying to me | God bless you | R B S

455. To Richard Peake

Add. MS. 35118, ff. 81–82. *Address*: June twenty eight 1802 | Richd Peake | Peake's Esqr. | Stafford *Fr.*: R B Sheridan *Pm.*: JUN 28 1802

28 June 1802
Monday
Private

Dear Peake,

Bravo!—had you said it was necessary before you went I could with ease have had a thousand more as Lord Thanet's[1] Letter will shew you but He is gone to Appleby. Consult with Tom and try Monckton with the enclosed seal it, after. I send a Bond, it is the first favour I ever ask'd him.[2] Fox certainly stands for Westminster | Yrs in great hast[e] | R B S

456. To Richard Peake

Egerton MS. 1975, f. 79. *Dock.*: Mr. Sheridan

[*1802?*]

Dear Peake,

Ten Pounds more will not break our back. Therefore by no means I beg most particularly fail to pay Keen[3] by a

[1] Sackville Tufton, 9th Earl of Thanet (1767–1825) was tried in April 1799 for helping to cause a riot at the end of O'Connor's trial at Maidstone. S. gave evidence there and his pause was thought to show uncertainty and to have influenced the jury. See *The Journal of Elizabeth Lady Holland* (ed. Earl of Ilchester, 1908), i. 246.

[2] Mr. Brian Ball owns a document binding S. to Monckton in the sum of £1,000. It is dated 28 June 1802, and witnessed by Burgess. S.'s address is given as Hertford Street, Mayfair.

[3] One of S.'s servants at Polesden. The only allusions to him in the D.L.Th. accounts concern a draft for £5. 18*s*. 0*d*. which he received on dates given as either 31 May or 2 June 1800.

Draught *to Day* the order I have given him—his wife is dying at Polesden and after *what has happen'd there* for him to be sent back without money would be the Devil.— | Yours 'till tuesday | R B S.

2 o clock

457. 'To the Worthy and Independent Electors of the Borough of Stafford'

Pub.: *Staff. Adv.*, 3 July 1802.

July 1802

Gentlemen,

The distinguished Honor we have enjoyed in being elected Representatives of your ancient and respectable Borough for four successive Parliaments, and the very flattering reception we have this day met with on our canvass, claim our most grateful acknowledgments.[1]

Be assured that our most earnest wish is to retain your good opinion,[2] and that your interests shall ever be the first object of attention with, | Gentlemen, | your obliged and devoted Servants | E. Monckton | R. B. Sheridan

458. To His Son Tom

McAdam MS.

[*Just before 4 July 1802*]

My Dear Tom

I am coming like Smoke considering I am still I assure

[1] The *Staff. Adv.* reported on 3 July 1802: 'Mr. Sheridan comes in for Stafford, without a contest. Strong application was made to Government to support a mercenary opposition; but much to the honour of Mr. Addington's liberality, he not only refused all countenance to the application but distinctly declared, that he should regret, as a public man, to see Mr. Sheridan out of Parliament, or even disturbed in his seat for a place, which he had represented honourably and independently for four successive Parliaments'.

[2] Their letter of thanks for election is in the *Staff. Adv.*, 10 July 1802. It is the same as that of 28 May 1796, except that 'a Fourth time' becomes 'a Fifth time'.

you an *invalid*—and travelling the worst thing for me—no other journey would I have undertaken at this moment—I have said to the Messenger

> 'Be thou as Lightning in the eye of Stafford
> For e're thou can'st report I will be there
> The Thunder of my Cannon shall be heard'[1]

Your's and all Friends | ever | R B S.

Your saying the Election is monday[2] I take to be fair fudge to hasten me

459. To Henry Burgess

N.L.I. MS. 3901, ff. 7–8. *Address*: Stafford June fifth 1802 | Mr. Burgess | Curzon-St. | May-Fair | London *Fr.*: Free R B Sheridan

5 July 1802

Stafford
Monday—one o'clock

My dear B.

The Election is over—I am just got out of the Chair.[3] Nothing could exceed the cordiality and unanimity of the Town—

Pray copy and get the enclosed[4] into the Herald—and

[1] Cf. *King John*, I. i. 24–26:

> Be thou as lightning in the eyes of France;
> For ere thou canst report I will be there,
> The thunder of my cannon shall be heard:

[2] S. arrived in Stafford on 4 July, to attend the election held on Monday, 5 July.

[3] After their election in 1790, S. and Monckton 'were carried through the town in triumphal chairs elegantly decorated for the occasion' (*Wolverhampton Chronicle*, 23 June 1790).

[4] In S.'s hand: 'Extract of a Letter from Stafford | Monday July 5th: 1802 | "The Election is just over.—Sheridan and Monkton returned again without opposition and with the completest Unaniminity—Your information and apprehensions respecting Captn. Whitby of the Navey were entirely groundless Captn. Whitby is not even in the Country and Mr. Whitby of his Father a Gentleman of an independent Estate in the Neighbourhood came into the Town only to contradict the Report and to offer Mr. Sheridan his Interest. The only attempt made was by your old Friend Dick Whitworth who publish'd a handbill taxing Mr. Sheridan with having been absent from the Borough ever since the last Election above six years and promising the Burgesses *a third man* it ended however in his proposing himself, which he retracted this morning on the Hustings and voted for our two esteem'd Members.

just call and say something to M. Chronicle and Times.[1] The Election dinner will not be 'till tomorrow—when I shall set out on my return—to Day the Principal Burgesses treat me— | God bless you | R B Sheridan

and get this into *Courier* and General Evening Post if you pay—I have a particular Reason—send the Papers with the accounts to Mr. S.

460. To Richard Peake

McAdam MS. *Address*: Mr. Peake *Wm.*: 1801

[*1802*]
Polesden
Wednesday

Dear P,

By Heaven you must get another £10 from G.[2] Edwards is so distress'd for money to pay the man our harvest will stop—if G. will make it £20 G. Edwards[3] shall undertake to repay it. H Ogle and Spouse[4] come to Day and go Friday when I shall return to Town—and let us come back together. Beside the money Pressure I am so anxious to know how R.[5] is I send Keen on Purpose. | Yrs ever | R B S

Crops famous!

I hope the Devil won't send rain

Mr. Sheridan made an admirable Speech in thanking his Constituents for this their fifth election of him and turned the charge of his long absence from the Borough so cleverly as to excite the most enthusiastic applause. Mr. Sheridan did not arrive here 'till yesterday but his Place was so ably supplied on the canvass by his Son Tom, that he lost nothing by the Delay, indeed had Mr. Sheridan stood for Westminster on Mr. Fox's retirement as was at one time reported young Sheridan would have been infallibly returned for Stafford with the same unanimity as his Father—Our County election comes on on Wednesday—all Quiet. The same at Litchfield—the Election on tuesday—Sir Niger has quitted the Field—at Newcastle also Mr. Smith has declined the contest—and Sir Robert Lawley is come in his Place."' (N.L.I. MS. 3901, ff. 9–10.)

[1] It appeared, with only trifling corrections, in the *Morn. Her.*, 8 July 1802, and *The Courier*, 7 July 1802. There is no hint in these reports that the passage was written by S. himself. The paragraph in *The Times*, 8 July 1802, resembles that of the *Staff. Adv.* of 10 July.

[2] John Graham?

[3] George Edwards ran Polesden for S.

[4] Henry Bertram Ogle and Anna Maria Raphael were married at Marylebone on 31 May 1802. See Ogle, p. 139.

[5] Richardson.

461. To Anna Maria Ogle[1]

Harvard MS.

[*1802?*]
Holywell
Sunday morning

Dear Malty

I think both Mrs. Sheridan and our little Boy require Sea-bathing, and I hear there is an improvement in the Baths at Southampton, in which case I should for many reasons prefer it to any other Place, will you have the goodness to enquire what decent house there may be vacant but as much out of Town as possible. I am told there is one near you which Mr. Smith had which is perhaps not taken. But I should wish a spare Best Room or two so as to be able to accommodate the Scotts and little ones should they come to Hester. I will not make any excuse for giving you this trouble as I know your Good nature will make you execute it with Pleasure.—A very quiet sleeping Room for ourselves is a very great object to me. | Your's very sincerely | R B Sheridan

direct to me at Polesden Leatherhead Surry

Is the Cutter alive?

462. To Anna Maria Ogle

Osborn MS.

[*1802?*]
Farnham
Tuesday Evening

Dear Malty,

I beg you a thousand Pardons for not having answer'd your obliging Letter—but I every Day thought either to set out for Hampshire or to give up the scheme. In this state of uncertainty I put off writing to you. I am now on the road to Holywell—and your last Letter I only caught at Polesden this morning—I like the Notion of the House in the Polygon[2]

[1] Anna Maria Cowlam was married in 1787 to Mrs. S.'s eldest brother, Nathaniel Ogle (1765–1813). Her pet name was 'Malty'; see Ogle, p. 157.

[2] This was to have been an elaborate building (planned by Leroux) of twelve

best of all—I shall certainly want room. My son Tom I think will join us[1]—and Stables are most necessary, as we bring six Horses with us—make a fair Bargain with your Friend Mr. Hoohey. I thank you sincerely for the offer of your House—but I would not have suffer'd you to have left it on any account | Your's truly | R B Sheridan

You are *right* in every thing you have done about *the child*.

463. To Richard Peake

Salt MS. *Address*: Mr. Peake *Dock.*: Mr. Sheridan

[*1802?*]
Sunday

My Dear Loggerheads[2]

Better give the Bearer another little Tip; and send him up to Polesden *to Night*—for fear Keen should be out in the morning—Keen has the double barrell'd Gun for you tell Burgess he is to put the *but-end* of the Gun to his shoulder, and the muzzle towards the Bird. We will not begin fishing till towards one—if Burgess hasn't the Homer *Mr.* S will kill him. H. Scott is here and Tom will be here in the morning | Yours ever | R B S

464. To William Adam

Adam MS. *Dock.*: R B Sheridan

Ellingham[3]
Monday 12[4] Septr. 1802

My Dear Adam

In reliance of the relief of at least the amount of one of R's

sides, with hotels in its wings and assembly and card rooms at its centre, but it was converted into a number of houses: see the description and plate in *The British Magazine*, ii (1783), 420; and *The Diaries of Mrs. Philip Lybbe Powys* (ed. Climenson, 1899), p. 273.

[1] Tom S. declined an invitation to stay with 'Malty' in his letter to her (Osborn MS.), postmarked 9 Nov. 1802.

[2] Apart from the sense of 'blockhead', S. may have intended allusion to the village of Loggerheads on the border of Peake's native Staffordshire.

[3] Three miles from Bungay. The Adam MSS. also contain a letter from Henry Smith to Adam, written from Ellingham on the same date and concerning the Committee of Shipping. S. was probably staying with Smith (afterwards M.P. for Calne, 1807–12) at Ellingham Hall, Suffolk.

[4] 13 Sept. S.'s mistake.

Debentures before this Day I find myself in the most distressing situation possible. I lose the letting of my House[1] if I cannot give Possession of it tomorrow—and I cannot move the Sequestration[2] without paying the cost which they have run up to £150! This is also the last Day allow'd by the Chancellor for any application to be made to him and with a little ready money I could prevent two or three Things being sent in to him in a litigious way—which indeed is promised by Burgess to be done. The Duke of Bedford is for the present out of the Question and indeed I have made up my mind that it should remain as it is—and for the present I trust there is Plenty. I know my dear Adam there is no want of friendly exertions on your Part—but such is my case | yours ever | R B S.

I have paid Walter

465. To Richard Peake

McAdam MS. *Address*: Southampton October twelve 1802 | Mr. Peake | Charlotte-St. | Rathbone Place | London *Fr.*: Free | R B Sheridan *Dock.*: Mr. Sheridan

12 Oct 1802
Southampton[3]
Tuesday

My Dear Peake

Fail not *by return of Post* to send me *five Days* Pay i.e. five and twenty guineas—not less. You can always manage a few Days advance and I shall never want more. We are living here most œconomically but pay house and all *every week*—I rely on your not delaying this—and then I shall set off to

[1] Grey wrote to Whitbread on 29 June 1804 (Whitbread MS.) to prove that theirs was not 'the only execution which kept him [S.] out of his house in Hertford St. on his return from the North'. This may refer to some later occasion, but it is worth noting that *The Times*, 17 Nov. 1801, reported that the Sheridans had left their house in Hertford Street for lodgings in Cork Street; and that *Boyle's Court and Country Guide* (1802), p. 257, gave S.'s address as 3 Cork Street. Probably S. wanted to return to Hertford Street and was prevented from doing so by the bailiffs.

[2] See p. 151, n. 3.

[3] *The English Chronicle*, 9–11 Sept. 1802, thought it surprising that the attractions as a watering-place, of this 'charming and fashionable spot' were so often passed over.

be among you, and bring home good Grist for the Mill with me[1]—which I should not have finish'd either in London or Polesden. Pray send me also a return of each Nights Receipt since I left Town. | Yrs ever | R B S

466. To John Graham

Pub.: Maggs Catalogue 386 (1919), item 3035.

30th October, 1802

I call'd on you this evening to have proposed to you the security for your retaining the deposit for the share which Mr. Burgess will now show you and which if sign'd by Mr. Wright must put all objection to compleating the business in Hartford St. out of the question; it is now declared both by Mr. Wright and Mr. Jennings that it never was understood that you were to have part of the money—this I confess surprises me as it certainly was very principally that you might obtain assistance from it that I consented to the sale of the share on such terms; however I trust no further difficulty will be made or I shall think myself strangely treated.

467. To William Adam

Adam MS. *Dock.*: Mr. Sheridan | 9th Novr. 1802

9 Nov. 1802

My Dear Adam,

We came to a unanimous resolution[2] to request the Duke[3] on his Declining to be Trustee, to recommend one to our choice who will be immediately appointed.[4]

[1] 'Mr. Sheridan's long promised opera of *The Foresters* is said to be that to which he is now putting a finishing hand' (*The English Chronicle*, 23–25 Sept. 1802). This was never completed, and it seems more likely that S. read over or revised work by others. The new pieces given before Christmas were James Cobb's *A House to be Sold*; and the anonymous *Love and Magic; or Harlequin's Holiday*.

[2] At the renters' meeting in the Crown and Anchor on 5 Nov.

[3] John Russell, 6th Duke of Bedford (1766–1839), succeeded his brother on 2 Mar. 1802.

[4] George Biggin, the Duke's friend, was duly appointed a trustee of D.L.Th. in place of Albany Wallis. See P.R.O. Chancery Procs. C 13/2325, and H. Holland to Biggin, 9 May 1803 (Gilmore MS.). Cf. Letter 475.

and now I have to finish the other business to your satisfaction—in the interim pray obtain Coutts to consent to the enclosed. I am selling the house for him infinitely better than it can otherwise be disposed of as I fear he is quite off his Proposal in regard to Richardson | yours | ever | R B Sheridan

468. To Thomas Creevey

J. R. Blackett-Ord MS. *Address*: T. Creevey Esq | Cumberland-Place *Dock.*: Sheridan

[*Nov. 1802?*][1]

My Dear Sir,

I return to Town on monday—when I can decide about the House. I am ashamed not to have called on you and Mrs. Creevey— | Yours in great haste | most truly | R B Sheridan

Friday morning

469. To William Adam

Adam MS. *Address*: W. Adam Esqr. *Dock.*: Mr. Sheridan | 16th Novr. 1802

Tuesday Evening—
Nov. 16th *1802*

My Dear Adam,

Richardson has communicated to me a very extraordinary Letter from O'Brien evidently intended to be shewn to me with an enclosure from you stating that there is £400 in your hands at my disposal. Mr. O'Brien as I understand desires to borrow this money. I should be very ready to serve him if I had any money to lend—my exigenc[i]es I know to be greater than his. However in the case of this money it is not mine but disposed of in the same order and confidence which you so properly attended to in all the preceding Payments—Mr. Burgess who is in advance for much more than this sum

[1] Creevey wrote to Currie from Great Cumberland Place on 8 Nov. 1802: see *Creevey Papers*, i. 4.

and who has my order long since for the first money in your hands will give you a receipt for the above | yours | R B Sheridan

470. To William Adam

Adam MS. *Dock.*: Mr. Sheridan | 5th Decr. 1802 *Wm.*: 1801

5 Dec. 1802
Sunday Evening

My Dear Adam

I have been unfortunate in missing you these two Days in Lincoln's-Inn. I will say nothing more on matters I must speak to you upon *after wednesday*—but the enclosed refers[1] to an hour—pray accomplish what I request in it and I will see all right in that quarter and many other[s]— | Yours ever truly | R B Sheridan

471. To Richard Peake

Add. MS. 35118, ff. 137–8. *Address*: Mr. Peake | Charlotte-St. | Rathbone Place *Dock.*: Mr. Sheridan *Wm.*: 1801.

[*1802–3?*][2]
Saturday morning

My dear Peake

A merry Xmas to you—but to make mine more merry, do follow up what you said very kindly last Night that you thought we were met to procure me some present accommodation. With this view do beg Heath[3] not to add the furniture £100 to the money for the share—but to let me have that advance. The furniture security is quite safe. Of the £50 you advanced on the Note—Mrs. Hall had £30 and Miss Palmer £10—Hall had also a draft for £20, dated to Day

[1] Manuscript 'prefers'.

[2] Christmas day fell on a Saturday in 1802, and on a Sunday in 1803.

[3] S. was friendly with James Heath (1757–1834), engraver, but appears to refer here to one Heath, a broker. D.L.Th. Receipts and Payments, 1801–2 (Folger MS.), notes £112.17*s*.0*d*. received from 'Mr. Heath Cash lent by him to pay Mr. Bannister's Arrears of last Season and this on 30 Oct. 1801'. It also records three payments of expenses to 'Heath Broker'. He is also mentioned in the accounts of 1803–4.

but which I suppose will not be presented 'till monday—it will be the devil not to be answer'd. Send it out of Heath's advance if you succeed as I trust you will and to me £50 at H. Scott's Esq. Holywell Bishop's Waltham Hants *by this day's Post*. Tell me where *you eat* your chop monday. | R B S

472. To John Fonblanque

Bodleian Library, Western MS. 35574, f. 117d.

Monday
Jan 3d. [*1803?*]

Dear Fonblanque

I am going very abruptly to ask you a very great Favor. I am on the road going to discharge matters at Southampton and most unexpectedly disappointed of a sum of money. Would you ask the Stratford-Place[1] bank to give Burgess cash for the enclosed or even one of them I cannot describe the favor it would be to me and as I am confident we shall come to have greater Dealings I pledge myself most positively to you for the punctual Payment of the Drafts | yours in haste | most sincerely | R B Sheridan

473. To Richard Peake

McAdam MS. *Address*: Southampton January fourth 1803 | Mr. Peake | Charlotte-St. | Rathbone Place | London *Fr.*: Free R B Sheridan *Dock.*: Mr. Sheridan | [another hand] I will accept 2 Bills for £40 each at a Month and 6 Weeks | *indeed* I have not any Money

4 Jan. 1803
Tue[s]day

Dear Peake

By Heaven you must assist me with an advance. B.[2] will explain how I am situated— | yours ever | R B S.

I am here to make excuses for the bills—but without some money I am stuck.

[1] Fonblanque's father was a banker. The only bank I can find at this address was that of Smith, Templer, Middleton, and Johnson.

[2] Burgess.

474. To James Perry[1]

Miss Emily Driscoll MS. [Ph.] *Address*: James Perry E | Strand | Near Exeter-Change *Fr.*: R B Sheridan *Dock.*: R. B. Sheridan Esq | 14 March 1803

Sunday Evening
March 13th. [*1803*]

My Dear Sir

Letters evidently containing printed Papers are often not hastily open'd by idle members of Parliament. I have only this evening broke the seal of one sign'd by you March 11th. respecting the Surrey Rail-way—.[2] I am an enthusiast on this subject, and a decided Foe to the stupid eagerness of extending the Plan of Canals where they can only be mischievous—above all in our County. I will certainly be at the House tomorrow[3] (the second reading as I understand from this Paper) and shall be happy to meet you there. | Yours ever | R B Sheridan

475. [To Richard Peake]

Add. MS. 35118, f. 159.

[*15 Mar. 1803?*]
Tuesday

Private

Dear P.

Canvass every one you can for the Trustee Friday[4] it will be either the Duke or his recommendation | R B S.

in Town tomorrow or early Thursday

[1] James Perry (1756–1821) was a proprietor of the *Morn. Chron.* between 1789 and 1821. He lived at Merton, Surrey.

[2] The railway from Wandsworth to Croydon, opened for goods traffic on 26 July 1803. As early as 25 May 1801 the *Morn. Chron.* had praised the iron roads as excellent substitutes for canals, noting that they were built at one-third of the expense.

[3] S. moved the second reading of the Surrey Iron Railway Bill in the Commons on 14 Mar. 1803.

[4] An election of a trustee for D.L.Th. (in place of Hammersley) was held at the Crown and Anchor on 18 Mar. 1803. George Shum received forty-three votes; Graham, sixteen. See Winston, 1801–4, and *The Times*, 21 Mar. 1803.

476. To Richard Peake

Add. MS. 35118, ff. 86–87. *Wm.*: 1801.

Sunday
May 8th [*1803*]

My Dear Peake

Burgess has let sleep to my great disappointment the substituted security for the £100 each advanced by yourself etc. It is not possible for me to describe the inconvenience and distress this has brought on me. I enclose you the Bonds etc. The Letters to Sir R. Ford Heath and Watkins Burgess I find has delivered. Do I entreat you bestir yourself so as to get this done for me and the notices to Drewe sign'd in the course of tomorrow. You cannot conceive the consequence it is of to me | Yours truly | R B Sheridan

I miss'd you to Day

477. To Henry Burgess

Harvard MS. *Address*: To Mr. Burgess—Curzon St. | May-Fair.

May 9th [*1803?*]

Please to deliver to Mr. Heath the additional £100[1] Share I have promised from my own. | R B Sheridan

478. [To Lady Bessborough]

Brinsley Ford MS. *Pub.*: Sichel, ii. 440–1. *Wm.*: 1801.

[*23 May 1803*]

I snatch a moment to obey your commands, half famish'd and ready to sink under Noise, heat and fatigue. Grey has just mov'd the amendment,[2] after a very able judicious and

[1] Possibly £200. The figuring is careless.

[2] The debate followed Hawkesbury's motion approving His Majesty's endeavours to preserve peace and deploring the restless ambitions of France. Grey's amendment sought the omission from the address of any approval of the government's conduct, and he argued that there was still an opening for negotiation.

argumentative Speech, in which he stated as the grounds for his amendment, the impossibility of his acquiescing (under the present unexplain'd circumstances) in a vote which went directly and positively to assert that the War was unavoidable. He spoke with great perspicuity and force and was most attentively listen'd to, which should be of itself a Proof of his Speech being uncommonly good, for he labour'd under the disadvantage of rising immediately after one of the most brilliant and magnificent pieces of declamation that ever fell from that rascal Pitt's lips. Detesting the Dog as I do, I cannot withdraw[?][1] this just tribute to the Scoundrel's talents.

I could not help often lamenting in the course of his harangue, as I have frequently done before, what a pity it is that He has not a particle of honesty in him.

He would be a great treasure, if he had a Grain. Lord Hawkesbury[2] began the business with a calm, temperate, and sensible Speech, and tho' I cannot say at all brilliant or satisfactory, (and with bad taste I thought in two or 3 of his state[3] quotations) was upon the whole a judicious imposing and statesmanlike Speech.

Erskine[4] follow'd, agreeing and disagreeing contradicting and confusing himself, and alternately entertaining and tiring and disgusting the House, and for the most part talking like the merest Jack Ass that ever was heard. He began by declaring that he was not nor even[5] would be the advocate and Apologist for France—and before he ended his object seem'd to be to persuade us that he would probably never again be employ'd as the Advocate of any Country or any Individual, and that no one would ever think of giving him 10 Shillings to advocate any cause upon Earth—

Pitt rais'd the War [w]hoop most vehemently and eloquently. And the Cry was loud. He took many sly opportunities as you may imagine of ridiculing poor Tom Erskine, whose nonsensical contradictions he treated with a degree of scorn and contempt that was possibly not quite so palatable to the learned Counsel as they were relish'd by the House.

[1] Sichel prints 'withhold'.

[2] Foreign Secretary.

[3] Possibly S. meant to write 'stale'.

[4] Thomas, afterwards 1st Lord Erskine. Creevey thought the speech 'the most confused, unintelligible, inefficient performance that ever came from the mouth of man' (*Creevey Papers*, i. 15).

[5] Sichel prints 'ever'.

Lord Castlereagh,[1] upon Grey's sitting down rose to speak. I got up immediately to go to dinner, in the Middle of which I write to you. What Castlereagh has said I have not enquir'd, nor do I mean to do so.

Here's submission to your Will!! | Yrs ever, | S[?]

House of Commons
Monday

We shall divide I suppose about 50 against 400.[2] I can't send you the words of Grey's amendment but the substance of it is to leave out all the Words that follow the assurances of supporting the dignity of Crown and Country etc. and adverting continually to the concluding part of the declaration which intimates a desire of cultivating and improving whatever opportunities may offer for procuring Peace.

I am half drunk and can write no more. Perhaps had better not to have written half so much.

479. To Lady Bessborough

Dufferin MS. *Pub.*: Sichel, ii. 440. *Address*: Ly. Bessborough. *Wm.*: 1801.

[*25 May 1803*]
½ past 1.

Dear Lady Bessborough

I have done what I would do for no one breathing but you—Left the House while Fox was speaking[3] to answer your note—The debate will I suppose be very short when he sits down. He has spoken not only wonderfully well, but with the greatest possible dexterity, prudence, management, etc., qualities he has not always at command—He began in the putting the House in the best possible humour with him, joking about the temporary *cessation of hostilities*[4] from Pitt's

1 Robert Stewart, Viscount Castlereagh (1769–1822), was President of the Board of Control.

2 The Address was carried by 398 against 67 (*Annual Register . . . 1803*, p. 141).

3 Fox spoke after Grenville, Whitbread, Canning, and Dallas, in the debate continued from the previous day. He made some defence of the French attitude and suggested that England should be more reasonable in her claims. W. B. Ponsonby though it the finest speech ever heard. See Sir J. Ponsonby, *The Ponsonby Family* (1929), p. 64.

4 War with France had been declared on 18 May.

friends Canning and such like, and he has gone on conciliating the House more and more. Taking the most judicious line too in abusing Bonaparte and his government and his 'Acts'—The first part of his speech and that to which he will of course recur was to enforce the propriety and necessity for the Amendment, which he did forcibly and I daresay will conclude irresistibly; at least to most people's conviction tho' it may make little or no difference as to votes—tho' indeed in this respect it will do some good with I think 3 or 4 persons—It has been hitherto a dry dull debate not worth detailing to you. Canning's Speech[1] had nothing I think good in it, even in point of declamation; and not even lively, which he generally is.

Tom Grenville spoke tolerably well, but not very. Upon the whole a sensible dull speech.[2] He made rather an odd avowal at one part of it, saying that he saw *nothing objectionable* in the Amendment—this raised a great cry of hear hear as you may imagine on our Part.

I won't write another word. I have lost 5 minutes. Adieu—

Here's obedience passive obedience with a vengeance!

480. To His Wife

Harvard MS. *Address*: London June thirty 1803 | Mrs. Sheridan | Deanery | Winchester *Fr.*: Free | R B Sheridan

30 June 1803
Thursday

By my Life and Soul if you talk of leaving me now[3] you will destroy me. I am wholly unwell—I neither sleep nor eat.[4] You are before my eyes Night and Day. I will contrive

[1] George Canning (1770–1827) was hostile to Addington's administration. The gist of his speech is to be found in his statement that the House must 'abandon the vain delusion that any safety was to be found in lowliness'.

[2] Grenville said that he could not see how the amendment differed from the original motion, lamented that it should be persisted in, and called for unanimity in opposition to France.

[3] Lady Bessborough wrote to Lord Holland (*c.* June 1803) to say that S. 'is never sober for a moment and his affairs worse than ever—*pour comble* he has quarrelled with Mrs. S. A sort of separation took place, but I believe it is partly made up again, at least they live in the same house again, but not very good friends' (Holland House MS.). Cf. Sichel, ii. 270.

[4] Quoted by Rae, ii. 216.

that you shall go to the North at all events, but don't leave me to myself. I would to God that you had told me that Bain thought you getting robust and strong—it is so far my first anxiety on this earth that for that I would compromise to give up every other Hope. I will set out on Saturday or Sunday to come to you—I think very ill of Arabella[1] and find that I have the truest regard for her in the World. But my mercurial bodings are not much to be regarded.

Pray let me hear from you by return of Post. What I have received from you is one Line to say you got safe, then a Letter with some sweet words in it, and this of yesterday.

Smythe[2] is fix'd otherwise. We will talk of this at Winchester. Dear Charles kiss your mother for me, if I live 'till you have mind to know me you will not cease to love me. | bless you Hecca | S

481. To Richard Peake

McAdam MS. *Dock.*: Mr. Sheridan

[*After June 1803*]
Sunday

Dear Peake,

Give my £31. 10. 0[3] to J. Edwards before you sleep for God's sake. I return with Mrs. S. Tuesday and then will work like a Horse for the Theatre | Your | R B S

Get £10 from some damn'd Tenant or other and give it Mrs. Richardson[4]

482. To Charles James[5]

Harvard MS. *Address*: Charles James Esqr.: *Dock.*: Sir Wm. Geary *Wm.*: 1798

Friday July 1st [*1803*]

My Dear Sir,

I have been so employ'd lately that I could not call upon

[1] Mrs. Bouverie. Lady Harriet Cavendish noted on 22 Nov. 1803 that she was much better in health. See *Hary-O* (ed. Sir G. Leveson Gower and Iris Palmer, 1940), p. 82.

[2] Possibly S. thought of engaging William Smyth as Charles Sheridan's tutor.

[3] His weekly salary from D.L.Th.

[4] After her husband's death on 9 June 1803, she drew ten guineas a week from D.L.Th.

[5] An attorney, and partner with Abel Jenkins at 8 New Inn.

you. The last time I saw you it was settled that our business should stand over for a *fortnight* or *three-weeks* and the share to be sold in the interval which I consented to at any Price. One Share is contracted for at a price which must prove my determination to pay Sir W. Geary's demand at any rate— and I am ready to submit to the same Loss on the other.[1] I am surprised to hear from Mr. Burgess that any hostile proceeding still exists. | Yours ever | R B Sheridan

on the other subject I will see you tomorrow.

483. To Andrew Bain

Pub.: Moore, ii. 448–9

July 31. [*1803?*]

My Dear Sir,

The caution you recommend proceeds from that attentive kindness which Hester always receives from you, and upon which I place the greatest reliance for her safety. I so entirely agree with your apprehensions on the subject, that I think it was very giddy in me not to have been struck with them when she first mentioned having slept with her friend. Nothing can abate my love for her; and the manner in which you apply the interest you take in her happiness, and direct the influence you possess in her mind, render you, beyond comparison, the person I feel most obliged to upon earth. I take this opportunity of saying this upon paper, because it is a subject on which I always find it difficult to speak.

With respect to that part of your note in which you express such friendly partiality, as to my parliamentary conduct, I need not add that there is no man whose good opinion can be more flattering to me. | I am, ever, my dear Bain, | Your sincere and obliged | R. B. Sheridan.

[1] In a list of £3,000 shareholders (Folger MS.) Geary is noted as possessing two absolute shares.

484. To Henry Addington

Viscount Sidmouth MS. *Pub.*: Pellew, ii. 224–6. *Address*: Right Honble. Henry Addington | etc etc etc | Downing Street | London *Dock.*: Mr. Sheridan *Pm.*: WOBOURN

Wobourn, Augst. 29th. 1803.

Dear Sir,

I trouble you with these few lines from a good intention or I should not expect your excuse for the liberty I take in writing to you.

When I first saw Lord Hobart's[1] letter to the several Lords Lieutenants, directing them not even to transmit to Government offers of Volunteer service to a greater amount than the number which together with all actually existing Corps of yeomanry and Volunteers, would be equal to six times the old Militia I felt great apprehension that the most unpleasant consequences would follow and that a great risk was incurr'd not merely of damping the spirit so generally rising and spreading, but of creating a temper of jealousy and discontent among the greater part of the Mass of the People. Nothing but finding to my conviction at least that the effect has already more than justified my fears could induce me to intrude on you any opinion of mine upon a subject which so entirely belongs to the direction and views of his Majesty's Ministers. But we must not overlook the language which as Members of Parliament we have all in common held on this point.[2] One pledge was to become as far as possible an armed Nation and the appeal both in the House and out of it has been to the spirit and loyalty of every individual Man in the Country capable of bearing arms in its defence—The phrase which I remember you referr'd to at

[1] Robert Hobart, afterwards 4th Earl of Buckinghamshire (1760–1816), was Secretary for War and the Colonies. His circular letter suggested limiting the number of volunteers because it was impossible to equip all who had come forward. S.'s reactions were common, but the Foxites distrusted his point of view and thought him deceived by and devoted to Addington.

[2] S.'s orations on the Defence Amendment Bill (4 Aug.) and on the Volunteers (10 Aug.) are in *Speeches*, v. 236–61. The gist of them is to be found in S.'s sentence, 'He rejoiced to find that a military disposition pervaded the land, and he wished that the effect of this military disposition might be visible in a general military appearance in the country'.

your Table of 'One and all' is become a powerful catch word since Lord Hobart's letter. In every District and Village they are ready to go forth 'One and all' in arms, but the mere mention of limitations and selections has wholly abated the general Zeal—I wish I may be misinformed in this respect, but I assure you I do not speak on light suggestions—accidental circumstances have brought to my knowledge a number of authentic instances of the change I lament—Lord Ossory who was here the other day and the Duke of Bedford think more of the matter even than I do.—Numbers of the Duke's own Corps are already desirous of retiring. It would indeed be unreasonable to expect that all the arms asked for could be now forth coming, but as to the expence of the clothing[1] it seems generally admitted that nothing would be more easy than to have County subscriptions for that subject. At all events my dear Sir excuse this intrusion on my part which I should not have ventured, did it not appear that the error of it has been one [that] may be now the Department is in Mr. Yorke's[2] hands be most easily rectified. I will trespass on your time no further at present, as I shall be in Town in a few days and shall very earnestly wish a short conversation on this subject. | I have the honor to be | with great esteem and respect | Your obedient Servant | R B Sheridan

485. To His Wife

Osborn MS. *Wm.*: 1801

[*31 Aug. 1803*][3]
London Wednesday

It was scarcely more than half past ten when I got to Town. The King very gracious but it is strange to think how he picked up every thing that is going on. The first thing he

[1] 'So expensive as to preclude altogether a certain class of individuals from joining the ranks' (*The Times*, 12 Aug. 1803).

[2] Charles Philip Yorke (1764–1834) had been Secretary at War, but was sworn in as Secretary of State for the Home Department on 17 Aug. 1803.

[3] This is the only date when S. and the Bishop of Rochester were together at a levee. S. presented an address from Stafford. See *The Star*, 1 Sept. 1803.

ask'd me was whether you had recovered the ill effects of your steps? 'tis fact what I tell you. He spoke a great deal on the subject, and seems a decided enemy to the new Capers, he said your Grandfather[1] advised him from a boy never to attempt to excel in Dancing, and that the Queens corns had providentially interfered with her early propensity to become a proficient in that frivolous and often mischievous accomplishment. He was very curious to know whether the Duchess of Bedford[2] intended to continue to assert her superiority in this art.—I answer'd that the Duke was particularly desirous that she should, and had even proposed that Mr. Holland should direct the Riding house[3] to be floor'd for a practicing room but that I doubted whether the Duchess had not formed a different idea on the subject. He commended her highly for it and said he was sure that Mrs. Whitbread[4] was of his opinion. This I think was chiefly all that pass'd on the subject of '*circuitous impious ambling*', which very much diverted him and he ask'd the Bishop of Rochester[5] whether he remember'd where the Passage was in Latin. The Bishop thought it was in Salust, but the King said Terence, and there the conversation dropp'd.

I am now going about business and to get my wench a mot of money! and then I will add a Line—no Letters for you whatever!

5 o clock. O my dearest beloved Hecca the Gloom sprite has hold of me so horribly that I have been near returning to Wobourn[6] to take care of you—would my heart were but truly known to you! Let me beseech you to take care. Be not sweet Hecca seduced about wine you were burning hot this morning. Let Humphrey be told that I have enclosed him some money to Wobourn—

I have no Place to dine at nor a Soul to speak to.

[1] John Thomas (1696–1781), successively Bishop of Peterborough, Salisbury, and Winchester. When George III was Prince of Wales, Dr. Thomas was his tutor.

[2] Georgiana, daughter of the 4th Duke of Gordon. She had married John, 6th Duke of Bedford, as his second wife on 23 June 1803.

[3] Built 1794.

[4] Elizabeth Whitbread (1765–1846), elder daughter of Sir Charles (afterwards Earl) Grey.

[5] Thomas Dampier (1748–1812), Bishop of Rochester, 1802–8.

[6] S. soon joined his wife at Woburn and they went on to visit the Whitbreads at Southill. See the *Daily Advertiser and Oracle*, 7 and 8 Sept. 1803.

486. To Sir Nathaniel Wraxall[1]

Pub.: Maggs Catalogue 353 (1917), item 659. *Dock.*: From Sheridan to me.

16 Sept. 1803

Without fail I will have the pleasure of waiting on the Duke of Queensberry[2] tomorrow and shall be particularly happy in the opportunity of meeting you.

487. To W. A. Downs

Pub.: G. Raymond, *Memoirs of R. W. Elliston, Comedian* (1844–5), ii. 227–8.

[*1803*]

Dear Major,—

I have called on you once or twice, and on *military* business; but I shall now say a word on what I think is pressing at this moment. No corps of volunteers should receive the communications of the Speaker of the House of Commons[3] without *returning a proper answer*, to be communicated through the lord-lieutenant[4] to Mr. Speaker. This has always been the practice when generals, admirals, and seamen, etc. etc., have been thanked;—the answers are read in the House by the Speaker, and entered on the journals. The record and its effect in the present case, will have the best consequences, and, *I can assure you*,[5] it is both expected

[1] Wraxall (1751–1831), the author of *Historical Memoirs of My Own Time.*

[2] William Douglas, 4th Duke of Queensberry (1724–1810): 'Old Q'. He supported Addington at this period: see his letters to Macpherson (14 Mar. 1803) and to Addington (23 Nov. 1803) in the Sidmouth MSS.

[3] S. moved in the Commons on 10 Aug. 'that the thanks of this house be given to the volunteer and yeomanry corps, for the zeal and promptitude with which they associated for the defence of the country, in this important crisis' (*Speeches*, v. 250). This was carried *nem. con.*, and the Speaker's letter of thanks was duly sent to the Lords Lieutenant (*The Times*, 30 Aug. 1803).

[4] See the next letter.

[5] William Augustus Downs, undertaker. 'Better known . . . as "Fat Major Downs" of the St. James's Royal Volunteers, a fellow of infinite humour. . . . Downs was the original "Two Single Gentlemen rolled into One", the actual "Will Waddle" of Colman's capital song' (R. B. Peake, *Memoirs of the Colman Family* (1841), ii. 330).

and desired by the Minister and the Speaker. I should have taken the liberty of writing to Lord Amherst,[1] but that I have not the honour of knowing him. You will make such communication on the subject as you think proper. I wish to see the example set by the St. James's Volunteers. I need not add that the answer should be *short* and *spirited*. I see no objection to its being signed by all the officers—certainly by the principal ones—and it will remain a record on our journals for their posterity to read to the end of time. | Yours truly | R B Sheridan

I shall return to town on Wednesday or Thursday at latest.

488. [To the Lord-Lieutenant of Middlesex, the Marquess of Titchfield?][2]

W.T. *Pub.*: Rae, ii. 346–7, from 'the draft, in his own hand'.

[*1803?*]

My Lord,

The Thanks of the House of Commons having been communicated to the St. James' Volunteers which I[3] have the Honor to command, I am authorized by the whole Corps to express the ardent Pride with which They have received at once the testimony and reward of the zeal which has call'd forth their exertions—The Feelings of the Corps on this occasion are shortly and easily to be express'd—They are most grateful for the high honor conferr'd upon them, They consider it as a proof of the confidence which the representatives of the People repose in their fix'd resolution

1 On 22 Sept. St James's Loyal Volunteers had a grand field day at Hyde Park—800 of them mustered at Burlington House, 'under the command of Lord Amherst and Major Downes' (*The Star*, 23 Sept. 1803). William, 2nd Lord Amherst (1773–1857), later became Earl Amherst of Arracan.

2 William Cavendish-Scott-Bentinck, Marquess of Titchfield (1768–1854), afterwards 4th Duke of Portland.

3 Was the letter written as a model for the Prince or Downs to follow? S.'s own association with the command is noted by his brother on 10 Oct. 1803: 'Richard is Lieutenant-Colonel of the St. James's Volunteers, the Prince's Own, so he will be obliged to keep early hours in spite of himself' (Rae, ii. 346). Yet the *Morn. Chron.*, 9 Feb. 1804, reported that S. had been proposed as a member of the St. James's Volunteers and was to be balloted for next day by a committee.

to make every sacrifice in support of their King[1] the constitution and their Country; but they cherish the eager hope that the hour shall come in which they may have the more glorious opportunity of proving that this confidence has not been ill-placed.

489. To William Adam

Adam MS. *Dock.*: Sheridan | 28 Sept. | 1803

Wednesday Night
Sept. 28th *1803*

My Dear Adam

I am rejoiced that you are come—you are my good Genius always tho' you have not g[r]eat reason to say the same of me.[2] I will try to get to you tomorrow if not at your own time and Place friday | your's ever | R B S

490. [To Richard Peake]

Harvard MS.

Octr. 1st. 1803

Mr. Graham[3] has this Day advanced me one hundred Pounds which I pledge myself to return to him in a fortnight and in the mean time I authorize Mr. Peake to charge it on my subsistance[4] money after the £250 advanced by him. | R B Sheridan

491. To W. Morland[5]

Ashley Library MS. B 4240. *Address*: Mr. W. Moreland | Dean-St. | Soho

Wednesday Evening
Novr. 2d. [*1803?*]

Dear Sir

Please to deliver to Mr. Burgess the books of mine in your

[1] W.T. 'being'.

[2] Moore, ii. 366, mentions 'the perpetual entanglements of the property [D.L.Th.] which Sheridan's private debts occasioned, and which even the friendship and skill of Mr. Adam were wearied out in endeavouring to rectify'.

[3] Probably John Graham.

[4] It amounted to £5. 5*s*. 0*d*. a day at this period.

[5] Morland had a considerable interest in D.L.Th., and exercised eleven

possession together with a copy of the List I have of them as you have obligingly promised to do for which Mr. Burgess will give you his receipt. | your's truly | R B Sheridan

To Mr. Moreland
Dean-St. Soho

492. To His Wife

Osborn MS. *Address*: London November ten 1803 | Mrs Sheridan | Worthing | Sussex *Fr.*: R B Sheridan

10 Nov. 1803

I dined yesterday at Guildhall where I met Lord Charles Somerset[1] of whom I shall tell you something—They drank Dan's health[2] and it was so rec[e]ived as would have gratified Hecca's heart, who endeavours to perswade that heart that it can distinguish its devotion to Sheridan's Fame and honor from affection to him—

Pray tell Humphrey[3] that that vile woman in the village instead of sending off the boy directly did not for three hours after—So James came in pitch dark and rode against a heap of stones so He should at least abuse her as He goes by—not fair dealing even with a Village woman!

493. To William Adam

Adam MS. *Dock.*: Mr. Sheridan | 16th Novr 1803

George-St.
Novr. 16th. *1803*

My Dear Adam

Altho' it is a week since I returned to Town I have been so taken up by some *necessary* exertions for Tom previous to

votes out of the fifty-nine cast in the election of a trustee in 1803. The 'books' are clearly account-books.

[1] Charles Henry Somerset (1767–1831), M.P. for Scarborough, 1796–1802, and for Monmouth, 1802–13 (Judd).

[2] Among the others present at the Lord Mayor's day dinner were the American and Danish Ministers as well as Castlereagh and Erskine.

[3] Humphrey Davies, S.'s coachman.

his Departure for the Defence of your Country[1] that I have not been able to attend to other matters however important or you should certainly have seen me, Tom goes this Evening and tomorrow I will come to you and be entirely at your command | yours ever truly | R B Sheridan

494. To W. A. Downs

Pub.: P. & S. C., 14 June 1861, lot 680. *Address*: Downs, undertaker, Lower James Street, Golden Square.

16 Nov. 1803[2]
Wednesday 16th 1803

[Will be responsible for the charges of the funeral of Willoughby Lacy's child, fifteen months old, who had died that morning, but which from not receiving his annuity from the theatre as usual Lacy was unable to pay. Sheridan was in a similar condition.]

495. [To Charles James?]

Harvard MS. *Dock.*: Sir W. Geary

[*20 Nov. 1803*]
Southill
Sunday

My Dear Sir

I return to the meeting of Parliament on tuesday[3] and

[1] On 26 Oct. 1803 Tom S. was presented at Court on his appointment by the Prince of Wales to a Cornetcy in the Prince of Wales's own regiment; likewise 'on his appointment as one of the Aids du Camp to the Earl of Moira, by the noble Earl'. The Earl of Moira was also presented 'on his appointment to the chief command in Scotland' (*The Star*, 27 Oct. 1803). Adam was a Scot.

[2] Given this date in P. & S. C., 16 Mar. 1852, lot 721.

[3] In a letter of 6 Dec. 1803 to Grey, Whitbread recalled that S. 'most unexpectedly came down here three days before Parliament met and made a great fuss about being up for an Hour's conversation with Fox before the Debate began . . .' (Grey MS.). Parliament met on 22 Nov. 1803, when Fox deplored the fact that the King's speech contained no mention of mediation by the Emperor of Russia, and criticized the administration's attitude towards Ireland. *The Star*, 23 Nov. 1803, reports that S. was present at this debate.

thence forward shall be wholly at your service with respect to the arbitration, Sir W. Geary's business and everything else—

I assure Mr. Link[1] that the Surry matters shall be settled in the course of the week— | Yours very truly | R B Sheridan

496. To Sir Robert Barclay[2]

Harvard MS. *Address*: Sir Robt. Berkeley | Bart.

[*1803*]

My Dear Barklay

I am extremely sorry that I could not get to you yesterday we had a meeting of the Drury-Lane Renters to chuse a Trustee in the room of poor Biggin[3] which lasted longer than I expected—tho' everything was done in the most handsome and satisfactory way to me that could be. I must see Sir Mathew[4] before the second: I think the matter in a train of certain success. I will call on you at three tomorrow or expect you at 12. | Yours truly | R B Sheridan

497. To Sir Robert Barclay

Harvard MS. *Address*: Sir Robt. Barclay, Bart. | Parliament St *Wm.*: 1801

[*1803–4?*]
Wednesday Night

My Dear Barclay

Not a word from Sir M. The suspence hurts me more than the accommodation could serve me— | Your's truly | R B Sheridan

[1] Richard Link, attorney, also of 8 New Inn.

[2] 8th baronet (1755–1839). He was M.P. for Newtown, 1802–7 (Judd).

[3] He died on 3 Nov. 1803, 'aged about 43'. He was a trustee, too, of the Opera House. See *Gent. Mag.* lxxiii, pt. 2 (1803), pp. 1093–4.

[4] Sir Matthew Bloxam (1744–1822), M.P. for Maidstone, 1788–1806, stationer and banker. He lent S. money thinking that S. could 'serve his views with Mr. Addington': see P. & S. C., 29 July 1861, lot 1134.

498. To Sir Robert Barclay

Harvard MS. *Address*: Sir Robt. Barclay | Bart.

[1803–4?]
House of Common[s]

My Dear Barclay

I have a Letter from Sir M. which makes it indispensable that I should see you pray if you leave the House before I return leave a Line with Mrs. Bennet to say where I can catch you | Yours | R B S

499. To Charles Ward

Egerton MS. 1975, ff. 123–4. *Address*: T. Ward[1] Eqr | Great-Queen-St | Lincolns Inn | lefthand side near the middle of the Street | deliver by 9 in the morn

[25 Jan. 1804?]
Wednesday Evening

My Dear Sir,

Pray be at the Crown and Anchor tomorrow—you should have Mrs. Linley's share with you. We will adjourn after the meeting.[2] Your last Letter was only ill-judged. Mrs. S. but very poorly | Yours truly | R B S.

Now or never is the Time for Rail way—

500. To the Prince of Wales

Windsor MSS. 40090–1. *Dock.*: R B Sheridan | Febry. 21 1804

21 Feb. 1804

Sir

I will not attempt to describe the strong impression of Gratitude[3] under which I address these few Lines to your

[1] C. W. Ward, Mrs. Linley's son-in-law, lived at 34 Great Queen Street from about Sept. 1802 (Black, p. 266). S. forgot his initials and supplied them in his usual way. For Ward's 'improved railroad', see S.C., 15 Dec. 1964, lot 526.

[2] A meeting of the renters of D.L.Th. was held on 26 Jan. 1804 to inquire into its state and property. See the report in Add. MS. 42720, ff. 13–62.

[3] For his appointment as Receiver-General of the Duchy of Cornwall. This was worth at least £1,402 a year. See Rhodes, pp. 257–61.

Royal Highness. No one but yourself Sir could have so greatly enhanced the value of a Favour and Honor by the manner of conferring it.[1] I trust that I feel and prize every word of your most gracious Letter as I ought. It was not possible to encrease the Devotion and Attachment to your Royal Highness's Character and Person which have so long been among the warmest Feelings of my Heart. But Diligence and exertion on my Part may be encreased—and they shall be. To the end of my Life I will strenuously employ every Faculty of my mind in your service.[2] And never can there arise any reward so grateful to my Feelings as will be the consciousness of contributing in the slightest Degree to the advancement of your Royal Highness's happiness and the maintenance of your renown and Power— | I have the Honor to be | with the truest sentiments | of Duty and attachment | Your Royal Highness's | most obliged and devoted Servant | R B Sheridan

February
21st 1804

501. To Henry Addington

Viscount Sidmouth MS. *Pub.*: Moore, ii. 320–2.

[*21 Feb. 1804?*]
George-St.
Tuesday Evening

Private

Dear Sir

Convinced as I am of the sincerity of your good-will[3] towards me I do not regard it to be an impertinent intrusion to inform you that the Prince has in the most gracious man-

[1] Edward Lord Eliot of St. Germans (1727–1804), the holder, died on 17 Feb. For the Prince's letter of 20 Feb., offering the office to S., see Rae, ii. 243.

[2] Lady Bessborough reported on 17 Oct. 1803 that the Prince had heard from Tom S. that after some provocation by Tierney, 'S. flew out again into a long Rhodomontade of attachment to the Prince, and belonging to *no* party' (*Leveson Gower Corr.* i. 437).

[3] Windham refers to S. and Tierney as 'the new allies of Ministry' on 29 July 1803 (*The Windham Papers* (1913), ii. 210). The qualified support which S. gave Addington's government increased Foxite suspicions of S.'s steadiness.

ner, and wholly unsolicited, been pleased to appoint me to the late Lord Elliot's situation in the Dutchy of Cornwall. I feel a desire to communicate this to you myself because I feel a confidence that you will be glad of it.—It has been my Pride and Pleasure to have exerted my humble efforts to serve the Prince without ever accepting the slightest obligation from him. But in the present case and under the present circumstances I think it would have been really false Pride and apparently mischievous affectation to have declined this Mark of His Royal Highness's confidence and Favour. I will not disguise that at this peculiar crisis I do feel greatly[1] gratified at this event. Had it been the result of a mean and subservient Devotion to the Prince's every wish and object I could neither have respected the Gift the Giver or myself. But when I consider how recently it was my misfortune to find myself compell'd by a sense of Duty stronger than my attachment to him wholly to risk the situation I held in his confidence and favour, and that upon a subject[2] on which his Feelings were so eager and irritable I cannot but regard the increased attention with which he has since honor'd me as a most gratifying Demonstration that he has clearness of Judgement and firmness of Spirit to distinguish the real Friends to his true Glory and Interests from the mean and mercenary Sycophants, who fear and abhor that such Friends should be near him. It is satisfactory to me, also, that this appointment gives me the title and opportunity of seeing the Prince on trying occasions openly and in the face of Day and puts aside the mask of mystery and concealment. I trust I need not add that whatever small Portion of fair influence I may at any time possess with the Prince it shall be uniformly exerted to promote those feelings of Duty and affection towards Their Majesties which tho' seemingly interrupted by adverse circumstances I am sure are in his Heart warm and unalterable, and that general union, as far as I may presume, throughout his illustrious Family which

[1] Moore reads 'I am greatly'.

[2] The Prince wrote to Addington on 18 July 1803, renewing his request for 'the responsibility of a military command'. After much correspondence, in which the King and the Duke of York were involved, the request was refused. 'On which occasion Sheridan coincided with the views of Mr. Addington somewhat more than was agreeable to His Royal Highness' (Moore, ii. 321).

every honest subject must look to as an essential Part of the Public strength at this momentous Crisis.[1] | I have the Honor to be | Sir, with the sincerest | Respect and esteem | Your obedient Servant | R B Sheridan.

Right Honble. Henry Addington.

502. To Colonel John McMahon

Sir Shane Leslie MS. Text from Sir Shane Leslie's transcription. *Pub.*: Moore, ii. 358–9.

[*1804?*]
Thursday Evening

Private

My Dear McMahon

I have thoroughly considered and reconsidered the subject we talked upon to Day. Nothing on earth shall make me wish the possibility of the Prince's Goodness to me furnishing an opportunity for a single scurrilous Fool's presuming to hint even that He had in the slightest manner departed from the slightest engagement.[2] The Prince's right in point of Law and Justice on the present occasion to recall the appointment given,[3] I hold to be incontestible but believe me, I am right in the Proposition I took the Liberty of submitting to His Royal Highness and which (so far is He from wishing to hurt General Lake) He graciously approved but understand me —my meaning is to give up the emolument of the situation to General Lake,[4] holding the situation at the Prince's Pleasure and abiding by an arbitrated estimate of General Lake's claim, supposing His Royal Highness had appointed him in other words to value his interest in the appointment

[1] Moore's version is probably from a draft, for the last sentence contains some changes in wording.

[2] On 5 Aug. 1795 the Prince had appointed his equerry, Major-General Gerard Lake, afterwards 1st Viscount Lake (1744–1808), to the office of Receiver-General in reversion of Eliot and during good behaviour.

[3] Lake's reversionary patent was said to be invalidated by his absence in India as Commander-in-Chief; but another reason for the withholding of the appointment was given by C. F. Sheridan's son, Charles, on 6 Mar. 1804, after seeing S.: 'Lake has behaved so ill to the Prince' (LeFanu MS.)

[4] See the full discussion of the circumstances in Rhodes, pp. 203–7.

as if He had it, and to pay him for it or resign to him. With the Prince's Permission I should be glad to meet Mr Warwick Lake[1] and I am confident that no two men of common sense and good intentions can fail in ten minutes to arrange so as to meet the Prince's wishes and not to leave the shadow of a pretence for envious malignity to whisper a word against his decision | yours ever | R B Sheridan

I write in great haste going to A[2]

503. To General Lake

Pub.: Moore, ii. 359–61.

[*1804?*]

Dear General,

I am commanded by the Prince of Wales to transmit to you a correct Statement[3] of a transaction in which your name is so much implicated, and in which his feelings have been greatly wounded from a quarter, I am commanded to say, whence he did not expect such conduct.

As I am directed to communicate the particulars in the most authentic form,[4] you will, I am sure, excuse on this occasion my not adopting the mode of a familiar letter.

Authentic Statement respecting the Appointment by His Royal Highness the Prince of Wales to the Receivership of the Duchy of Cornwall, in the Year 1804, to be transmitted by His Royal Highness's Command to Lieutenant-General Lake, Commander-in-chief of the Forces in India.

The circumstances attending the original reversionary

[1] Lord Lake's brother (d. 1821). Farington (ii. 194) states that Lake 'actually advanced money or became security for the General upon the credit of that reversion'. He now sought to receive the income of the office as the General's deputy.

[2] William Adam was Attorney-General to the Prince from 1805.

[3] Moore, ii. 359, describes this as 'a rough and unfinished sketch . . . of a statement'.

[4] Rhodes, p. 205, quotes a parliamentary speech by S. of 1812, in which he stated that the Prince's legal advisers agreed that General Lake could not accept the office of Receiver-General when absent from the country. S. had then met Warwick Lake and, in the presence of the Duke of York, had stated that he (S.) would resign the office on Lake's return. S.'s letters patent for the Receivership are dated 6 March 1804.

Grant to General Lake are stated in the brief for Counsel[1] on this occasion by Mr. Bignel, the Prince's solicitor, to be as follow: (No. I.) It was afterwards understood by the Prince that the service he had wished to render General Lake, by this Grant, had been defeated by the terms of it; and so clearly had it been shown that there were essential duties attached to the office, which no Deputy was competent to execute, and that a Deputy, even for the collection of the rents, could not be appointed but by a principal actually in possession of the office, (by having been sworn into it before his Council,) that upon General Lake's appointment to the command in India, the Prince could have no conception that General Lake could have left the country under an impression or expectation that the Prince would appoint him, in case of a vacancy, to the place in question. Accordingly, His Royal Highness, on the very day he heard of the death of Lord Elliot, unsolicited, and of his own gracious suggestion, appointed Mr. Sheridan. Mr. Sheridan returned, the next day, in a letter to the Prince, such an answer and acknowledgment as might be expected from him; and, accordingly, directions were given to make out his patent. On the ensuing —— His Royal Highness was greatly surprised at receiving the following letter from Mr. Warwick Lake. (No. II.)

His Royal Highness immediately directed Mr. Sheridan to see Mr. W. Lake, and to state his situation, and how the office was circumstanced; and for further distinctness to make a minute in writing. . . .

504. To His Wife

Yale MS. *Address*: London February twenty | seven 1804 | Mrs. Sheridan | Mrs. Ogle's[2] | College | Durham *Fr.*: Free R B Sheridan

27 Feb. 1804
Monday

Dear sweetest Hecca

Do not think it neglectful that I do not write more to

[1] Moore, ii. 358, notes that 'measures were even in train for enforcing the claim by law'.

[2] Mrs. S.'s father, Dean Ogle, had died on 4 Jan. 1804, and had been buried in Durham Cathedral (Ogle, p. 135).

you—if you saw the worry I live in and the *really unavoidable* bad hours I keep you would rather wonder that I can write at all.—There never was known before anything equal to the agitation of Peoples minds at this moment,[1] and the Prince just recovered from an illness in which his Life was despair'd of for two Days is so nervous and anxious that it is not easy to thwart him tho' He runs a great risk of making himself ill again. I now see him openly, but till lately I never saw him till after twelve at Night,[2] and He has often kept me till 5 in the morning not supping or with a drop of wine but in his bed-room.[3] Then I see Fox every Day—and Addington almost every evening—I met Grey at Fox's this morning. He was I thought particularly *Hearty* and *cordial* to me and indeed he ought to be so, but my poor Hecca He tells me you will not be able to walk these two months and I happen to care more about your ankle than all the Politics on earth—.

I must tell you another time of a droll Scene at Fox's[4] where were assembled the *new coalition*[5] Lord Grenville[6] etc. etc. which was the last Place a blundering Servant should have shewn *me* into. Here is also a great bustle about my appointment which, I have insisted on not accepting but on Terms which I know *you* will approve—for they shall be dictated by disinterestedness and honor to the extreme Point.

There will be a bustle in both Houses to Day[7] but I shall not attend. I enclose you a copy of my Letter to Addington after I had received the Prince's which will help to explain

[1] The King had had another fit of madness.

[2] Cf. the Duke of Portland's letter to Addington of 19 Feb. 1804: 'It is asserted by Mrs. Fitzherbert that since the P. of Wales has returned to Town, He has not seen any body, except yourself and Lord Thurlow and that he is perfectly reconciled to The Queen. He has avoided caballing with every description of people and has dined every day at Mrs. F——s *what she calls quite alone* viz. with only such people as Tom Tyrrwhitt, or McMahon' (Sidmouth MS.).

[3] Rae, ii. 249, prints all but the first sentence of this passage.

[4] Described in full detail in *The Diaries of Sylvester Douglas, Lord Glenbervie* (ed. F. Bickley, 1928), i. 370.

[5] Of Fox and the Grenvilles. It 'is not called a coalition but an approximation . . . it is more likely to approximate Mr. Pitt towards Government' (*Beresford Corr.* ii. 273).

[6] W. W. Grenville, 1st Baron (1759–1834), had been Foreign Secretary under Pitt from 1791 to 1801, and had resigned over the Catholic question.

[7] The Commons debated the King's indisposition, and the Volunteer Consolidation Bill.

Things. I will write every Day—bless thee Dear Hecca and for Heaven's sake let me know that you are doing well | S

505. To Richard Peake

McAdam MS. *Address*: *Private* | Mr. Peake | Charlotte-St | Rathbone-Place

[*1804?*]
C[arlton] House
Thursday morning

Most confidential

Come to the Door in the Park—and shew this card—and then come in at the side door—not the great Porch | R B S

506. To Richard Peake

Osborn MS. *Address*: Mr. Peake

[*1804?*]

Dear Peake

twenty or fifteen Pounds for the Irish[1] instantly or there will be the Devil to pay—it shall be stop'd for you from the subscription in the morning | R B S

Wednesday

507. To ——

Harvard MS. *Wm.*: 1801

[*1804?*]

My Dear Sir,

I have settled with the Expectants of the Mornington to wait no moment longer than monday next—when I shall certainly give notice—and for a short Day. Pray apprize

[1] The Benevolent Society of St. Patrick helped poor Irishmen and their children, and usually met at the London Tavern on St. Patrick's Day. S. was a Vice-President and was frequently present. *The Star*, 18 Mar. 1807, reported that over the years he had contributed £341 to the society. His donation was normally twenty guineas, but the *Morn. Chron.*, 19 Mar. 1804, noted that it was now £20.

Mr. Hall of this with my apologies for not having answer'd his Letters. | your's ever truly | R B Sheridan

I hear the Chancellor is all favourable on the Prince's Question.[1]

508. To Richard Wilson

National Library of Wales MS. 15238 E. *Address*: Richd. Wilson Esq. *Dock.*: Sheridan

Sunday
August 5th: [*1804?*]

My Dear Wilson,

you damp'd me a little this morning by not seeming so sanguine about getting me a good Lift to THE LOAN[2] as you were the other evening—but I really think the earnest exertions of a few Friends will accomplish it, for there is not a possible risk. The Blank after Graham's name was left to the discretion of your Eminence—£100 I owe you already—and may be thus secured. I need not say that any addition with your name[3] would be a signal for success— | yours ever truly | R B Sheridan

But Time! Time is everything to me!

509. To the Prince of Wales

Windsor MSS. 40270–1. *Dock.*: Mr. Tierney | Aug 20 1804

London
August 20th 1804

Sir

Before this can arrive at Brighton I take it for granted an

[1] The Prince of Wales wrote to his mother on 4 July 1804, seeking to dispel the King's coldness towards him. The Queen placed her trust in the Lord Chancellor, Eldon, as mediator between father and son. See H. Twiss, *Life of Lord Chancellor Eldon* (1844), i. 460–1.

[2] This was eventually made in 1806. See Peake's letter to the contributors in Winston, 1808–9, and J. Adolphus, *Memoirs of J. Bannister, Comedian* (1839), ii. 196–7. In 1802 Wilson became a member of the board of management and auditor of the accounts of D.L.Th.

[3] In a letter to Grey of 16 Nov. 1804 Creevey noted that Wilson had been lucky enough to win £5,000 in a lottery and to receive a bequest of £15,000. 'I saw him yesterday in Town between Sheridan and Fonblanque and I hope before this they had turned him to some account'. (Grey MS.)

Express will have reach'd your Royal Highness to announce the intelligence, I trust the fortunate intelligence, of the intended meeting between his Majesty and your Royal Highness on wednesday next. His Majesty's Letter to the Chancellor, as stated to me is full of cordiality and affection.[1] This is a momentous Crisis in your Royal Highness's Life—a crisis which calls for, what I am sure will be bestow'd on it, all the Judgement Penetration and Decision which belong to your Royal Highness's mind. It has been hinted to me that it is probable that his Majesty means to proceed to measures *far beyond domestic reconciliation*.[2]

Lord Grenville is in Cornwall.[3] However I judged it best to address a Letter to him at Dropmore[4] in order that He may be apprized of your Royal Highness's intentions had his Lordship been accessible, which I trust your Royal Highness will approve of.

I shall have the Honor of paying my Duty to your Royal Highness at Bushy tomorrow[5] | I am ever your Royal Highness's | most devoted and faithful Servant | R B Sheridan.

[1] It is querulous in tone: see H. Twiss, *Life of Eldon* (1844), i. 462–3. Moira and Tierney tried to bring about a reconciliation, in which the Prince was to indulge the King's whim of becoming Princess Charlotte's guardian. On 20 Aug. the King agreed to receive the Prince on the following Wednesday at Kew.

[2] A flight of fancy.

[3] Busy with his plantations at Boconnoc, where politics were 'no more alluded to in conversation than astrology' (*Auckland Corr.* iv. 314).

[4] Grenville's Buckinghamshire home, two miles west of Burnham Beeches.

[5] The Duke of Clarence was Ranger of Bushy Park and lived there. All the princes, except the Dukes of York and Cumberland, gathered at the house on 21 Aug. to celebrate the Duke of Clarence's birthday. 'They separately and together joined in saying that the King had on the previous day used the following expressions of the Prince: "Wednesday I am to see him, I will not see him at Windsor for there he would stay, but I will see him at Kew for there he must go about his business when it's over. I know him. The opposition have all left him, and now he is paying Court to my Minister and trying to be reconciled to me. He is a Second Edition of Lord Lansdowne. . . ." ' (J. McMahon to the Duke of Northumberland, 25 Aug. 1804 Alnwick MSS., LXII, ff. 48–53.) The meeting with the King did not take place: S.'s draft expressing the Prince's regrets is among the Yale MSS.; and George III suspected that S. had tried to counteract Moira's negotiations: see Rose, ii. 169.

510. To William Chisholme[1]

Hyde MS. [Ph.] *Address*: Lymington August third 1804 | Mr. Chisholm | R. Wilson's Esqr. | Lincoln's-Inn-Fields | London *Fr.*: Free | R B Sheridan *Dock.*: Sept. 3d. 1804 | Mr. Sheridan | R. B. Sheridan to W C. respecting the engagement of Master Betty then called the Young Roscius[2] *Pm.*: SEP 4 1804 [Endorsed] Put in September 3rd.

3 Sept. 1804
Lymington
Monday

Dear Sir,

You have done every thing as well as possible, and all your arguments were right, but I fear all will be vain, I wish to Heaven you could have gone at first instead of Mr. Graham. Is it possible that to the Lad who was getting £100 per week his offer for 12 Nights could only have been *half a Benefit*! Pray explain this to me. He assured me he had a positive promise of the Refusal. He never consulted me about the Terms—my vexation is beyond measure—this Loss will be the Perdition of the Season. I would answer for his voice.[3] A Boy is always better heard than a man. The *Children* in Richard are heard every word. I hope if you found it necessary you did not stand for the charges of the Benefit. I am sure you would not. I shall be most anxious to hear from you tomorrow. Should he be engaged for the 12 Nights at Convent-Garden your Next step must be to have him pursued to Liverpool,[4] and engage him for 12 Nights for us on the same Terms. | your obedient Servant | R B Sheridan

[1] William Chisholme became solicitor to the Grand Surrey Canal and the Lambeth Water Works, and was in partnership with Richard Wilson at 47 Lincoln's Inn Fields. He was probably the 'William Chisholm' who signed the declaration of the Friends of the People on 26 Apr. 1792. See *The Oracle*, 30 Apr. 1792.

[2] William Henry West Betty (1791–1874) made his first appearance in Aug. 1803, at Belfast. His success was so great as a boy actor that, in the following year, Aaron Graham went to see him act at Birmingham but could not persuade him to accept the terms D.L.Th. offered. It seems certain that after Graham's return, Chisholme was sent there to pursue the point. See Add. MS. 29710, f. 302: 'Expenses to Birmingham Chisholm—£8. 13*s.* 6*d.*' Eventually Betty was engaged to act in Dec. at both C.G.Th. and D.L.Th.

[3] Betty's voice was 'rather thick and clouded' (*Colchester Corr.* i. 545).

[4] 'As the friends of the boy now

better perhaps enclose this Letter of mine to you to Mr. Wilson as I only write him a Line

I enclose my Line to Mr. Wilson for fear the Direction should be wrong

511. [To William Chisholme]

Pub.: S.C., 27 Nov. 1889, lot 212.

4 Sept. 1804

Certainly have him[1] at any rate if you can

512. To Anna Maria Ogle

Brinsley Ford MS.

Wednesday Sept. 12th [*1804*]

Dear Malty

One Line on my [way] to Town to beg you will send me a Line by return of Post to George-St. to tell me what money will set us clear at Southampton. I hope to see you soon.[2] God bless you. | Yours truly | R B Sheridan

513. To ——

Historical Society of Pennsylvania MS. *Pub.*: *The Dreer Collection of Autographs* (Philadelphia, 1890), ii. 107.

[*1804?*]
Mr Budd's[3]
Pall-Mall

Dear Sir

Mr Budd is heartily welcome to print that little Pamphlet

demanded 50 guineas per night, and a whole clear benefit, the Drury Lane managers began to deliberate, and Mr. Harris [of C.G.Th.], in the interim, engaged him on the terms proposed. This roused the Drury Lane managers, who immediately sent their deputy (Mr. Wroughton) to Liverpool . . . to outbid their rival' (*The Thespian Dictionary* (1805), *sub.* Betty).

[1] Betty.

[2] S. has scribbled the names of 'Mr. Ebdon Organist Durham' and 'Mr. Aynsley Kirkley Newcastle upon Tyne', with some figures, on the sheet.

[3] On 13 Sept. [1804], Francis Horner stated that he had permitted his name 'to be put down in the list of a new club to which Fox, Windham, Sheridan, etc.

of mine on the India-Bills,[1] but I can no where get it—Perhaps you will be so good as to meet me here at half past one tomorrow | your obedient Servant | R B Sheridan

514. To W. L. Bowles[2]

Pub.: *A Wiltshire Parson and his Friends: The Correspondence of W. L. Bowles* (ed. G. Greever, Constable, 1926), p. 93. Directed to Bowles at Miss Costello's Haymarket. Cf. S.C., 23 Mar. 1936, lot 421.

Carlton House, October 12th, [*1804*]

Dear Bowles

I received yours this morning being luckily in town, as is also the Prince for a few days. I have this moment seen him, and most graciously will he receive your dedication.[3] I certainly should wish you to present your morocco yourself, but I must apprise you of his motions. Upon your question of the manner of dedicating I will write a few lines to-morrow or next day. You date only Donhead[4] and I forget whether it be your new or old residence, but I will enclose to John's.[5]

515. To Richard Peake

Add. MS. 35118, f. 163. *Address*: Mr Peake

[*29 Oct. 1804*][6]
Merton
Monday morning

My Dear Peake

For Heaven's sake get the enclosed done and send it to

belong. . . . this club meets at Budd's in Pall Mall, where Cobbett's works are published, under the sign of the Crown, Bible and Mitre' (*Memoirs . . . of Francis Horner* (Edinburgh, 1849), p. 144). John Budd was imprisoned for libel in 1805 and 1810.

[1] *A Comparative Statement* . . . (1788).

[2] The poet (1762–1850). Moore states (ii. 254) that Bowles was a frequent companion of S. on his sailing excursions on 'Southampton river', and quotes a poem by Bowles on the subject. The lines 'were much admired . . . by Sheridan, for the sweetness of their thoughts, and the perfect music of their rhythm'.

[3] Greever notes that Bowles's dedication of *The Spirit of Discovery* to the Prince of Wales was dated 'Donhead, Nov. 3. 1804'.

[4] He had been appointed Vicar of Bremhill.

[5] J. S. Ogle's rectory at East Knoyle was some six miles from Donhead.

[6] See Black, p. 268, for Charles

me by *tomorrows Post* to Lymingt[on] where I shall arrive with one halfpenny | Yours ever | R B S

Pray send me at the same time a *great-coat* and a foot-ball for Charles.

516. [To the Creeveys or Mrs. Ord]

J. R. Blackett-Ord MS.

[*29 Oct. 1804*]
Merton
Monday morning

I should have been very happy to have been of your Party had I not been going out of Town. I am this moment proceeding to Lymington. I enclose two orders for the Box. I return in a week, and hope to bring Hester with me tho' she finds the air and bathing agree with her particulars and also with the Boy | Yours faithfully | R B S.

make them give you the Key [?] of Hesters Tea.

517. To Mrs. Lacy

Shuttleworth MS.

[*1804?*]
Hertford bridge[1]
Monday Night

Dear Madam

After I call'd at Seniors[2] yesterday I received a Letter informing me of a fall my little Boy has had from a horse. I am on the road to see him—but before I left Town I again saw both Mr. Graham and Mr. Wilson and I trust it is not possible that any thing can prevent Mr. Lacy's Liberation.

Ward's account of his excursion with S., and their overnight stay at Merton on their way to Lymington.

[1] Hartfordbridge, on the main road between Bagshot and Basingstoke.

[2] D.L.Th. Nightly Accounts, 1799 to 1800 (Folger MS.) contains entries of payments of £10 on account by Lacy to Senior on 14 June and 4 Nov. 1800. John Senior was an attorney of 4 Charles Street, Covent Garden.

Should any new difficulty arise give me a Line to Lymington Hants. I shall be back in three or four Days when we will apply to a general settlement | yours truly | R B Sheridan

518. To Anna Maria Ogle

Osborn MS.

[*1804?*]
Tuesday

Dear Malty

I enclose the Franks. I wish Mary[1] was at Southampton. I will send a man over for Red Mullets early tomorrow morning.

—Nat is in great disgrace with the four Ladies here—Sailing absolutely prescribed for their health, Hester not riding since her fall, and Mrs. C. Ogle[2] with little chance of recovery without it, yet Nat deaf to all their entreaties refused them the accommodation of the *Phaedria* for a month! tho Scott and Henry and Captain Ogle[3] guaranteed the most exact care of her. We mean to engage the Brothers. Pray what sort of a Vessel is it? | Yours truly | R B S.

519. To Richard Peake

McAdam MS. *Address*: Lymington November second 1804 | Mr. Peake | Charlotte-St | Rathbone Place | London *Fr.*: Free | R B Sheridan *Dock.*: Mr. Sheridan

2 Nov. 1804
Friday

My Dear Peake,

I was obliged to give Nicholl at Farnham a Draft for £5[4]

[1] Nathaniel Ogle's daughter (d. Aug. 1819). She married Henry Gaulter.

[2] Charlotte, daughter of General Thomas Gage. Her ill-health suggests the possibility that the letter belongs to just before Sept. 1814: see iii. 201.

[3] Charles Ogle (1775–1858), afterwards baronet and admiral. Rose, ii. 170, writes on 4 Oct. 1804, 'Mr. Sheridan came here to dinner with Captain and Mrs. Ogle (with whom he was staying at Lymington) . . . somewhat unexpectedly'.

[4] D.L.Th. Salaries, 1804 to 1806 (Folger MS.), lists on 3 Nov. 1804 a payment, 'Mr. Sheridan £5'.

which sum I beseech you will not fail to send to Biddulphs and Cox on receipt of this and send word for what and give me a Line *by return of Post* to satisfy my mind that I may leave Lymington at ease on Sunday | Yours ever | R B S

520. To Anna Maria Ogle

Osborn MS. *Address*: Lymington November 3d 1804 | Mrs N. Ogle | Orchard Place | Southampton *Fr.*: Free | R B Sheridan

3 Nov. 1804
Saturday

My Dear Malty

I am very sorry for poor Briar and his Family if there is any subscription made for them I will send something.

Yes mullets if they are to be had | Yours ever | R B S

all well
very bad of Nat

521. To Richard Peake

McAdam MS. *Address*: Mr. Peake | Charlotte-St | Rathbone-Place | *Dock.*: Mr. Sheridan *Wm.*: 1801

[*Nov. 1804?*]
Wednesday Night

I have a cold and shall stay at home all tomorrow morning —pray don't fail to call on me | Yours truly | R B S.

The £5 draft to the Innkeeper at Farnham was disgraced and returned—I fear'd it would be so, notwithstanding the earnest manner in which I wrote

522. To His Wife

Osborn MS.

Thursday[1]
Nov. 15th [*1804*]

I felt very much obliged by your little kind fif of yesterday

[1] S. wrote 'Wed.' but crossed it out.

short tho' it was, and it drove Gloom-Spright away who had got very fast hold of the collar of my heart. And today your Letter told me something about your self which is what I always like to hear and to know when you are at sea or on shore and diverted or dull. I should very much have liked to have been of the Party to the Tribune[1]—by the wind I presume They are all gone.

Well Ma'am as to Politics in the first Place be assured there is no need, nor ever can be, to exhort me to do right and go straight forward—my Price is not on this earth to do otherwise.[2] How matters will end I cannot yet venture to predict. There are great apprehensions afloat respecting the Princes steadiness—and what must divert you is that the confidence of *certain Ladies*[3] that he will prove steady is in great measure founded as themselves declare on his constant communication and associating with me—. Besides my morning visit I have din'd and supp'd with him three Days running at Melbourne-House: only ourselves and the Family and one Day Charles Fox. All this interferes terribly with my other matters—however I know it is right—and no effort of mine shall be wanting to keep him so—all this is well known to Fox's *new allies*,[4] and now it is droll to think what a favourite I am with them all. Lord Moira was to see the King by appointment to[5] Day at three o'clock at *Windsor*—and the Prince goes there tomorrow—but I shall know nothing 'till saturday. I go to Polesden at six o'clock tomorrow morning.—There is a meeting on the business of enclosing all the Commons—Ranmore, Bookham etc. etc. and if I am not on the alert they will cheat me egregiously and perhaps ruin the beauty of Polesden—but they cannot and shall not move an inch without me and so I have given Sumner and Laurell to understand.[6]

[1] Presumably a boating excursion.

[2] Rae, ii. 366, quotes S. as writing, here or elsewhere: 'My price is not on this earth to do otherwise than what was right and go straight forward.'

[3] Not the Devonshire House ladies, if Lady Bessborough's reports in the *Leveson Gower Corr.* (i. 477) accurately express their feelings.

[4] The Grenvilles.

[5] A meeting between George III and the Prince took place on 12 Nov. at Kew. By agreement, politics were ignored at the interview. On 13 Nov. Pitt sent for Moira and informed him that the King would see him on 15 Nov. at Windsor (*Dropmore Papers*, vii. 240–2).

[6] This sentence is quoted by Rae, ii. 206, but he makes an addition that is

I am now writing to you in the evening—and accident has given me the opportunity. The case is I was to have gone to Polesden to dinner to Day with Wilson and Burgess—but something detain'd Wilson till past 4 while I was waiting for the Prince. Then you know a stretch-Leg with orders for the Carriage to follow down Grosvernor Place after they had got lights. Of course they chose to prefer Sloane-St. and after Wilson and I had kick'd our heels 'till past six at the Kings-road Gate we gave it up and returned—and must positively be off in the morning

523. To His Wife

Osborn MS. *Wm.*: 1795.

[*Nov. 1804?*]
Monday Night
G. St.

My Dearest one, Here am I so melancholy and so solitary that I know not how to look out for a ray of Light, sunshine or moonshine but by turning to you and writing a few Lines —I have never been out of the House nor moved from my table from 12 this morning 'till now 12 at Night and entirely alone the whole time. My three Days absence at Polesden stopt me in my other matters for the Theatre and I was resolved to pull up lost time for the Theatre's sake but this solitariness will not do with me—especially after I have been bustling about in worldly matters, and the thoughts cross me as they never cease to do on such occasions of the precariousness of accomplishing what we aim at, or if obtain'd the disparity between the exertion to reach it and the little *mot* of time for which one can enjoy it. How un-

not in this MS.: 'Nothing can be more for our interest than the enclosure if I have my due; but I will see real justice done to the cottagers and the poorest claimants. Timber-Toe Wood is the village Hampden'. Mr John H. Harvey, who is writing a history of Bookham, informs me that Ranmore and Bookham common wastes still remain unenclosed, but that the open fields of Great Bookham were enclosed by private act of 1821. James Laurell was Lord of the Manor of Great Bookham, 1801–11, and lived at Eastwick House, 1788–1809. George Holme Sumner was Lord of the Manor by 1811/12, but Mr. Harvey can find no direct evidence that he had interests in the parish before 1811.

ceasingly do I meditate on Death, and how continually do I act as if the thought of it had never cross'd my mind. Life is no first object with me for my own sake, tho' I hate Pain or Peril, yet things that have been dearer to me I have appear'd careless of and felt a perverse satisfaction that it should be so. I have been always fond of Popularity too indiscriminately and jealous of the worlds good opinion yet have forever risk'd the former, in society I mean, by negligence nor ever pursued the latter with common Prudence but have even felt gratified at setting it at Defiance—but I will not go on egotizing and moaning, because observe Ma'am there is a Tinge of red above in my ink owing to this affecting cause—that I dipt my Pen in the wrong ink-stand and thence you are to learn that with red ink have I been compleating in this Day my alterations of the new comedy[1] and that brings to me a gratified feeling, for nothing does it more strongly than to catch myself breaking thro' my indolence and earning my brown bread. If anything could rebrace my nerves always irregular and dispel increasing Gloom it would be to fix that effect on Practice and habit—I ought to do so, and always mean to attempt it, but how easily do we compromise our engagements to ourselves. In just now speaking of the objects we pursue eagerly but may never accomplish or enjoy I was led away from explaining that what was in my mind was the *Bookham-Enclosure* which I had been attending, delighted to find that I had so great an interest and should have so great a share—that I was called to the Chair to resist Sumner's unpopularity, the poorer Claimants putting their cases entirely into my hands—I look at Maps and Plans am congratulated on the acquisition to Polesden,[2] but

[1] Cf. *The Times*, 15 Nov. 1804: 'The new Comedy, which has been erroneously ascribed to Mr. Sheridan, was yesterday read in the Green-room' of D.L.Th. The same newspaper stated (13 Dec. 1804) that 'the Epilogue to Mr. Holt's new Comedy comes from the pen of Mr. Sheridan'. This refers to F. L. Holt's *The Land We Live In*, given at D.L.Th. on 29 Dec.

[2] Mr. John H. Harvey suggests that this refers to the purchase of Yewtrees Farm and belongs to the period July–Nov. 1805. S. was congratulated because the acquisition was, in a later phrase, 'reputed and considered to be essential to the enjoyment of Polesden' (Recital in Declaration of 27 Dec. 1817, Polesden Lacey deeds, Surrey Record Office, Kingston), and because all the difficulties of the purchase had been overcome. I have not accepted this interesting argument because I incline to believe that S. is referring to a scheme of enclosure that would have benefited him but which did not come off.

then comes the silent hour and the thought which is but how long will you want expanse of Space on Earth?

524. To Thomas Grenville

Add. MS. 41856, f. 189. *Address*: Right Honble. | Thos: Grenville | upper-end of | Charles St: Berkley-Square. *Dock.*: Mr. Sheridan | 20 Novr. 1804

George-St.
Tuesday Evening
Novr. 20th:—*1804*

Dear Grenville

I have great satisfaction in informing you[1] that all the Negotiations proposed to or proceeding from Carlton-House closed *this morning* by the Prince's adopting the only Line of conduct which anyone who really regards his interests or his honor could wish to see him adopt. This was formally communicated to Mr. Pitt by Lord Moira. I know not whether this will find you in Town, if so I will call and tell you particulars. | your's sincerely | R B Sheridan

525. To Eleanor Creevey

J. R. Blackett-Ord MS. *Address*: Mrs. Creevey

[*Nov. 1804?*][2]

You are so forgetful that I am afraid you do not recollect that you are to give me some Dinner on Sunday! | With great Pleasure | R B S.

[1] S.'s letter is paraphrased in a note from T. Grenville to Lord Grenville of 21 Nov. T. Grenville adds: 'The whole matter therefore seems finished for the present, though I cannot conceive why in that case the P. should be gone to Lord Thurlow to Bath, as to-day's papers inform us'. See *Dropmore Papers*, vii. 242.

[2] Dated from Creevey's letter to Charles Grey of 30 Nov. 1804: 'Sheridan dined here on Sunday in *Buff and Blue*. He is a perfect Foxite. . . .' (Grey MS.)

526. To Mrs. Lacy[1]

Shuttleworth MS. *Address*: Mrs Lacy | No. 9 Duke St. Lincoln's Inn *Dock.*: Sunday Nov 25 1804 | Whether Mr. S. alludes to Govt. or treasury cruelty I don't know | 18 Guineas due on Saturday[2]

25 Nov. 1804

Pray send one to Lacy. I will settle everything tomorrow or break finally with these People—it is shocking usage to us both

527. To Thomas Grenville

Clements MS. [Ph.] *Dock.*: Mr. Sheridan 27 Novr. | 1804

27 Nov. 1804
Tuesday morning

Dear Grenville

I have told the Prince that Lord Grenville will be in Town on thursday—and He wishes him yourself and Wyndham[3] to dine with him. Fox is in Town but returns to Dinner. He will have done at Carlton House by one | Yours truly | R B Sheridan

528. To Thomas Grenville

Clements MS. [Ph.]

[*29 Nov. 1804*]
Charles St.
Thursday
4 o'clock

Dear Grenville,

I have just call'd at Lord Spencer's Door by command of

[1] Willoughby Lacy's second wife. He had married her ('Miss Jackson of Hanwell') in Aug. 1789.

[2] D.L.Th. Salaries, 1804 to 1806 (Folger MS.), notes on 1 Dec. 1804, 'Mr. Lacy by Mr. Sheridan's Order £5. 0*s*. 0*d*.' Lacy drew a guinea from every performance.

[3] On 29 Nov. 1804 Grenville wrote to Windham: 'Altho' I find by a note from Sheridan that he is ordered to invite you to meet Lord Grenville and me at dinner at Carleton House to-day, I write this line to ensure your doing so. . . . You are expected at the *small house next to Carleton House at six*' (*The Windham Papers* (1913), ii. 245).

the Prince to say that *his Royal Highness* requests his Company at Dinner to Day to meet Lord Grenville and you—not finding you at home for fear of mistake I leave this Note— | ever your's | R B Sheridan

529. To His Wife

Osborn MS. and Sir John Soane's Museum MS. *Address*: London December fourth | 1804 | Mrs. Sheridan | H. B. Ogle's | Little Testwood[1] | Southampton *Fr.*: Free | R B Sheridan *Dock.*: [Soane's Museum passage] Part of a Letter from Mr. Sheridan to the 2nd Mrs. Sheridan whose name was Hester and who was called by Mr. Sheridan Hecca

1–4 Dec. 1804
Saturday Night

I was in hopes of hearing from you to Day. I find it difficult to get by myself[2] to write to you of a morning and I don't like writing at Night because I am then often in a melancholy mood. I left many things untouch'd on in my last which I meant to say a few words upon—particularly on the subject of money and expences in which you suppose your manner of replying to me had *affronted* me. I assure you it had not but I should be false if I did not own that I had been extremely hurt at it. But a word or two on this tomorrow and I promise you with no unkind impression left—and then too another word about the horse.

You cannot conceive how the Prince has occupied my Time 4 times Fox has been sent for to Town[3] to meet me

[1] Kate Ogle, J. S. Ogle's wife, was descended from the Sneyds of Testwood, Ireland (Ogle, p. 139). On 14 July 1803 Jeremy Sneyd, late of the Secretary of State's office, died at the age of eighty-five at 'Titwood House in Hants.' (*Europ. Mag.* xliv (1803), 158).

[2] Charles Ward noted on 'Friday 30th' [Nov.] that S. was 'now fighting with his Pen both Pit[t] and the Chancellor . . .' (Black, p. 270). I take it that this means that S. wrote the Prince's letters. See *Dropmore Papers*, vii. 353–5.

[3] On 26 Nov. the Prince wrote to Fox to ask him to put off his journey to Lord Robert Spencer's and to be at Carlton House on 27 Nov. The Prince wrote to him again on 28 Nov. to say that he had had a letter from the King and one from the Lord Chancellor: 'the most impudent, barefac'd and foolish productions that ever yet were penned by Man'. The Prince wanted to discuss them with Fox on the following day: see Add. MS. 47560, ff. 83–84.

and five hours at a time have we spent at Carlton House. On Thursday tho' I ought not to have left the House I was obliged to go to a meeting at Dinner with the P. with Lord Spencer Lord Grenville and Wyndham—the Party and Proceeding having been of my own advising. However I have set my heart on his not being the Dupe of the Knavery that has been entrapping him or of his own irresolution, to the ruin of his own character and consequence and to the great injury of our Party.[1] Yesterday I could not stir out for my cold and the P came here for 4 hours, to Day the same and you may judge not very well when I have not been to see the first appearance of Young Roscius[2] but this is by Bain's advice and I am better tho litterally have not slept 5 hours in the last 3 Nights. I have left off opiates but touch not one drop of Wine—only sleep will not come near me—and yet I am sure I have had no Fever. So much for an uninteresting subject—myself[3]—now respecting the *Boy*. I believe I did not tell you that I had dined with him at Wilson's—He is the most lovely creature that ever was seen, and the most unlike any other human being that ever I saw.[4] He is the reverse of what I had heard he was a little boisterous Pickle, or like Pinto[5]—tho He faces an audience so confidently in a private room or at least with strangers his bashfulness and diffidence makes it distressing to you to notice him. Great bickerings and discussions between Convent-Garden and us about the double engagement[6]—however we shall strictly maintain our Share. Harris wants to try to cajole me however He being luckily laid up as well as I, we don't meet. The Crowd tonight at C.G. was beyond[7]

[1] The Prince made it plain that he would not release his daughter if she were to be placed under the care of her mother, the Princess of Wales; and could not support Pitt's administration. See P.R.O., 30/8/105, ff. 238–47; and *Dropmore Papers*, vii. 245.

[2] Betty's first London performance was at C.G.Th. on 1 Dec., as Achmet in John Brown's *Barbarossa*.

[3] The passage from 'I am better' to 'myself' is quoted by Rae, ii. 214.

[4] S.'s enthusiasm can be gauged from Egerton MS. 1975, f. 16: 'Mr. Sheridan bets Peake One Guinea that on one Night that Master Betty Plays there will be £50 more Recd than the first Night. | 13th Decr. | to be spent'.

[5] George Frederick Pinto (1786–1806), precocious musician.

[6] According to *The Times*, 11 Feb. 1805, Betty had been engaged to play for twelve nights at both C.G.Th. and D.L.Th. Renewal for twelve nights more was optional. He began with six at C.G.Th.

[7] The Soane's Museum MS. begins with this word.

anything ever known—They say a man or two has been kill'd. I have had People with me of all sorts with accounts of the Performance. He was applauded beyond measure—but expectation was work'd to so high a Pitch that many were or affect to be disappointed on the whole—The Part however and the Play (Barbarossa) are both execrable and all the other characters heinously ill-acted, and the play shockingly got up. It is strongly imagined that the Policy at C G is to make the most of the first Spurt of Public curiosity but ultimately to run him down if they can finding that any future engagement is to be with us. This is the Fathers persuasion, who remonstrated earnestly that he might be advertised as he had been at Edinburg[h] and all over the Kingdom—[1] but they would have it '*Master Betty*' The Revival of the Report that He was a Girl having been traced to Kemble.[2] After the three Nights more he is to play at C.G., I'll answer for it He will shew superior Powers at D.L.

would I could feel the least tendency towards Sleep in my eyes or mind but it is past 3 oclock and so good Night and Heaven bless thee Hecca—!

Sunday Night

About ten this morning I got to sleep for 4 hours sound—which has done me infinite good, and I trust my cold will be gone tomorrow. I shall only say good Night and hope a kind Letter tomorrow for one Night, I will try not sitting up. Bless you Dear I have done everything you wish'd respecting the Horse, and Mr. Cambell has got him and returned the money. But when you are acquainted with circumstances about it all, which were not with[h]eld from any mystery I know you will be sorry my Hecca that it has happen'd as it has. The whole talk of the Town nothing but Young Roscius Young Roscius Young Roscius. He has been with me and the Father a long time to Day and I introduced Bain to him who apprehends that if they continue to work him so They will destroy him.[3]

[1] As 'The Young Roscius'. His father was William H. Betty (d. 1811).

[2] The Kembles were contemptuous of this thirteen-year-old tragedian, and Mrs. Siddons referred to him as '*the Baby with a Woman's Name*' (John Rylands Library MS., Eng. 574).

[3] So S. arranged that he was not to act at D.L.Th. more than three times a week: *Morn. Her.*, 6 Dec. 1804.

Monday—No Letter. I fear you must be ill or the Child—you would not otherwise neglect me so—! I can not go on writing what I meant.

Tuesday
Theatre

I would scarcely believe my senses when they brought me word here that the Post had come in and no Letter!—Surely surely you or the child have met with some accident—I will wait tomorrow.

530. To Henry Holland

Gilmore MS. *Address*: Henry Holland Esq. | Sloane-Place *Wm.*: 1803

[*1804?*]
Wednesday Evening

My Dear Sir

I should think it strange indeed if *you* should ever find such difficulty in obtaining a Box in Drury-Lane Theatre. I hope[1] to have secured a side-box for you tomorrow for Douglas[2] as you desire—and beg that you and Mrs. Holland will always command my interest in this respect without ceremony | yours ever truly | R B Sheridan

H. Holland Esq.

531. To C. J. Fox

Add. MS. 47569, ff. 190–1. *Dock.*: Mr. Sheridan *Wm.*: 1802

Monday
Decr. 17th [*1804*]

My Dear Fox

Taylor is never to be seen but on a sunday and I have tried two sundays without success—however I saw Gould on Saturday who has the real management,[3] but he is implacably

[1] Manuscript 'I hope happy'. S. may have intended to write 'I am happy'.

[2] Possibly to see Betty as Young Norval in Home's *Douglas*, at D.L.Th. on 10 Dec. 1804.

[3] Taylor conveyed the King's Theatre to Francis Goold on 7 Sept. 1804. Goold was 'well suited for the management of an extensive theatre, and knew music scientifically' (Kelly, ii. 192–3). See

bent on paying the Performers of all descriptions as little as possible.—Mighty civil of course as to you but He had begun by refusing the Prince on a similar application and was determined to adhere to his plan of paying no attention to any interference of the kind.

Of Politics I have little to say and may defer that little as I understand I shall have the Pleasure of seeing you so soon in Town. I believe no mischief has been renew'd in one Quarter tho' attempted. The King certainly desired Lord Moira to be sent for, and as certainly Lord Moira has never heard anything of it from Ministers, nor has any reference of any sort been made to him, nor has the least idea of coming to Town.[1] The Prince remains at Brighton in hourly expectation of Moira's arrival. The Letters from Edinburgh by this Days post will undeceive him. This is certainly all very strange and puzzles the P. who always particularly wants to be *doing*, when he can do nothing better than to be Quiet. The King has *certainly* sent to Pitt to *insist* in very strong terms that He and Addington shall shake Hands before the meeting of Parliament.[2] The Duke of Cumberland[3] is the Negotiator, but this is not to be mention'd on account of the Channel we have the intelligence from.

Now one word upon what the Public deem a much more interesting and important subject—Master Betty. I hear you mean to be at the Play on tuesday. I need not say how entirely Mrs. Sheridan's Box will always be at Mrs. Fox's service, but as it is bad for seeing I spoke to the Duke of Bedford yesterday and he reserved his Box for Mrs. Fox and will meet you there. The Boy is certainly something extraordinary and the manner People flock after him equally so.

T. Gilliland, *The Dramatic Mirror* (1808), i. 163. He died in 1807.

[1] McMahon's letter to the Duke of Northumberland of 17 Dec. (Alnwick MSS., LXII, f. 75) amplifies this by stating that the King had ordered Moira to be sent for on 2 Dec. with the words 'there is an unaccountable misunderstanding somewhere and it can only be explained by Lord Moira. Let Lord Moira be immediately written for'. On 14 Dec. Moira wrote to McMahon (who received the letter on 17 Dec.) to say he had not been ordered to go to London. Next day, however, Moira received the message from Pitt and left Edinburgh at once: ibid. ff. 75, 96.

[2] They did so on 23 Dec., and Addington agreed to become Viscount Sidmouth, and Lord President of the Council.

[3] Ernest Augustus, Duke of Cumberland (1771–1851), fifth son of George III.

I shall be curious to know your opinion[1]— | Your's ever sincerely | R B Sheridan

532. To Richard Peake

Egerton MS. 1975, f. 73.

24 Dec. [1804?]

Dear Peake,

I really must make a Point that you take up your acceptance for Lacey. It distresses him beyond measure[2] | R B S.

Dec. 24th.

533. To Richard Peake

Osborn MS. *Address*: Mr. Peake *Wm.*: 1804

[1804?]
Tuesday

Sad sad sad Poverty pray send as enclosed!!! | Yours ever | R B S.

I have seen Glossop[3] both yesterday and to Day—

534. To Richard Peake

McAdam MS. *Address*: Mr. Peake *Dock.*: Mr. Sheridan *Wm.*: 1804

[1804?]
Thursday
Evening
near 9

Dear Peake

I am waiting in great anxiety that you should send me

[1] Fox saw Betty and thought him finer than Garrick.

[2] The D.L.Th. account book contains the entry: '31 Dec. 1804: Lacy to making good salary before on list £35. 10' (Add MS. 29710, f. 287).

[3] Glossop was paid £1,333 in 1804, but when he received no more money he thought himself tricked by S. So he supported Burdett in the Westminster election of 1807: see Add. MS. 27850, f. 76. This brought him a payment of £79. 10*s.* from D.L.Th. on 16 May 1807: see Pay Book, 1806–8 (Folger MS.). S. had given him a bond on 10 Aug. 1805 for a rent charge of £1 a night.

what I desired—every five minutes is of consequence to me —don't let any one know that you send it for I shall want it every shilling if I don't see you to Night pray don't be later with me than eleven tomorrow morning—it must be *before* you think of going to the Theatre | yrs | R B S

535. To Samuel Whitbread

Whitbread MS. 4127. *Address*: S. Whitbread Esq *Wm.*: 1804.

[*c. 1804*]
Saturday

My Dear Whitbread,

From what pass'd last Night I hoped Burgess would have had the remaining £100 this morning. He has pledged himself in a material Quarter and is absolutely undone without. I will begin Enquiry for the Lawyers without Delay. I do not recollect that I undertook to send Burgess to you this morning.—I cannot tell you how hard it is on him, or what ruin to our cause in his quarter. Send to Curzon St. by return of Post pray— | yrs | R B S

536. To C. J. Fox

Add. MS. 47569, ff. 214–17.

Private—

Thursday Evening
Jan. 3d.—[*1805*]

My Dear Fox

I was with the Prince to Day from one 'till near seven which must account for and excuse my not writing to you as I promised. You ask'd me if I thought any mischief was done, I think a great deal is *now* done. Erskine alone was with us a great Part of the Time, and, tho' I had no opportunity of talking apart with him, He must be I am sure of my opinion. There is certainly a perverse Fatality that compels the Prince to injure himself and lose his object when he thinks he is using the greatest dexterity to foil his opponents. When I left Town on the monday every thing was right—and the King declining on so inconsistent a Pretence to see Moira, and he having applied for Permission to go to Leicestershire[1] I thought every thing well over. What brought Moira the Chancellor and Pitt together on the tuesday when a *written memorandum* was *mutually agreed to* has not been satisfactorily explain'd to me—or what brought the Chancellor and Moira to Carlton-House on the wednesday morning, tho' I have of course heard all the history and motives from the Prince. However when He sent for me on tuesday last[2] the result I found was a very crafty and well considered Paper from the King, which The Prince as I told you yesterday declined answering 'till Moira should come to Town. This morning the King's Messenger returned with Moira's answer to the Chancellor and an *outline* for the Prince's answer to the King's last Paper which with *some alteration* is *gone* to the Chancellor. The Prince at my very pressing request decides to have the Princess Charlotte's *home* under his own Roof in the adjoining House—and has given orders to prepare it accordingly[3]—yet it will end in her entirely belonging to the King. And all the great Point he has stood upon that the Princess should not visit her too often will end in nothing, and any future stir of his upon this subject,

[1] From a further letter by McMahon to the Duke of Northumberlnad of 1 Jan. 1805 (Alnwick MSS., LXII, ff. 96–99), it appears that Moira saw Pitt on reaching London. No word came from the King (for Pitt, according to McMahon, had not reported Moira's arrival) so, on 24 Dec., Moira wrote to the Duke of Kent stating that he was in London as directed and now awaited orders. If he was not wanted he would go to his Leicestershire home at Donnington and remain there until his leave ended in March. The King then replied that there was no just reason to stop Moira joining his family at this particular season.

[2] The Prince's letter is dated 31 Dec. 1804, and complains that S. had broken his promise to be in London by the previous Friday. The Prince added, 'I have just receiv'd this moment a Letter from the Chancellor that demands a very smart reply from me, and I therefore write to You, in the hopes that you will *instantly* come to Town . . . as I should be sorry to send an answer . . . without availing myself of your advice' (Osborn MS.).

[3] In his letter to Northumberland of 1 Jan. 1805, McMahon also stated that it had been made clear to Pitt and the Lord Chancellor that the Prince would not allow his daughter to live at Windsor as the King desired, though the Prince had no objection to her visiting Windsor and seeing her mother at any time. The nomination of Charlotte's household was also to remain in the Prince's hands, though he was prepared to consult the King's wishes about the appointments.

which he reserves and speculates on, will be as foolish as unpopular.—Now what is effected is this, and Pitt never could have hoped the Game to have been so play'd for him. The Prince blind to the sheer Roguery of Tierney,[1] and encouraged by the deluded vanity of Moira has establish'd for Pitt a channel of influence over the King much greater than He ever had thro any source before. The Queen is now out of the Question. The ascendency of the Princess is not to be described. It is settled that she is to have Kensington Palace—and to reside in the House with her Daughter when she visits Windsor. She will become a different character in the eye and estimation of the Country. She is to be at all the Fetes etc.—from which the Prince on that account decides to exclude himself. She thinks herself injured and provoked by the Prince so as to justify resentment and vengeance to every extent, with this I don't meddle. She feels herself obliged to Pitt (and to him *alone*) for the manœuvre which shall have placed her in this new situation both as to personal character and political importance. And I see no motive for her using ungratefully the decided influence she already has over the King. Her greatest Friend at this moment is Lady Hester Stanhope,[2] Pitt's Niece who lives in his House. And so there is the Kettle of Fish, which all these mysteries and negotiations have produced. At the same time I must tell you that the Prince was never more fair stout and honourable in his Political Path and attachments than at this very moment. At the same time he entertains in his own mind ill views and *Purposes* respecting the Princess (his wife) which I am sure you or I shall never countenance or meddle with but to dissuade him from.—But of this hereafter.

My letter is not very long but I don't know when I have written so long a one. But I am very much struck with what I consider to be the likely consequences of this Day's settlement.

Of common News there is little worth writing.—The Prince appears and professes to be very cold and reserved

[1] S. seems to have suspected that Tierney was ready to sacrifice the Prince's interests to secure his own ends and serve Pitt, but S.'s attitude may have been dictated by jealousy of Tierney's 'independence' and standing with the Prince.

[2] 1776–1839. In later life she travelled in the Middle East and adopted eastern ways.

towards Tierney. Addington is certainly to be a Peer,[1] and it is said with the blue Ribband—Lord Chesterfield[2] and Abercorne[3] the other two.

Lord Hawkesbury[4] carried on the negotiation between Pitt and Adington by the Kings Command. Hily Addington[5]—Braggs[6] Bond[7] etc. are to be provided for—and Lord Buckinghamshire[8]—Lord St. Vincent[9] entirely clear of the whole business. Lord Rosselyn[10] died last Night— | Yours ever | R B S.

537. To Mrs. Ord

J. R. Blackett-Ord MS. *Address*: Mrs. Ord.

[*15 Jan. 1805?*]
Tuesday Night

The enclosed you should have had tonight—but it is just returned by a Porter who mistook the Direction and so bethumb'd that Hecca, in bed, desires me to put it in another cover that it may go in the morning. | yours truly | R B S.

Verily and truly the answer to Bunoparte's Letter[11] is a most bloodthirsty, murderous and foolish Performance.

[1] Created Viscount Sidmouth on 12 Jan. 1805. He was not given the Garter.

[2] Philip Stanhope, 5th Earl of Chesterfield (1755–1815). He was Master of the Horse 1798–1804 and was well liked by George III.

[3] John Hamilton, 9th Earl and 1st Marquess of Abercorn (1756–1818). Apart from Abercorn and Chesterfield, Garters were also given to Pembroke, Dartmouth, and Winchilsea.

[4] The reconciliation between Pitt and Addington on 23 Dec. took place at Hawkesbury's house, Coombe Wood.

[5] Hiley, Henry Addington's brother. He was M.P. for Harwich, 1803–18, and died in 1818.

[6] Charles Bragge-Bathurst (*c.* 1754–1831), M.P. for Monmouth, 1790–6, and for Bristol, 1796–1812 (Judd). He was Addington's brother-in-law.

[7] Nathaniel Bond (1754–1823), M.P. for Corfe Castle, 1801–7 (Judd). He was appointed Judge Advocate General, 15 Jan. 1805.

[8] Formerly Lord Hobart. He became Chancellor of the Duchy of Lancaster in January 1805, and entered the Cabinet.

[9] John Jervis, Earl of St. Vincent (1735–1823), admiral; and First Lord of the Admiralty in Addington's administration. S. said of him on 2 May 1805, 'The honour of that noble lord [St. Vincent] was a part, and a proud part, of the glory and the honour of the country' (Hansard, 1st Ser., iv. 584).

[10] Alexander Wedderburn, 1st Earl of Rosslyn, formerly Lord Loughborough.

[11] His letter, stating that his 'first sentiment is a wish for peace', was dated 2 Jan. 1805. The British government's reply, through the Foreign Secretary, Mulgrave, was dated 14 Jan. 1805. Both are to be found in the *Annual Register . . . 1805*, pp. 615–16.

538. [To Sir Richard Ford]

Brinsley Ford MS. Copy.

Monday Jan. 28th [*1805?*]

Dear Ford,

Graham being now returned, whose presence I deemed essentially necessary, I will appoint the earliest evening most convenient to the Trustees for the meeting of counsel in order that we may carry our last resolutions into the speediest effect.[1] | Yours truly, | R. B. Sheridan.

539. To His Wife

Pub.: Rae, ii. 228.

[*7 Mar. 1805?*]

I did not speak till 12 o'clock . . . for as I did not look at any of the materials which belonged to the question, I was obliged to wait till others furnished something to remark on. . . . The Ministerial *Times* does me the honour to put my speech in the first person.[2]

540. To Richard Peake

McAdam MS. *Address*: Mr. Peake | Charlotte-St. | Rathbone-Place *Dock.*: Mr. Sheridan *Wm.*: 1804

[*11 Mar. 1805*]
Carlton-house
Monday morning

Dear P.

Send me by *this Day's Post* £10 direct to me at Lord

[1] When the case of Ford *v.* Sheridan was heard at the Court of Chancery on 14 Aug. 1805, counsel declared that the managers of D.L.Th. had been informed in Nov. and Dec. 1804 by the trustees that if arrears of £16,000 were not paid in one month, the management must be placed in other hands. The Lord Chancellor then said that the Court would do its utmost to relieve the petitioners when they brought before it competent evidence of the mismanagement of the theatre. See *The Times*, 15 Aug. 1805.

[2] *The Times*, 7 Mar. 1805, gave other speeches in the parliamentary debate of 6 Mar. on the Additional Force Bill, in reported speech. S.'s is the only one in direct speech. Whitbread, Pitt, and Lord H. Petty had all spoken before S. rose. S. made much of Pitt's figures showing that comparatively small numbers had been recruited under the General Defence Act.

Moira's Donnington Park[1] Loughtorough Leicestershire—for which Place I am this moment setting off with the Prince[2] | Yours ever | R B S.

Pray pray be brisk in the Trustee business[3] I will write Graham

541. To William Adam

Adam MS. *Dock.*: Mr. Sheridan | from | Carlton House | March 1805

[*11*] *Mar. 1805*
Carlton-House
Monday, one oclock

Private

My Dear Adam

I am this moment setting off with the Prince for Donnington (Moira's), I shall be greatly obliged to you to express my Regret to the Sheriffs for my unavoidable Absence[4]—but had I an opportunity to explain to you the motives and circumstances I am confident you would see that it is unavoidable— | yours ever | most truly | R B Sheridan

542. To His Wife

Osborn MS. *Wm.*: 1804

[*1805?*]
Saturday Night

I left my bed as soon as I had written you a few Lines to

[1] Ten miles from Loughborough.

[2] *The Times*, 12 Mar. 1805, noted that S. had gone to Moira's seat, and on 19 Mar. it stated that S. and the Prince had returned on 16 Mar. At the dinner of the St. Patrick's Society on 18 Mar., S. had said he had 'the honour, a few days since, to be in Leicestershire, on a visit to the Earl of Moira, in humble attendance on his Royal Highness the Prince of Wales, and it was with pleasure he witnessed the friendship which subsisted between that illustrious Personage and the Noble Earl . . .'.

[3] One of the trustees of D.L.Th., George Shum, had died in Feb. 1805. A successor was not elected, however, until 28 May, when John Hosier accepted the trust: see *The Times*, 30 May 1805.

[4] On 11 Mar. the Commons debated the conduct of the Sheriffs, Sir William Rawlins and R. A. Cox, at the Middlesex election of 1802. They were accused of favouring the return of Burdett, and in spite of Adam's three-hour speech in their defence, were committed to Newgate.

catch the Post, and have been sitting by my self most melancholy and gloomy ever since but much better of my complaint. Great Pain is a very bad thing but I think a fit of very low Spirits in solitude as bad. And my dearest Hecca I swear to you it is owing to your Letter this morning, and the constant anxious thoughts that follow me respecting your health with at times the most unreasonable apprehensions that have put my heart so down this Night. For otherwise I should rather have felt glad and grateful at finding myself so suddenly better after having according to my usual foolish and nervous superstitions put myself down for dying yesterday morning but your applying that word to yourself undoes all care about myself—think as you will my Hecca but I would with the hand I am now writing with I would cut off the other to ensure your health and Life. Do not ask me whether I should take care of Charles were anything to happen to you—look to me with no reliance—

Monday

I would not go on in my Gloom Saturday Night. I have only a moment to thank you from my heart for your Letter—I am getting quite well to Day tho I thought myself worse than ever yesterday which was a mistake

I will write tomorrow—

Heaven bless you—upon my soul Bain says you must only walk the Horse[1] | Your's ever| R B S

543. To His Wife

Dufferin MS. [Ph.] *Address*: London April eighteen 1805 | Mrs. Sheridan | S. Whitbreads Esq. | Southill | Biggleswade *Fr.*: Free | R B Sheridan *Pm.*: Free

17–18 April 1805
Wednesday Night

I must write to you tho' you do not to me. You bid me say exactly what was my disorder—indeed it was not wine tho' I own I drank that night too much which was Whitbread's and Grey's fault as I can demonstrate tho' they were not in

[1] Just possibly 'House'.

company. It was in fact a violent cold attended by sudden inflammation. This inflammation was of the phlegmonous kind and began in the intercostal muscles from whence it spread to the interior Parts of the Thorax thence with unusual rapidity to the Pleaura, mediastenum pericardium diaphragm and to the Parenchymatous substance of the Lungs causing a very formidable Peripneumony—. I am interrupted but this is but one of the several disorders that attack'd me at once which I only select as most easily to be explain'd

Thursday

I have received your two Letters, tho' you dont give me much encouragement I cant help thinking Whitbreads will be glad to see me—I must have two quiet Nights and a little country air for the chance of sleep. I find it very hard for me to do anything right—you made a Point—of my getting Charles from Oxford[1] without Delay and now, I have been in too great a hurry. I had order'd his cloathes—but I have now unorder'd them. I am sorry you care so much about such trifles. God bless you—

Pray say that at any rate I have no thought of being at Southill to dinner to morrow

544. To Richard Peake

Add. MS. 35118, ff. 141–2. *Address*: Mr. Peake *Dock.*: Mr Sheridan about A Johnstone's[2] Money *Wm.*: 1803.

[*15 Aug. 1805*]
Thursday morning
Hatfield[3]

My Dear Peake

I beseech you explain to Johnson how greatly he will

[1] In an undated letter (probably of 1805) Mrs. S. mentions the advantages of Charles's being tutored at Oxford: 'A House taken by the Year, and the Woman who letts it a person I can depend on for giving Charles the little attendance he requires keeping his clothes right . . . and means of getting without expence or trouble books globes maps etc with perhaps the cheapest (tho' excellent) mode of living ever heard of owing to the dinners going on in the colleges the superintendence of which in some manner . . . belongs to a friend of Mr. Baker's and also of my brother John's' (Mr. J. R. Blackett-Ord's MS.).

[2] Alexander Johnson, the machinist, 'who ruined himself . . . by assisting

[*Footnotes 2 and 3 continued on facing page.*

oblige and pay it to Biddulph and Cox.[1] I am undone else. Would not his acceptance do?

and pray see instantly Mrs Lownds[2] and let her have her press ready tomorrow when the Post gets in—to print a short circular Letter[3] which you will receive from [me] and which must be delivered tomorrow | Yours ever | R B S

545. To Richard Peake

Add. MS. 35118, ff. 91–92. *Address*: Biggleswade August fifteen | 1805 | Mr. Peake | Charlotte-St. | Rathbone-Place | London *Fr.*: Free | R B Sheridan *Dock.*: Mr. Sheridan

15 Aug. 1805
Thursday morning

My Dear Peake,

A Line on the Road. Not to waste Time I shall write from wherever I sleep to Night—so you will not get it tomorrow—but have the press and messengers ready for Saturday morning. | Yours ever | R B S

546. To Richard Peake

Add. MS. 35118, f. 93. *Address*: Stamford August sixteen | 1805 | Mr. Peake | Charlotte-St. | Rathbone-Place | London *Fr.*: Free | R B Sheridan *Dock.*: Mr Sheridan's Instructions to Peake

15 Aug. 1805
Stamford
Thursday Night

My Dear Peake

You are to *sign* nothing but the envelope which should be printed on a separate Paper from the Note—but take care it

Sheridan to get into Parliament . . .' (C. Dibdin the Younger, *Professional and Literary Memoirs* (1956), p. 43). But it is also worth noting that Mr. Bertram Shuttleworth owned a letter in which John Johnstone claimed to have lent S. £200 on 8 Aug. 1805.

[3] S. was on his way to Scotland to visit the Duke of Atholl.

[1] The bankers, of 43 Charing Cross.

[2] The printing office of D.L.Th. had been run by C. Lowndes of 66 Drury Lane, 'next the Stage-Door', and Marquis Court.

[3] See p. 246, n. 2.

is all accurately printed, and circulated as fast as possible. [Send][1] me a couple of both[2]—

I will have no advice on the subject. I know I am doing what is right and just by the Renters. | Yours ever | R B S

I shall write constantly for my mind is in the business and I have leisure to think without being worried. I shall *certainly* be back before the opening.[3]

Sir or Madam of course as the case is

547. To Richard Peake

Add. MS. 35118, ff. 94–95. *Address*: Hexham August twenty one 1805 | Mr. Peake | Charlotte-St. | Rathbone-Place | London. *Fr.*: Free | R B Sheridan *Dock.*: Mr. Sheridan *Pm.*: NEWCASTLE-U-T FREE AUG 24 1805

20 Aug. 1805
Whitfield[4]
Tuesday

My Dear Peake

I send you some Moor-Game, and will more, so dispose of the surplus as may be best for the common cause | on more important matters by the next Post— | yours ever | R B S.

548. To Richard Peake

Salt MS.

[*27 Aug. 1805*][5]
Whitfield Tuesday

My Dear P

Thank you for yours and for your diligence in getting

[1] Manuscript torn.

[2] Among the Harvard MSS. is a printed note from the Proprietors of D.L.Th. dated 16 Aug. 1805, together with S.'s drafts of this note and of Peake's letter that accompanied it. They were addressed to the Theatre's renters who were asked 'not to be influenced by an ex parte statement made upon, or in support of, a late Petition in the court of Chancery, so as to lead any of them in the smallest degree to under-rate the value of their Shares'. For the petition of 14 Aug. see p. 241, n. 1.

[3] He must have changed his plans, for he had not returned when D.L.Th. opened on 14 Sept.

[4] Whitfield Hall, Northumberland, was the home of William Ord, son of Mrs. Creevey.

[5] A cover in the collection of Mr. and Mrs. Donald Hyde reads: 'Newcastle August twenty-eight N.B. 1805 | Mr. Peake | Charlotte-St. | Rathbone Place | London | Free R B Sheridan FREE AUG 31 1805.'

Johnson's—Think you whether you could not pick up another. What say you to old Moody,[1] properly *incensed* as we say in Stafford? it would be very convenient indeed.

Direct your next to me at N. Ogle's Esq Kirkley Newcastle on Tyne. But tell anyone else to send to George St. and they will be forwarded. My mind and resentments are very much in the Theatre or I should feel most pleasantly here—it is a delightful Spot and society and I am remarkably well. I set the Trustees at utter Defiance—but Mum for the Present. I hope you go to Polesden. | Yours ever | R B S.

549. To Richard Peake

Add. MS. 35118, f. 96. *Address*: Hexham August twenty nine 1805 | Mr. Peake | Charlotte-St. | Rathbone-Place | London *Fr.*: Free R B Sheridan *Dock.*: £20 Mr. Sheridan *Pm.*: NEWCASTLE-U-T

29 Aug. 1805
Whitfield
Thursday

My Dear P

Send me the enclosed[2] to Kirkley Newcastle on Tyne | Yours | R B S

I will write again tomorrow.

550. To Richard Peake

McAdam MS.

Kirkley
Tuesday
Sept: 10th [*1805*]

My Dear P

direct your next to me at the Honble C Grey's[3] Howick

[1] John Moody (1727?–1812) had retired from D.L.Th. in 1796. His acting is eulogized in Churchill's *The Rosciad*. When he sought payment in the Court of King's Bench on 28 Nov. 1800 of salary owing to him from D.L.Th. since 1794, Lord Kenyon praised him as 'a frugal and prudent man' (*The Times*, 29 Nov. 1800).

[2] An acceptance for the amount mentioned in the docketing?

[3] Grey wrote to Fox from Howick on 22 Sept. 1805 to say: 'Sheridan stopped here a day in his way to Scotland' (Grey MS.). The *Morn. Chron.*, 18 Oct. 1805, reported that 'Mr. and Mrs. Sheridan went last Friday from Edinburgh to pass a few days with Mr. and Mrs. Grey in Northumberland, on their way back to London'.

Alnwick Northumberland. By your account I stand very safe at Biddulph and Cox's. I have drawn for ten Pounds for mine and my Son's mourning[1] in favour of Dixon a Newcastle Tailor—on Biddulph and Cox date the 14th. I need not say that it would be death and damnation to me not to have the Draft answer'd. I rely on your taking care there shall be no mistake— | Yours ever truly | R B S

551. To Richard Peake

Add. MS. 35118, ff. 97–98. *Address*: Dunbar September sixteen | 1805 | Mr Peake | Charlotte-St. | Rathbone Place | London *Fr.*: Free R B Sheridan *Dock.*: Mr. Sheridan *Pm.*: FREE SEP 19 1805

16 Sept. 1805
Lord Lauderdales
Dunbar
Monday

My Dear Peake

For Heavens sake send me the enclosed to *me Post Office Edinburgh.*[2] The Post is just going—I will write to Graham tomorrow. His last letter only caught me to Day | yours ever | R B S.

552. To Thomas Creevey

J. R. Blackett-Ord MS. *Pub.*: *Creevey Papers*, i. 39. *Address*: T. Creevey Esq | Park-Place | St James-St. *Dock.*: Poor Sheridans note | T. C.

[*c. Nov. 1805?*]
Thursday Evening

My Dear Creevey

If you don't leave Town tomorrow come and eat your Mutton with me in George St. and meet Adam and

[1] For Dean Ogle's funeral in 1804?

[2] Moira wrote on 20 Sept.: 'Sheridan, his wife and a large party are at present here. They dine with us tomorrow' (H.M.C., *MSS. of the late R. R. Hastings* (ed. F. Bickley, 1934), iii. 243). Cf. Rae, ii. 264; and S.C., 15 Apr. 1896, lot 417: A.L.s. by S., from Holyrood, Tuesday.

McMahon and more than all my Son and DAUGHTER.[1] Mrs. Creevey will excuse you at my request. And you will be a Piece of a Lion to have seen so early Mrs. T. S. whom I think lovely and engaging and interesting beyond measure, and, as far as I can judge with a most superior understanding | yrs ever | R B S

553. To Eleanor Creevey

J. R. Blackett-Ord MS.

[*Nov. 1805?*]
Saturday

My Dear Mrs. Creevey

I have only one moment to say that I am more obliged to you than I can express respecting Charles.[2] I'll tell you all my meaning and feeling about [him] on monday—when He will arrive at Brighton—and pray let the good old Lady expect him.

To your kind Daughters I know I shall have a thousand thanks to pay also— | most truly yours | R B Sheridan

554. To Eleanor Creevey

J. R. Blackett-Ord MS. *Address*: London November nine 1805 | Mrs. Creevey | Brighton *Fr.*: Free R B Sheridan *Dock.*: Mr. and Mrs. Sheridan

9 *Nov. 1805*
Saturday

My Dear Mrs. Creevey

A Line only to request that if Hester has written to you that you will suspend answering till you receive a Letter I shall have time to write to you tomorrow when I will explain

[1] Sichel, ii. 303 (alluding to Egerton MS. 1975, f. 162), states that Tom S. was married to Caroline Henrietta Callander on 21 June 1805. Lady Bessborough suggests that they were married *c.* Oct. 1805: see *Leveson Gower Corr.* ii. 139.

[2] Following a promise by Mrs. Creevey to keep an eye on Charles at Brighton?

my meaning. Has my boy arrived safe and well?[1] perhaps you will favor me with one Line to tell me.— | Your obliged | R B S

555. To His Wife

Osborn MS. *Wm.* 1804

Wednesday evening
Decr 25th, Xmas-day! [*1805*]

I exhausted my Paper last Night and writing late could get no more or I believe I should have inflicted on you another tremendous Epistle—for I was then in a mood to have gone on writing to you,[2] and to day tho' no want of *Leisure* heaven knows! I have been employ'd otherwise. It ought to melt a heart of Scotch Pebble to have seen how I pass'd this *my* X Day—There is no Peer, no Gentleman no christian Sweep that does not make something social out of it, and I suppose I am the single Person not manacled who has spent it in my cell without communion with any fellow-creature[3]—but such is the fact—I have not stirr'd out of your Drawing room, indeed I had no where to go, and I am pleased to find how much better my nerves endure solitude than used to be the case. The particular object of my occupation to Day being to find some Papers of consequence immediately wanted. I lit upon a parcel of vouchers which I enclose to you one happens to be the first note Henry left on my Glass and which my *Establishment* conceiving it, and not unnaturally to be the bit of Paper allotted to assist the broken skrew had stuck again in the Frame and there I found it the monday after. Well they play'd the Rivals[4] really extremely

[1] Charles Sheridan went to stay at Brighton with his tutor, George Baker. After meeting them there, Mrs. Creevey wrote (10 Nov.) to her husband: '. . . I am very civil to the poor Man who seems very humble and I ask'd them to dinner today but he refused on the ground of its being better for Charles as he had not been well lately to dine at an early hour. . . . If you see Mr. Sheridan tell him his Boy is quite well—I have not got the second Letter he promised me'. (Mr. J. R. Blackett-Ord's MS.) S. himself was at Brighton on 23 Nov.: see *The Francis Letters* (ed. B. Francis and E. Keary, n.d.), ii. 630.

[2] Mrs. S. appears to have been still in Northumberland. She was at Howick with the Greys on 5 Dec. (Mr. J. R. Blackett-Ord's MSS.).

[3] Quoted by Rae, ii. 215.

[4] At the amateur theatricals in the Marquess of Abercorn's home, Bentley Priory, Middlesex.

well indeed, Lady Cahir[1] very good, and a Mrs Hasseltine a great Priory Personage and a very pretty woman admirable. She sings too I understand excellently with the finest voice in the world. I don't know when I have sat out a Play before[2]—it made me very nervous I don't mean the writing or sentiments of the Play but the recollection of the Days, when, just past twenty one, I wrote it—many years before I knew some *dear Friends*! who sat on the Bench with me or their world or their system. You wish'd me not to go unless I was press'd, such cautions are never necessary to me—and I had heard from Lady Melbourne[3] that *your Friend* had repeated to Lady A.[4] some things you had told her of my saying and with due fidelity of course I don't mean that Lady M knew that *you* had anything to say [about] it, but no matter I had resolved not to go tho I had wish'd it very much for the opportunity before the particular set of shewing every attention and respect to my daughter in Law—to Lady Cahir's invitations I made no answer at all but on sunday morning Lady A. sent up a servant with her Note which with a Letter from Tom decided me. I found her apparently as cordial as ever and on the Chapter of beds there really were scarcely sufficient to accommodate the Dramatis Personae and their immediate connexions. I believe I was the only highly favour'd Person and a very good Room I had. The Duchess[5] Lady Bessborough[6] etc. etc. all returned to Town at 4 in the morning—I was very much press'd to stay on or to return for tomorrow when they perform a musical Piece of George Lamb's[7] in which they say Mrs

[1] Lady Bessborough reported that 'Lady Cahir look'd very pretty in Lydia Languish, but was rather too violent for the Character; Mrs. Hesseltine perfect in Julia' (*Leveson Gower Corr.* ii. 151). Lady Caher was the wife of the Irish peer, Richard Butler, Lord Caher (1775–1819), of Tipperary.

[2] Lady Harriet Cavendish wrote that '*The Rivals* was acted even to satisfy Mr. Sheridan who was forced to laugh at all his own jokes and applaud all his own sentiments' (*Hary-O* (ed. Sir G. Leveson Gower and Iris Palmer, 1940), p. 140).

[3] Elizabeth, Viscountess Melbourne (1752–1818).

[4] The Marquess of Abercorn married in April 1800, as his third wife, Lady Ann Hatton. She was a great friend of Lady Bessborough, and was the subject of some occasional verse by S.

[5] Of Devonshire: see *Georgiana*, p. 275.

[6] She wrote, 'I am out of favour': see *Leveson Gower Corr.* ii. 146.

[7] Fourth son of the 1st Lord Melbourne. He was a good actor, and his two-act comic opera, *Whistle Me First*, was later (10 Apr. 1807) produced at C.G.Th. See Mabell, Countess of Airlie, *In Whig Society*, pp. 68–71.

Hasseltine and Tom sing famously[1] but I had resolved not and my principal inducement for going was out of question as poor Caroline was confined to her Room by a bad cold and certainly would not appear for some Days—you see I have taken pains to satisfy you on this subject and I have done it the more as I quite agree with what you felt respecting *Tom* and *her*. He insists that what you have written to him on the subject was at *my* suggestion—you know the contrary

556. [To T. N. Longman?]

W.T. From a copy.

George Street[2] Hanover
Square Decr. 26th [*1805–6*]

Sir,

I am apprehensive that some particular circumstances which have made it impossible for me to give a decisive answer to your proposition[3] may have led me to appear rudely negligent of your application—this I assure you was far from my intention—the subject is very interesting to the little vanity I have as an author, and your offer is frank and gentlemanly—I can only say that I am now at liberty to meet you in that subject, I will if agreable to you, appoint an early day for that purpose | Your obedient Servant | R. B. Sheridan

557. To Eleanor Creevey

J. R. Blackett-Ord MS. *Wm.*: 1804

Saturday
Decr. 28th. [*1805*]

My Dear Mrs. Creevey

I am infinitely obliged to you for the kind interest you

[1] Tom S. was a good comic actor and sang well.

[2] *Rider's British Merlin* (1806) gives S.'s address as 9 George Street.

[3] W.T. contains the following unsigned note: 'When Messrs Longman and Co. were about publishing Mrs. Inchbald's Rn. [British ?] Theatre, they made a proposition to Mr. Sheridan for the purchase of the School for Scandal, the copyright of which they considered to be still his property, but they receiv'd the above answer too late [to] enable them to use the play for the purpose they desired it—to be the first number of the series'. Longman advertised in *Bell's W. Mess.* of 1 June 1807, that Nos. 1–67 of *The British Theatre* had appeared and that publication was continued weekly.

take in Charles and for your Letter respecting B.[1] You may rely on his not having a hint from me of any such communication. I will say nothing on the subject now as I shall have the Pleasure of seeing you in a few Days, meaning to pay my Duty to the Prince to wish him all manner of good from the approaching new year. I hope Creevey keeps good hours and is abstemious in the article of wine, any other course of Life 'will not do', 'it will not do', 'it really will not do!' | your sincere and obliged | R B Sheridan

remembrance to my young Friends

558. To His Wife

Price MS.

Sunday Evening
Decr. 29th: [*1805*]

Yesterday I never moved from the House nor saw a human creature but stay'd alone the whole of the Day. To Day I was out very early, have seen many but refusing many invitations have dined alone again—it is clear to me that I shall become a Zimmermanian[2]—a Hermit only that I shan't have beard enough—I know a nice spot in Ranmorwood for my cell only there is no *chrystal Spring* near it. I shall do the same tomorrow tho' ask'd to Lady Melbourne's and Holland House. I should tell you that I have changed my bad hours—and now constantly ring up the house before Day-light and read and breakfast by candle-light and Ma'am I mean this shall positively last notwithstanding the treachery of my former resolutions to the same effect, but I know this *last* to be an honest deliberate trust-worthy Resolution whom I can depend on. Mark the event.

I return you, as you desired Stockdale's verses, very fine

[1] George Baker, Charles Sheridan's tutor, matriculated at Corpus Christi, Oxford, 6 May 1794, aged seventeen, and was registered as the son of the Rev. Philip Baker of Micklemarsh, Hants (Foster). He took his Master's degree in 1802. The good impression he had made at first on Mrs. Creevey had changed to dislike towards him, and Creevey thought him a 'coxcomb in society'.

[2] See ii. 132, n. 2. Cf. Rae, ii. 215, 363. *Solitude* was republished in 1805.

indeed. I think I knew a Percival Stockdale[1] once but I forget when where or how—but tho' I swear you deserve your stanzas far more than I do mine I think by his notice of 'the Tyrants of the East' as applied to me, and still more 'of Afric's mournful genius' they were *not* written at the date he puts to them. But at any rate I perceive you have been singing too much or he would not have been reminded of them—and with your cough too—you know this is the fact—how dare you do so. Now being on the chapter of verses I remember you demanded my opinion upon those you sent me of Bakers, declaring that you were *determined* to like them.[2] I admire your *resolution*, and the more for its having subdued your Taste, and therefore I will keep you company and admire them too.

> How softly on yon infant's couch are shed
> The *gracious dews* of sleep! the moon *meanwhile*
> Her *wanton* beam diffusing round his head
> Lingers as *amorous* of his rosy smile.[3]

Now a fastidious critic not determined to admire the Lines as we do would be apt to exclaim 'Oh fie Mr. Baker where did you learn to apply such terms as "*wanton*" and "*amorous*" to the poor dear chaste innocent moon who for ages has maintained the most unblemish'd character and of whom untill she came to be handled by *you* no one could say that "black was the white of her eye".'

For my part however I believe the whole proceeded from a mistake and that the '*amorous* moon' blunder'd about the rooms, and really meant to send her '*wanton* beams' in search

[1] Stockdale (1736–1811) was rector of Lesbury, Northumberland, and had the use of Grey's library at Howick. See his *Memoirs* . . . (1809), ii. 324.

[2] Mrs. S.'s letter is in my possession and bears the postmark 'DEC 20 1805'. It reads: '. . . I am *much* pleased with a letter I have had from Baker he sends me too some lines he wrote on Charles asleep. I am *determin'd* to think them pretty because they show affection to him—he calls them a few straggling lines written at Oxford.' She goes on to refer to the Greys, and it seems clear that her letter was written from Northumberland, either from Howick or from her brother's home at Kirkley Hall.

[3] In her letter Mrs. S. quotes George Baker's ten-line poem 'Tranquillity' and it is printed, with some corrections, in his *Tenby, The Navy of England, and Other Occasional Poetry* (1807), p. 59. This volume also contains (pp. 31–51) a poem called 'The Navy of England', which is dedicated to S. as 'the Eloquent and Accomplished Advocate of the Naval Interests of Britain'. The 'Advertisement' was written from 'Polesdon, Surry' in Aug. 1806.

of that naughty Endymion Baker. One thing yet I own I learn from the verses, and a fact is sometimes better than Poetry namely that Charles's sleeping room at the Oxford-Taylor's had neither *curtains* or *window shutters to it*—else could not the amorous moon have effected the intrusion so beautifully described but I also have a right to conclude that the wind and the rain took the same delicious Liberty.

No He must not form Charles's taste in Poetry.—Now with all my real partiality to Baker I am vex'd at a bit of intelligence received some days since from Brighton—I enclose you Mrs. Creevey's Letter as the shortest way—but burn it as I ought to have done only I like that you should be acquainted with everything. Her first note I received by McMahon only a few Days before. The fact is I suppose that they have not taken much to Baker, especially *Creevey*, nor seem'd desirous of *his* Company—and Baker finds the Boy a pass-ticket that mends his reception in other Places. All this is partially unlucky but it must be made the best of, I can neither ask Baker to live in solitude nor would I for the Boy's sake nor can I cure his being a coxcomb in Society. Since I received Mrs. Creevey's Letter I search'd and search'd and found a Letter from Baker at the end of which was a passage I had overlook'd proposing this *hop* to Warwickshire indeed Dear Hecca you must not giggle tho you say this hopping makes you do so for this would have been a very serious hop, such a one as I should have thought would have render'd his upper-grass[h]op[p]er-Springs really incapable—ask any coachmaker else.—But to do him justice in his last letter to me which I also enclose he does not repeat the subject, and indeed it would have been a foolish trip, expensive and taking the child away from the healthy course of exercise and regularity of application He is now engaged in—and my dear Hecca you must receive 'cum grano' as Nat and you say any want of partiality towards Baker from your own particular Friends—recollecting your own example you must allow that where you have shewn yourself so intolerant of his society you cannot expect others to make sacrifices which they have so much less motive to make. One of the things I wanted to tell you of the Dear one is that when McMahon was coming away He call'd at his door and took him into the chaise to him and on taking leave put a guinea into his hand which Charles very politely but very positively refused but Mac saying all boys took Xmas boxes shut his hand upon it and put him on the step when the boy with a good natured laugh bid him good bye dropping the money into the bottom of the chaise and ran into the house. I wrote to him on this to say how right he was. Good Night. God ever bless you—

559. To Richard Peake

Osborn MS. *Address*: Mr. Peake *Dock.*: Receavd One Pound N Collins *Wm.*: 1805

[*1805?*]
Thursday

My Dear P

Pray give poor N. who has nothing to get his Dinner, £1

560. To His Wife

Pub.: Rae, ii. 362.

[*1806*]

I continue my early hours and industrious exertions. All connected with me will be the better for it, perhaps even myself.

561. To His Wife

Pub.: Sichel, ii. 225.

15 Jan. 1806
Wednesday night,
January 16, 1806

I have been to-day at Iver attending poor Jane's funeral[1] with Tom. It was particularly decent and affecting. If you remember, she lived directly opposite the church of that very

[1] Jane Nash Linley, fourth daughter of Thomas Linley, and wife of C. W. Ward, had died on 8 Jan. 1806. Ward's brother, Edward, was rector of Iver from 1803. See Black, pp. 266, 272, and S.C., 16 Dec. 1964, lots 526–8.

neat and seemingly innocent village, and like that was her burial—no hearse or coach. Her sister's[1] was a gaudy parade and show from Bristol to Wells Cathedral, where all the mob, high and low, were in the church surveying and surrounding the vault. The recollection of the scene and of the journey has always pained me, independently of the occasion itself, and has decided me, who am a friend without superstition to attention and attendance on these occasions, to prefer the mode I witnessed this morning—and so shall be my own passage to the grave[2]

562. [To Viscount Sidmouth]

Osborn MS. *Dock.*: Mr: Sheridan | Recd: Jany: ye 23d: | at Richmond Park | [another hand] Mr. Sheridan | Jany: 1806.

22 Jan. 1806
Wednesday Evening

My Dear Lord

I am *commanded* to have a confidential communication with you. If you are not coming to Town tomorrow I will wait on you at Richmond Park[3]—or attend your appointment in Clifford-Street—if you are to be in Town.— | I have the honor to be | with the greatest respect | your Lordship's | obedient Servant | R B Sheridan

563. [To Viscount Sidmouth]

Viscount Sidmouth MS. *Dock.*: Mr. Sheridan | 1806

[26 Jan. 1806]
Sunday morning
10 o'clock

My Dear Lord,

I am commanded to see you *this morning*.[4] I shall have the

[1] S.'s first wife.

[2] His funeral (ending in interment in the Poets' Corner) was an elaborate one: see *Speeches*, v. xlvii–xlviii; Moore, vii. 460–1.

[3] Cf. Pellew, ii. 412.

[4] Following the death of Pitt, a new administration was likely to be formed. The King sent a message to Lord Grenville on 25 Jan.; and the same day

honor of waiting on you before one— | with the greatest respect | your's faithfully | R B Sheridan

564. [To Viscount Sidmouth]

Viscount Sidmouth MS. *Pub.*: Pellew, ii. 412. *Dock.*: Mr. Sheridan | Jan. ye 29th. *Wm.*: 1804

29 Jan. [1806]
Wednesday Evening

My Dear Lord,

I have something to communicate to you from the Prince[1] and Mr. Fox, and will have the honor of waiting on you tomorrow at twelve. | your's very faithfully | R B Sheridan

565. [To Viscount Sidmouth]

Viscount Sidmouth MS. *Dock.*: Mr Sheridan | Thursday Evening | Jan 1806

[30] Jan. 1806
Thursday Evening.

My Dear Lord,

I trouble you with one line after a conversation of nearly three hours with the Prince and the Marquess of Buckingham.—It has been most satisfactory, and when I say that, I mean to say that not a word pass'd which it would not have been grateful to *you* to have heard.

I have only to add that you have not only the Prince's permission but his most ready assent to your communicating

the Prince sent for Fox and S.: see Rae, ii. 247. Nicholas Vansittart reported that the Prince had told him at the Opera he intended to keep faith with Sidmouth. Vansittart added: 'Sherry then came out (very drunk). . . . He said that Lord Buckingham and Fox were determined to stand by you, and that the more certainly to engage the P.'s honor he would either bring or send you tomorrow a letter from H.R.H.' (Viscount Sidmouth's MS.)

[1] When the King saw Grenville on 27 Jan. he demanded the plan of a new Cabinet to be laid before him by Friday morning (31 Jan.) at latest. The Prince claimed that the three separate interests (followers of Fox, Grenville, and Sidmouth) in the projected administration were only reconciled by his mediation (Alnwick MSS., LXIII, f. 55). S. was his negotiator with Sidmouth.

to Lord Buckinghamshire[1] everything that I was authorized to state to you. His Lordship I understand is to see the Marquess in the morning. There can be no better channel—I will wait on you again in the course of tomorrow. I think, (perhaps over-sanguinely), that everything is in a train for the good of the Country, and I feel no risk in pledging myself to the honor of These, who deputed me to speak to you and to the fidelity with which *they* will fulfill every measure or idea I referr'd to.— | I have the Honor to be | with sincerest regard and respect | your Lordship's | faithful Servant | R B Sheridan

566. To Richard Wilson

Salt MS. *Dock.*: Febry. 11th 1806 Sheridan. *Wm.*: 1804

Tuesday Evening
Feb. 11th [*1806*]

My Dear Dick—

Put your best Foot forward and fill up that Paper but from a respectable quarter—a friend good and true and such a one as I ought not to be ashamed to be obliged to—observe only £200 remains unfill'd, but if it is not done in the course of tomorrow or *before 4 on thursday* it will be of no use. I kiss hands tomorrow and must be off for Stafford[2] on thursday Evening, I have written to your *new master*,[3] rather a serious Letter on the subject of *Burgess*. He *promised* me after my first suggestion, of you and equally in the Prince's presence that he should have preference in the Patronage, and I hear of everything going and nothing thought of for him—putting my personal Friendship with Erskine out of the question, there are 26 years of Patronage due to me from

[1] Sidmouth wished Buckinghamshire to be in the Cabinet with him, and argued the matter with Fox and Grenville until late on 30 Jan. He then agreed to accept the suggestion (apparently coming from S.) that Ellenborough, the Lord Chief Justice, should be his nominee and associate in the Cabinet. See *Auckland Corr.* iv. 273.

[2] On taking office as Treasurer of the Navy, S. had to contest his parliamentary seat again. His appeal to Wilson seems to concern the theatrical loan. See p. 218, n. 2.

[3] Wilson was principal secretary to the Lord Chancellor, Thomas Erskine.

every department and so Fox admits.[1] | Yours ever truly | R B Sheridan

There is no finding you at home—and still less the Ladies

567. [To the Duke of Bedford]

N.L.S. MS. 4001, f. 11. Copy by R. D. Richardson.

Wednesday Feby. 12th 1806

My Dearest Lord

I cannot easily express (for without affectation I am a very unprofessing Man,) the Gratitude I feel for your Grace's most kind acceptation of my recommendation of my Son to your Patronage and Protection[2] I have reason to think that my Brother is hurt (and your Grace told me today that you were to see him tomorrow with General Fitzpatrick[3]), that I have not forwarded as far as any Interest I possess his claim, whatever it may be. I have the greatest good will to my Brother but The Object of my heart is my Son. Having been Thirty years a Whig Politician and Six and twenty years in Parliament, and having expended full £20,000 of my own money to maintain my seat there and in all the course of Political life struggling thro' great di[f]ficulties and risking the existence of the only Property I had, I am certain I have only to state the short preceding sentence to make your Grace to understand me distinctly on this subject. I have only to add that it ought not to have been left to me to make this application to the personal Friendship with which you have long honored me. But great indeed will be my gratification to owe the object I pursue *to that* and *that Alone* | I am Ever your Graces | most sincere and Devoted Friend and Servant | R B Sheridan

[1] Rae remarks (ii. 254): 'If the following passage in the *Biographical Index to the House of Commons*, published in 1808 be correct, then there was nothing mercenary in Sheridan's expectations: "Nor ought it to be forgotten, that it was proposed by Mr. Fox to render him independent for life, by the offer of a patent place of £2,000 per annum, which he had the magnanimity enough . . . to refuse".' S. said (Hansard, ix. 213) Fox proposed for S. the Chancellorship of the Duchy of Lancaster for life, but colleagues objected.

[2] The Duke of Bedford became Lord-Lieutenant of Ireland on 12 Feb.

[3] Richard Fitzpatrick was Secretary at War in All the Talents.

568. To C. J. Fox

W.T. There is a further copy (by R. D. Richardson) in N.L.S. MS. 4001, ff. 12–13. *Pub.*: W. F. Rae, 'More about Sheridan', *Nineteenth Century*, xliii (1898), 260–1.

[*17 Feb. 1806*]
Monday Night

Dear Fox,

I have seen this Evening Sergeant[1] and then Vansittart[2] and afterwards Lord Grenville—it is clear that that seat may be managed very easily—but not in time to be of any use to *me*.—I am a very uncomplaining person and seldom intrude on you but where I think it is for *your* service—but I do not like to have a dissatisfied thought in my mind respecting you unrevealed to you. I deny that Pigott[3] or any attorney General had a claim with *you* that ought to have superseded mine for a seat in parliament without expence but the present case is peculiarly hard and unjust. The Duke of Norfolk first applied thro' me that a provision should be made for Lloyd,[4] and in doing it he said (having always as you know, professed the greatest good will towards me) that '*then* there would be a vacant seat which I might take, if I wished to avoid the expence of Stafford, or it should be open to any of Mr. Fox's friends'—I told him that I thought the proposition perfectly reasonable, but that as[5] to myself it being understood that I would spend no more of my own money at

[1] John Sargent (*c.* 1750–1831) had been Joint Secretary to the Treasury in 1804.

[2] Nicholas Vansittart (1766–1851), Joint Secretary to the Treasury in All the Talents. He was one of Sidmouth's supporters, and later 1st Lord Bexley.

[3] Arthur Leary Pigott was appointed Attorney-General on 12 Feb. Romilly, Solicitor-General, wrote on 10 Feb.: 'Pigott told me today, that Mr. Fox had desired him to say that the administration would bring us both into parliament without any expense on our parts' (S. Romilly, *Memoirs* (ed. cit.), ii. 135).

[4] James Martin Lloyd (1762–1844), M.P. for Steyning, 1790–2, 1796–1818, was appointed Clerk of the Deliveries in the Ordnance Office. A new writ was issued for Steyning on 14 Feb. 1806. The Duke of Norfolk wrote to S. on 19 Feb.: 'The alteration proposed at Steyning is now impossible. Before I left London I suggested to Mr. Fox the pract[ic]ability of substituting *your* name for Sir A. Piggot but it is now too late for that. The election is fixed for Friday when Lord Ossulston and Sir A. Piggot I expect will be returned. . . . If Sir A. Piggot does not take the seat Mr. Loyd must resume it'. (N.L.S. MS. 4001, f. 9.)

[5] Richardson reads 'is'.

Stafford I relied on *you* that my seat should be properly managed.[1] The seat at Steyning in consequence became yours, but how? Not in consequence of your *administration* making a provision for Lloyd as they must have done to bring in their *attorney General* but in consequence of Lord Moira's giving up a place in his own immediate patronage which if he could otherwise have promoted Lord Forbes,[2] I have every reason to believe he would have given to my Son.—So rests the matter.—The House is to adjourn to-morrow (and would have adjourned today but for my accidentally hearing of Sir J. Newport's writ)[3] without the slightest thought of me who am now out of Parliament on a reliance which I thought could not possibly fail me, without pretence or means to keep Stafford any longer at my beck[4] and sincerely sorry that I have vacated my seat.[5] The pressing[6] *hurry* to bring in Pigott I venture to say is felt only by yourself—I know it is not by Lord Grenville and that he and Vansittart understand[7] that it is *their* business to provide him a seat, and I am sorry to say appear to feel the priority of my claim more than you do. I have now done with this subject respecting[8] which I shall not utter another word nor take another step. But being on the chapter of grievance which believe me Dear Fox with you is a very hateful discussion to me I will unpack my mind at once and once for all. I am allotted a place to which I think there is allotted a Duty if a part[9] is to be fairly supported, I mean of receiving and entertaining members whom the Cabinet cannot open

[1] The Stafford election expenses were paid by the Prince. See p. 284.

[2] George, Viscount Forbes (1785–1836), son of the Earl of Granard and nephew of Moira. S. wrote him some verses entitled, 'On being asked the Reason for the Author's Absence from Church'. See *Notes and Queries*, 11th Ser., x (1914), 83.

[3] John, 1st Baronet (1756–1843), was Chancellor of the Exchequer of Ireland in All the Talents. New writs for his constituency, Waterford, and for Stafford, were ordered on 18 Feb.

[4] R. D. Richardson reads 'back'.

[5] Fox tried to prevent Newport's writ being moved until the Prince had been consulted. Thomas Grenville correctly interpreted this as 'a new intrigue of Sheridan's to make the Prince's name a bar to Newport, and an introduction to Tierney' (*Dropmore Papers*, viii. 33–34). The Prince threatened to withdraw his support from the administration on 16 Feb., but Lord Grenville did not give way. See N.L.S. MS. 4001, f. 5.

[6] W.T. 'pregoing'.

[7] R. D. Richardson reads 'understood'.

[8] Omitted by R. D. Richardson.

[9] R. D. Richardson reads 'party'.

their houses to—of course if I mean to serve you fairly out of my office I cannot save one guinea. I tell you frankly that I take that office without the slightest feeling of obligation to anyone living perhaps I might say more—it is seventeen years since when you professed to me that I should not be content to accept that alone[1]—I come directly to my point—and that is *my Son*—I will not recapitulate to you the motives that independently of the dear affection I bear him influence me on this subject. In the Kings last illness,[2] when perhaps I was deemed of more *use* than the present *famed*[3] administration may estimate, I had a very distinct pledge from you that Tom should be taken care of.—All our *mutual friends Men and Women* cried out Tom must be provided for—how does it end? You turn me over with a note to Lord Grenville,[4] which ends by a letter from him to ask a place from me for a friend of his, meaning no doubt to inform me that he had no patronage that could serve my son. In one word if nothing can be done for my Son The *Grenville Administration* are perfectly welcome to dispose of my office[5] | Yours ever Sincerely | R. B. Sheridan

On the subject of Sir J. Newport I have spoke with Lord G —it *must* remain as it is. I need not say his object will be to reconcile the Prince to it.

569. To Lord Grenville

Pub.: *Dropmore Papers*, viii. 37.

February 18, 1806

I wish to have the honour of waiting on your Lordship to-morrow between two and four, wherever you shall appoint. It is with great satisfaction that I have it in my power to assure you that the business respecting Sir John Newport's appointment was terminated at Carlton House in a manner that I think must be pleasing to you. You will probably have

[1] See i. 207, n. 1.

[2] Feb.–Apr. 1804.

[3] Richardson's reading. W.T. has 'formed'.

[4] Printed in *Dropmore Papers*, viii. 32.

[5] In his reply of 'Tuesday' (Osborn MS.) Fox said that S'.s letter vexed him exceedingly. Fox intended to look about him for a way of serving Tom S. but had 'no hopes of doing it instantaneously'. Cf. *Nineteenth Century*, xliii. 262–3.

received an account of it from Mr. Grattan, or Mr. G. Ponsonby;[1] but in the humble and sincere hope that these differences, so vitally mischievous in their report, may at once and finally be put an end to, I feel that I am serving the general cause in requiring a short, frank, conversation with your Lordship.

I am ashamed to have forgot when I saw you to have said that your recommendation respecting Mr. Ottey[2] shall be attended to by me with the most respectful consideration.

570. 'Instructions to my Canvassing Representatives Messrs T. Sheridan W Downes and R Peake'

Robert H. Taylor MS. *Pub.*: *The Princeton University Library Chronicle*, xxi (1960), 213. *Dock.*: Sheridan

[*1806?*]

Let the Billets be given into every *man's own Hand* after Promise on the Canvass—but let it be understood that what is further necessary will also be done—

You are to convey to me a List each Day of the Men receiving the Billets—

Make the Billets up as you travel—

Take the Bull-Ring[3] nightly if nobody opposes you—

Be careful on no account to get tipsy unless it be with Wine Punch or Ale—

571. To Richard Peake

McAdam MS. *Address*: Mr. Richd. Peake | Stafford *Fr.*: R B Sheridan *Pm.*: FE 18 806 *Wm.*: 1805

Tuesday
Feby. 18th: *1806*

My Dear Peake,

Ward and his *Drops*[4] set out by tomorrows mail and with

[1] George Ponsonby (1755–1817), Lord Chancellor of Ireland.

[2] P. E. Ottey is named as chief clerk in the Allotment office of the Navy Office, in *Rider's British Merlin* (1806), p. 160; and in the *Royal Kalendar* (1807), p. 161.

[3] At Stafford.

[4] Money to pay the burgesses £5 each for a vote? On this and 'billets' (for dinner and ale), see Rae, i. 354–5.

the writ also. I should go with them but am settling into Somerset house,[1] but shall follow as fast as possible—bravo Major! Remember me warmly to all Friends if practicable we *will* have a Day at Ricatscourt[2] | Yours ever | R B Sheridan

my writ was moved to Day

572. To Richard Peake

Osborn MS. *Address*: Mr. Peake

[*26 Feb. 1806*]

Again not a Line from you or Burgess

Ward will explain the absolute impossibility of my coming—let me see how well you manage. Fast Day no money to be got[3] you shall have enough to leave not a shilling due in Stafford | R B S

573. 'To the Independent Electors of Stafford'

Pub.: *Staff. Adv.*, 1 Mar. 1806.

London, February 26, 1806.

Gentlemen,

[It i]s[4] with feelings of the sincerest regret and [m]ortification, that I find myself unexpect[edly] prevented from the pleasure of paying my [respe]cts to you at Stafford, and personally [beg]ging your suffrages for the approaching [elec]tion. The duties of my Office render my [atten]dance at the Bank of England on Friday [   ] the 28th instant, absolutely indispensible.[5] [I h]ave endeavoured by every means to pro[vide] against this disappointment to my wishes, [but] find it absolutely impossible.

[I] need not express how much I am flattered [by t]he

[1] The residence in Somerset Place attached to the office of Treasurer of the Navy.

[2] Rickerscote, Stafford, was the home of Thomas Perkins, S.'s warm supporter.

[3] 26 Feb. 1806 was observed as a general fast: see *Gent. Mag.* lxxvi (1806), 176.

[4] Faulty printing.

[5] On 18 Mar. 1806 the Earl of Essex wrote to Viscount Lowther: 'I heard of Sheridan appearing before the Bank Directors to open his Navy office account, the joke is that they all ran out of the room carrying away their books and papers, etc.' (H.M.C., *13th Rep.*, VII, p. 181).

anxiety of so many steady Friends to [have] had me among them; at the same time I [am] confident that my unavoidable absence under [these] circumstances will not lessen me in your [estee]m, nor abate from that cordial support and [hono]rable zeal in my behalf, which I have [const]antly experienced from you thro' the [tim]e of five successive Parliaments.[1]

[At] an early period in this summer, you may [count] upon my visiting Stafford, when I shall have [the le]isure, as well as the satisfaction to prove [to yo]u the unalterable regard, with which I [shall] ever remain, | Your obliged and devoted Servant, | R. B. Sheridan.

574. To George Tierney

Mrs. L. A. H. Wright MS. *Address*: The Right Honble. | George Tierney | Hertford-St *Fr.*: R B Sheridan *Dock.*: Mr. Sheridan

March 2d:
1806

Dear Tierney

I write you a short Letter with great Frankness, and have since we met destroy'd with Pleasure a detail'd remonstrance very painful to me to make and which I fear would not have been satisfactory to you to have received.[2]—I acted under the impression that there was something little short of intentional incivility to me the Day I call'd at your Door three times and would have waited your coming in the last time if your servant had not discouraged me, but I am willing to suppose I was mistaken. The accidental yet I trust satisfactory explanation that we had in the Street, renders it unnecessary for me to say more respecting myself than to repeat that you ought to have known me better than to have believed for a moment that I could have given you reason to consider me, as far as my wishes were of any importance, as one earnestly[3] desirous that you should ally with us, under

[1] He was re-elected, without opposition, on 28 Feb.

[2] H. K. Olphin (*George Tierney* (1934), p. 102) states that Tierney was disappointed when Petty became Chancellor of the Exchequer in All the Talents, and that his only resource was to appeal to the Prince (through S.) for support.

[3] From this point, H. K. Olphin (op. cit., p. 102) quotes four sentences of the letter.

the Prince's auspices, upon the new arrangements in the manner most satisfactory to yourself, and at the same time to have done any one thing inconsistent with my Professions.[1] I was as I told you the first Person to set right the false idea of the Duke of Bedfords objecting to you, and to state the reverse to be the Fact. And with the sincerest alacrity I endeavour'd to execute the Prince's commands to obtain such a re-modelling of the arrangements as might have met his Royal Highness's most anxious and eager desire that he should be gratified by obtaining what was so near his heart, the fulfilment of your claim upon his Friendship. I can only add to this that (which I did not tell you when I met you), impress'd with this conviction I took upon myself to go down to the House of commons on the monday when I had accidentally heard that Sir John Newport's writ was to be moved, and procured its being postponed and the adjournment too, with the hope that even a Day's Delay might produce the accomplishment of the Prince's wishes on this subject, and of your own.[2]

Putting myself out of the Question, I have only to add one observation which is better done abruptly than ceremoniously—if you doubt the entire Friendship of the Prince's conduct *towards you* misinformation will make you appear most unjust and ungrateful which I am sure is not in your nature or character—It would be presumption in me to offer you advice, but I sincerely hope to see you again together as I have seen you. | with great esteem and regard | yours very truly | R B Sheridan

575. To Sir Robert Barclay

Harvard MS. *Address*: Sir Robert Barclay Bart. | Parliament St. *Wm.*: 17/

Sunday
March 9 [*1806?*]

My Dear Barclay

Sir M B[3] promised to discount me £500 the enclosed is

[1] Cf. p. 262, n. 5.

[2] Probably Tierney would have been contented with Newport's office, Chancellor of the Exchequer of Ireland. The *Morn. Chron.*, 10 Mar. 1806, reported a rumour that Tierney was to be Governor of the Cape of Good Hope.

[3] Bloxam.

as good as the Bank—a Gentleman of £3000[1] per ann Petitioner for Boston[2]—my wifes relation. The service to me will be my having the money in the course of tomorrow morning— | Yours ever | R B S

I have received Sir M's Letters and do not lose sight of the business

576. To the Duke of Bedford

Pub.: W. F. Rae, 'More about Sheridan', *Nineteenth Century*, xliii (1898), 260. Rae's text is from a rough draft. Cf. S.C., 25 May 1954, lot 278.

[*Mar. 1806*]

With regard to my personal feelings on this subject and the motives which make it to me such an object, I have spoken to you with frankness and sincerity, and greatly was I gratified to perceive that your private friendship for me took an interest in them; and to that and to the Prince's unbounded goodness to me on this as well as every other occasion did I hope alone to owe the accomplishment of my wishes with regard to my son, without pressing them as a claim on political connexion, or to an Administration upon so leading a part of which I have no claim at all. But when, my dear Lord, 'political considerations essential to be attended to'[3] are urged against my plea, and what indeed I thought I had your Grace's authority to consider as my accepted claim, I feel it would be a baseness in me not to

[1] The figuring is careless, and the '3' may be a '9'.

[2] John Ogle petitioned against the return of Thomas Fydell, junior, as member for Boston, on 27 May 1803. Consideration of the petition was eventually deferred to the following session, but it was not then renewed. See T. H. B. Oldfield, *The Representative History of Great Britain and Ireland* . . . (1816), iv. 150.

[3] On 26 Feb. the Duke of Bedford informed S. that he had been with Fox and had arranged everything to S.'s satisfaction: 'Tom will have what you wished for *him*'. On 10 Mar. Bedford wrote to S. to say that '. . . political considerations essential to be attended to, will stand in the way of Tom Sheridan's having the situation I designed and wish'd for him, viz. the half of Lord Lincoln's Place. I wish to know whether he or you would object to a Situation for him which would make a residence in Ireland necessary . . .' (N.L.S. MS. 4001, f. 10). See also *Dropmore Papers*, viii. 84.

assert my confidence that no mark of *Irish* favour conferred on *me* or any of *my family* would be unpopular in *Ireland*,[1] or considered as a distribution of patronage hostile to the 'political considerations essential to be attended to' for the honour and interests of that country.[2]

I bow with all possible respect to the pretensions of the great families in Ireland who, *previous to the Union*, possessed or contended for the patronage of her government, and no man living can feel more strongly than I do the claims of the few who have faithfully acted with the Whig party in England. At the same time I feel it no boast or conceit to say, adverting to the change made by the Union and the manifest disposition of the Irish to look now to the Prince, that any person honoured with his confidence and understanding his purposes on this great subject, and being himself an Irishman, is not guilty of great presumption in wishing to connect himself more manifestly with Ireland, or at least in being desirous to know the merits which are to supersede his pretensions.

As to poor Tom's personal claims, let them pass. He refused without consulting me,[3] and while indeed I was in the country, a friendly offer from Lord St. Vincent in Addington's Administration, that perhaps might have made his fortune, because he would not thwart what he knew to be my principle to receive no favour directly or indirectly from that Government. If I were to die to-morrow, worth however little, he would be at least £20,000 the worse for my election expenses in thirty years' party service, and that my line of party politics having placed me in a[4]

[1] *The Times*, 5 Mar. 1806, reported that 'Captain Sheridan, (the Son of the Treasurer of the Navy) is the new Muster-Master-General in Ireland. It is something about £1000 or £1200 per annum.' This was obviously what S. wanted for his son, but the office was actually taken with Denis Bowes Daly.

[2] See *Nineteenth Century*, xliii. 259.

[3] In 1803 St. Vincent offered Tom S. the valuable post of Registrar of the Vice-Admiralty Court of Malta, but S. persuaded his son to decline it. See Hansard, 1st Ser., xxiii. 611, 618; Moore, ii. 313. For the other place that S. made Tom S. refuse, see Moore, *Journal*, ii. 318.

[4] The draft ends here.

577. To Richard Fitzpatrick

Add. MS. 47582, ff. 245–6. *Address*: Right Honble: | Richd. Fitzpatrick

[*12 Mar. 1806?*]
Wednesday Evening

My Dear Fitzpatrick

If you will go to bed at ½ *after* eleven which was precisely the time I was at your door to Night—I have a right to assume that I do not interrupt your rest by directing the inclosures[1] to be delivered to you at *nine* tomorrow morning.—Your running your eye thro' them however hastily will explain all I could say in an interview. Pray see Fox *before the meeting* at *Lord* Spencer's. I need say no more to you, who cannot but understand me at a word.—I will give up and sacrifice everything rather than embarrass *him* or the *Duke of Bedford*, but if my son is to be sacrific'd to Ponsonby-rapacity it is a different case—and that alone I conceive to be the question. I know I have done honourably in avoiding any commu[n]ication with the Prince on this subject. It could lead only to irritation which might perhaps secure my individual object, but be of public mischief. All I desire of you is to request of Fox to stay out the meeting tomorrow which I understand was not the case at the last.

excuse my intruding on you this my private business—and sure I am that you will not consider it as an ill compliment that I do so.

I need not add that I commit to you the enclosures in the exclusive confidence of Friendship | yours ever truly | R B Sheridan

[1] Probably S.'s correspondence with Fox and Bedford on finding a position for Tom S. Bedford's third letter (W.T.) is dated 'Wednesday Morn: 8 oClock A.M.' and seems to belong to 12 Mar. He acknowledges a note from S. received on the previous day, and is sorry that S. has been misled into thinking that his son had been given a post: '. . . it could not be so, until the meeting for definitely settling the Irish arrangement had taken place. . . .' He also apologizes for forgetting that S. had told him it was impossible for Tom S. to reside in Ireland, and congratulates S. on now allowing his son to take a leading share in the management of D.L.Th. He adds a postscript: 'We have another meeting at Spencer House tomorrow, and it will afford me heartfelt satisfaction if I have anything pleasing to communicate to you.'

578. [To Richard Fitzpatrick?]

Pub.: Morrison Cat., vi. 127.

[*13 Mar. 1806?*]
Thursday evening[1]

Until an hour after I call'd on you this evening I did not receive your note. I thank you for it. It is very grateful to me to feel that I have only to intimate anything interesting to my happiness to assure your assisting my object. Pray send me back the papers I enclosed to you. I have occasion for them *early in the morning*.

579. To His Wife

Pub.: Rae, ii. 255–6.

[*1806?*]

I saw that the only way to effect it[2] was through the Prince, and I went immediately to him. You know that there has been always a distance not to say dislike between him and Grey. I never omitted an opportunity to remove this. I urged to him the good on every account of convincing Grey of his good-will towards him and gaining his personal attachment. Whitbread had stated that the thing would be most grateful. I represented to him that if anything were to happen to Fox and me, both as his Minister and private friend, he would look nowhere for anyone to be put in competition with Grey. The P. adopted the whole idea most cheerfully, and assured me he would propose it to Grey at D House in the evening and afterwards make a point of it.

[1] Cf. S.C., 18 Jan. 1877, lot 209: 'To Robert Fitzgerald: Tuesday evening. "Is very grateful to feel that he has only to intimate anything interesting to his happiness, to assure his having his object assisted." '

[2] Rae declares (ii. 255) that S. 'was personally active in the advancement of Lord Grey, who had been created Baron Grey de Howick on the 27th of June, 1801, to the rank of Viscount Howick and Earl Grey, and who would not apply to Fox for the promotion desired'. This refers to Sir Charles Grey (1729–1807), who became Viscount Howick and 1st Earl Grey on 11 Apr. 1806: but S.'s allusions in his letter are to Charles Grey, who succeeded to the peerage after his father's death in 1807.

Observe he was not asked for one tittle for anyone himself. This he has accordingly done, and I have no doubt it will succeed. He must have the exclusive merit of it with Grey, who of course must know nothing about me in the matter.

580. [To Benjamin West?][1]

Hyde MS. [Ph.]

[*1806?*]
Somerset Place
Sunday

My Dear Sir

I am confident the Prince will be greatly gratified in going to Newman St. for the Satisfaction of seeing your admirable Picture for such it is represented to be by all who have had that Pleasure. And if you are not afraid of a latish hour Mrs. Sheridan will be happy to see you tomorrow evening when we shall have an opportunity of fixing a time with His Royal Highness. | Your obedient Servant | R B Sheridan

581. To W. L. Bowles

Pub.: *A Wiltshire Parson and His Friends: The Correspondence of W. L. Bowles* (ed. G. Greever, 1926), p. 92. Cf. S.C., 23 Mar. 1936, lot 421.

April 10th [*1806?*]

Dear Mr. Bowles,

I have spoken to Tom[2] who says you are too late for this year, as all the glees have been presented some time, but that for another year all you have to do is to send whatever you wish to be presented to Knyvett,[3] and it is certain of taking

[1] Benjamin West, P.R.A. (1738–1820), lived in Newman Street and exhibited there, in 1806, his painting 'The Death of Lord Nelson'. Farington reported (iii. 269) a conversation with West in which the painter claimed that by 2 July 1806 thirty thousand people had been to see the picture.

[2] By an indenture dated 1 Mar. 1806 S. sold Tom S. a quarter share in D.L.Th. 'in consideration of the natural love and affection he had for his son, and in consideration of five shillings'. See the indenture made between S. and the D.L.Th. Company of Proprietors on 5 May 1813 (New York Public Library MS.).

[3] Either Charles Knyvett (1773–1859) or William Knyvett (1779–1856). Both organized concerts and sang glees.

its fair chance. I am particularly disappointed at this, as I shall not now be at liberty to sing the glee which after all I *stole*, and which I think quite beautiful, but which upon my honor I have shewn to nobody, nor will I without your express permission. I am still at Fenton's Hotel, St. James St.,[1] consequently have not yet been able to make use of my dear Purcell. When I do get settled, I will make up for time lost. Pray give my best regards to Mrs. Bowles, and believe me, | Yrs. very truly, | R. B. Sheridan.

582. To Earl Spencer

Earl Spencer MS. Text from Lord Spencer's transcription.

April 19th 1806.

My Lord

At the request of the Callico-Printers I take the liberty of informing your Lordship that I have more than once had an opportunity of thoroughly considering the case of the Callico-Trade and the differences which have so long existed between the Journeymen and the masters[2]—and that in my humble judgement it is a matter well deserving your Lordship's attention and if necessary the interposition of Parliament. I have twice brought the subject before the House of Commons and I had hoped that I had succeeded in bringing about a compromise and a good understanding between the parties, but finding that that has not been effected I beg leave earnestly to recommend to your Lordship's kind consideration the Petition of the Poor men whose cause I had espoused, conceiving it to be a properer course than under the present circumstances renewing my individual exertions in their behalf in Parliament | I have the honor to be | with great respect and esteem | your Lordship's obedient Servant | R B Sheridan

Earl Spencer

[1] S. stayed there in Oct. 1806. See p. 286, n. 2.

[2] The journeymen sought to prevent the masters from taking on too many apprentices, because they provided the masters with an excuse for turning out men who had spent seven years in the trade. See S.'s speeches in the Commons on 27 June 1805 and 23 Apr. 1807 (Hansard, 1st Ser., ii. 858: ix. 534–7).

583. To His Son Tom

Add. MS. 42720, ff. 7–8. *Address*: T. Sheridan Esq. *Dock.*: Agreement with C.G.

Somerset-Place
May 14th 1806.

My Dear Tom,

In consequence of a very serious discussion which took place not long since between Mr. Graham and me respecting the absolute necessity of adhering strictly to the honourable Performance of the agreement so solemnly enter'd into[1] and renew'd between the Theatres I have received from him the enclosed Paper. I imagine that he must have conceived from what pass'd that my mind was not entirely free from apprehension that owing to his zeal for Drury-Lane some aberration from the compact might have arisen on his Part. This was not my meaning at the same time I confess I was reluctant to believe that without the slightest Provocation on our Part Convent-Garden Theatre could have broke all faith and treated us as it has done—The case now speaks for itself. I send the Paper to you, as I hear you are to have a meeting, to use as you please. | yours ever[?] | R B Sheridan

584. To Richard Wilson

Robert E. Keighton MS. [Ph.] *Address*: R. Wilson Esq Lincoln's Inn Fields *Fr.*: R B Sheridan *Dock.*: Given to me by Mr. Wilson to whom it is (by Mr. Sheridan) Addressed. J.D. 1806.

1806
Somerset Place
Sunday

My Dear Dick

Tom gives a small theatrical Dinner here tomorrow to the Harris's[2] and John Phillip,[3] reconciliation the order of the Day | Yours ever | R B S

[1] On 25 Sept. 1803, at Kemble's house, S., Tom S., and A. Graham for D.L.Th., and Thomas Harris and J. P. Kemble for C.G.Th. renewed the managers' pledge of 1788 to act together to maintain their just monopoly. They had also agreed about free admissions and one form of articles to be used in engaging performers. See Add. MS. 42720, f. 5.

[2] Thomas Harris, manager of Covent Garden Theatre, and his son Henry.

[3] Kemble.

585. To Nathaniel Ogle

Yale MS.

[*1806?*]

Dear Nat,

leave off Wine ale and spirituous Liquors. To bed by Times and rise early.[1] Addict yourself to Tonics in short follow the example of Yours | truly | R B S

Be your disorder fix'd or chronic
In either case your cure's a Tonic
Instead of scottish Drawling be laconic.
But what can aid the change—a Tonic
Corinthian peers scorn mass Ionic.
Yet noble nerves require a Tonic
Tho' no great Songster—be harmonic
Your voice and ear but need a Tonic.
Reply in verse—in verse Adonic
Then I shall know you've ta'en a Tonic.

586. To John Graham[2]

Pierpont Morgan Library MS.

[*13 Sept. 1806*]
Saturday Night

Dear Graham.

I am now both well enough[3] to see you and open to speak on the subject of the Vacancy in Westminster by our irreparable Loss[4] the slightest hopes of whose recovery have seal'd my Lips. There have been scandalous tricks play'd too long to explain now—but we must be alert if we wish to

[1] Lady E. Foster noted shortly after Fox's death that S. limited himself to a pint of Port wine at dinner, and had reproached Fitzpatrick for being in bed at 10.30 a.m. See D. M. Stuart, *Dearest Bess* (1955), p. 152.

[2] He was the unsuccessful candidate (against Fox) at the Westminster election of 1802, and after Fox had been re-elected on 13 Feb. 1806, eulogized S. and Tom S. as suitable representatives. See *The Times*, 14 Feb. 1806.

[3] Creevey reports that S. had a sore throat, was shivering, and had a 'frightful' pulse late at night on 11 Sept. (*Creevey Papers*, i. 84).

[4] Fox had died at 5.45 p.m. on 13 Sept.

have a chance that Fox should be succeeded by a Foxite. You will greatly oblige by laying other things aside and meet a few Friends at my House tomorrow (*sunday*) at *one*. I shall send this by express to be given you by 8 in the morning. | R B S

587. [To Richard Wilson][1]

W.T. *Pub.*: Moore, ii. 340–3.

Somerset Place,
September 14 [*1806*]

Dear ——

You must have seen by my manner yesterday, how much I was surprised and hurt at learning for the first time, that Lord Grenville had many days previous to Mr. Fox's death, decided to support Lord Percy[2] on the expected vacancy for Westminster, and that you had since been the active Agent in the Canvas actually commenced. I do not like to think I have grounds to complain or change my opinion of any friend without being very explicit and opening my mind without reserve on such a subject, I must frankly declare that I think you have brought yourself and me into a very unpleasant dilemma. You seemed to say last night, that you had not been apprized of my intention to offer for Westminster on the apprehended vacancy, I am confident you have acted under that impression, but I must impute to you either great inattention to what fell from me in our last conversation on the subject, or great inac[c]uracy of recollection, for I solemnly protest I considered you as the individual most distinctly apprized, that at this moment to succeed that

[1] As the Duke of Northumberland's 'solicitor and confidential man of business' (Kelly, ii. 250) Wilson was the intermediary between Grenville and Northumberland. On 12 Sept. the Duke wrote to Howick: 'Lord Grenville having signified it to me thro' Mr. Wilson, that it was the wish of Government that Lord Percy should offer himself as a Candidate for the representation of Westminster, I consented to it. . . . I have sent an express to the Moors, where Lord Grey now is, and trust he will reach Town at latest on Tuesday next' (Grey MS.). Northumberland and Grenville both thought they were obliging the other, and Grenville was under the impression that S. would not stand. See Moore, ii. 339.

[2] Hugh Percy, afterwards 3rd Duke of Northumberland (1785–1847).

great Man and revered Friend in Westminster should the fatal event take place, would be the highest object of my ambition,[1] for in that conversation I thanked you expressly for informing me, that Lord Grenville had said to yourself upon Lord Percy being suggested to him that he, Lord Grenville '*would decide on nothing untill Mr. Sheridan had been spoken to and his intentions known*' or words precisely to that effect—I expressed my grateful sense of Lord Grenvilles attention and said that it would confirm me in my intention of making no application, however hopeless myself respecting Mr. Fox while life remained with him, and these words of Lord Grenville you allowed last night to have been so stated to me, tho not as a message from his Lordship. Since that time I think we have not happened to meet at least sure I am we have had no conversation on the subject. Having the highest opinion of Lord Grenvilles honor and sincerity, I must be confident that he must have had another impression made on his mind respecting my wishes before I was entirely pass'd by—I do not mean to say that my offering myself was immediately to entitle me to the support of Government, but I do mean to say that my pretentions were entitled to consideration before that support was offered to another without the slightest notice taken of me, the more especially as the words of Lord Grenville reported by you to me had been stated by me to many friends as my reliance and justification in not following their advice by making a direct application to Government—I pledged myself to them that Lord Grenville would not promise the support of Government[2] till my intentions had been asked, and I quoted your authority for doing so, I never heard a Syllable of that support being promised to Lord Percy untill from you on the evening of Mr. Fox's death. Did I ever authorize you to inform Lord Grenville that I had abandoned the idea of offering myself? there are points which it is necessary for the honor of all Parties should be amicably

[1] These statements prove that Cobbett's suspicion that there had been a secret understanding between S. and Wilson was unfounded: and that the Duke's supporters were wrong when they thought (as in Alnwick MSS., LXIII, f. 256) that Percy's nomination was 'an Electioneering Trick, merely to save Sheridan an useless Expence'.

[2] The words, 'would . . . Government', are missing in W.T. and are supplied by Moore.

explained, I therefore propose as the shortest way of effecting it, wishing you not to consider this letter as in any degree confidential that my statements in this letter may be submitted to any two Common Friends, or to the Lord Chancellor alone, and let it be ascertained where the Error has arisen, for Error is all I complain of, and with regard to Lord Grenville I desire distinctly to say that I feel myself indebted for the fairness and kindness of his intentions towards me.

my disappointment of the Protection of Government, may be sufficient excuse to the Friends I am pledged to should I retire,[1] but I must have it understood whether or not I deceived them when I led them to expect that I should have that support | I hope to remain | Ever yours sincerely | R B Sheridan

The sooner the Reference
I propose the better.

588. To Viscount Howick

Grey MS. *Dock.*: Mr. Sheridan | Septr. ye 16. 1806.

Somerset-Place
Sept. 16th. 1806.

Dear Grey,

I enclose you a Copy of my Letter to Wilson which cer-

[1] At a meeting at the Crown and Anchor on 18 Sept., S. seemed to be the probable choice but, after eulogizing Fox, he withdrew in favour of Lord Percy. The Prince had instructed McMahon 'to exercise all my influence over Mr. Sheridan to preserve every thing quiet at a moment like the present' (*Dropmore Papers*, viii. 339). The manner in which this was done is to be gathered from the Duke of Northumberland's letter to Howick of 20 Sept. 1806: 'I understand . . . from Lord Moira, that he has persuaded Mr. Sheridan not to offer himself' (Grey MS.). The following passage in S.'s hand seems to have been written out by him for this occasion and the voice of a friend: 'That the long and faithful services of Mr. S. in Parliament, his uniform support of all the Principles and measures which recommended our late illustrious Mem[b]er to our confidence and affection, his almost unrivall'd Talents and his devoted attachment to his great departed Friend do eminently qualify him—to succeed Mr. Fox as Member for Westminster. At the same time this meeting cannot but acquiesce in the motives which induce him to withdraw himself on the present occasion in the sanguine hope that upon a future opportunity they may be enabled to manifest the high sense the[y] entertain of his merits. . . .' (Osborn MS.)

tainly contains what pass'd between *him* and *me*. I could have remark'd the other day, but that it would have been an ill opportunity, when you informed me that Lord Grenville had ask'd you, previous to sending to Lord Percy,[1] whether you knew if I wish'd to offer myself, and that you had answer'd that you believed not for you had not heard me mention it I could have remarked that had I been in your Place and You in mine I should have answer'd 'I do not [know] but I will send to him and ask him'. This would have saved me very great embar[r]assment and mortification However believe me I am convinced that you did not intend me any slight or that my Pretensions, such as they were, should be pass'd by with contempt and disregard.

I shall endeavour to see Lord Grenville to Day to convince him that I never can or will be the cause of any mischievous difference of opinion[2] being formed respecting the Proceedings of his Government even on so unimportant a subject as its conduct towards me.[3] | ever Your's Faithfully | R B Sheridan

589. To Lord Grenville

George Fortescue MS. Text from Dr. Arthur Aspinall's transcription. *Pub.*: Moore, ii. 343–5.

Somerset Place, 16th September 1806.

My Dear Lord,

Since I had the honour of your Lordship's letter I have received one from Mr. Wilson in which I am sorry to observe he is silent as to my offer of meeting in the presence of a third person in order to ascertain whether *he* did or not

[1] In his letter to the Duke of Northumberland of 10 Sept. Howick had said he had 'heard it intimated that Lord Percy might possibly have a view to the representation of the City of Westminster. should this be so, not a moment should be lost in his appearing in Person . . . he may depend upon receiving all the assistance that I can give him'. (Add. MS. 31158, f. 199.)

[2] Lady Bessborough reported that S. made a great merit of his withdrawal and that he believed he could have carried the election 'against Lord Percy and all the Ministers put together' (*Leveson Gower Corr.* ii. 212).

[3] Lord Holland thought there was too much disposition among the leaders of the administration to defy S. and blamed Grey, who had 'perhaps, neglected *consulting* persons somewhat too much' (Holland, ii. 62).

so *report* a conversation with your Lordship as to impress on my mind a belief that my pretensions would be considered before the support of Government should be pledged elsewhere; instead of this he only[1] does not admit the *precise words* quoted by me, but does not state what he allows he did say: if he denies that he ever gave me reason to adopt the belief I have stated be it so, but the only stipulation I have made is that we should come to as explicit an understanding[2] on this subject, not with a view to quoting words or repeating names, but that the misapprehension whatever it was may be so admitted as not to leave me under an unmerited degree of discredit and disgrace. Mr. Wilson certainly never encouraged me to stand for Westminster, but on the contrary advised me to support Lord Percy, which made me the more mark at the time the fairness with which I thought he apprised me of the preference my pretensions were likely to receive in your Lordship's consideration.

Unquestionably your Lordship's recollection of what passed between Mr. Wilson and yourself must be just, and were it no more than what you said on the same subject to Lord Howick I consider it as a mark of attention, but what has astonished me is that Mr. Wilson should ever have informed your Lordship, as he admits he did, that I had no intention of offering myself. This naturally must have put from your mind whatever degree of disposition was there to have made a preferable application to me, and Lord Howick's answer to your question, on which I have ventured to make a friendly remonstrance, must have confirmed Mr. Wilson's report. But allow me to suppose that I had myself seen your Lordship and that you had explicitly promised me the support of Government and had afterwards sent for me and informed me that it was at all an object to you that I should give way to Lord Percy, I assure you, with the utmost sincerity, that I should cheerfully have withdrawn myself and applied every interest I possessed as your Lordship should have directed.

All I request is that what has passed between *me* and Mr. *Wilson* may take an intelligible shape before any common

[1] Moore reads 'he not only does not'.

[2] Moore reads 'to an explicit understanding'.

friend or before your Lordship. This I conceive to be a preliminary due to my own honour and what he ought not to evade:[1] I shall write to him again on the subject and I trust the proposal may have the sanction of your Lordship's recommendation.

I beg you a thousand pardons for so long intruding on your time, and have the honour,

590. To the Prince of Wales

Windsor MSS. 40724–5. *Dock.*: Mr. Sheridan | Septr. 22. 1806

Monday
Sept. 22d. 1806

Sir,

It is impossible for me to express my gratitude for the manner in which your royal Highness has been graciously pleased to express yourself concerning me in some passages of your late Letters to Colonel McMahon. The Devotion of my Life would not repay all I have long owed to you and it is a Debt you are pleased to continue to encrease. I shall humbly take the Freedom to touch on this subject again tomorrow or next Day as well as to say a word or two on the Westminster business—a subject on which no human consideration should have induced me to have occasion'd your Royal Highness one moments uneasy sensation.

As I know the Ministers write by this Post to your Royal Highness I need not recapitulate the new arrangements. Wyndham[2] positively refusing the Peerage it would have been difficult to have made another Arrangement—As Grey could not but have the Lead in the House of Commons. If Tierney goes to the Board of Controul[3] I presume the Salary will be mended—I shall be very glad to find that he is entirely satisfied. Whitbread's understood reason for declining to be secretary at war is curious indeed![4] Lord Howick and

[1] Moore's version breaks off here.

[2] Windham refused three times before the matter was dropped: see *Dropmore Papers*, viii. xxxvi–xxxvii, 340–5.

[3] He did.

[4] Sidmouth wrote to Bathurst on 26 Sept. to say that Whitbread was now disposed to become Secretary at War without the Cabinet, 'on which he had before insisted' (Viscount Sidmouth MS.).

Lord Grenville were particularly civil to me in their manner of communicating what was going on.

I entreat your Royal Highness to excuse my breaking off abruptly and with the most ardent wishes for your health and happiness | I have the honor to be | ever Your faithful and dutiful Servant | R B Sheridan

His Royal Highness The Prince of Wales.

591. To Viscount Howick

Grey MS. *Dock.*: Mr Sheridan | Septr. ye 23d 1806

23 Sept. 1806
Somerset Place
Tuesday morn 8 oclock

Dear Grey

I really cannot say how you will oblige me by turning a favourable eye on my two little jobbs.[1] McMahon will tell you that the Prince interests himself very much in young Harris—so it will please *him* too—and Graham will get a Fortune for his Children.

I saw Lord Grenville after I left you. I think every thing seems tight and strong.[2] I wish you joy on very many accounts— | Yours faithfully | R B Sheridan

592. To the Prince of Wales

Windsor MSS. 40731–2. *Dock.*: Mr. Sheridan *Wm.*: 1805

Somerset Place
September 24th 1806

Sir

It may not be immaterial to your Royal Highness to know that Mr. Fox's Funeral,[3] which I am informed your Royal Highness has an intention of honouring with your attendance, is postponed from tuesday the 7th of next month

[1] Howick was First Lord of the Admiralty, but now became Foreign Secretary.

[2] Changes in the ministry were settled on 21 Sept.

[3] S. was in charge of all the arrangements for the funeral.

to Friday the 10th. That being the anniversary of his first election for Westminster. I know not on what Day your Royal Highness proposed returning[1] but I apprehended that the time fix'd for this solemnity might in some degree regulate it. We have had a long meeting this morning respecting the arrangement of the ceremony and Procession —and they have referr'd it to me to form a plan for that purpose, I should think it fortunate were I in the way of explaining my ideas to your Royal Highness, and having the advantage of your advice and superior Judgement, but your Royal Highness's Letters are just going so that I must defer submitting to you the Plan which it is in my mind to propose until tomorrow, when I may also have the opportunity of informing your Royal Highness of the manner in which the new arrangements are received by the Public in general and particularly by the Foxites.— | I have the Honor to be | with the truest Devotion | Your Royal Highness's | Dutiful Servant | R B Sheridan

His Royal Highness
The Prince of Wales

593. To Richard Peake

Salt MS. *Address*: Winchester October first 1806 | Mr. Peake | Charlotte-st. | Rathbone-Place | London *Fr.*: R B Sheridan

1 Oct. 1806
Winchester[2]
Wednesday

My Dear Peake

Here I am in high health and Spirits—pray pray manage not to damp me on the Score of the Renters, getting me thro' with credit in this is of boundless importance. Keep all Friends back you can till next Payment—and don't scruple

[1] The Prince had left London on 25 Aug. to visit Wroxton Abbey, Ragley, and Knowsley. When the above letter was written he was with Earl Fitzwilliam at Doncaster. See *Dropmore Papers*, viii. 356.

[2] S. and Mrs. S., with Tom S. and his wife, were staying at Sir Chaloner Ogle's and attending the Winchester Music Meeting, 'with a numerous circle of the amiable and accomplished Ogle family' (*Morn. Chron.*, 4 Oct. 1806).

a £200 acceptance *if necessary*—by Heaven I will see all safe. Send me a Line—I dine at Creeveys in St. James['s] Place on saturday | yours ever truly

I will see the Major[1] justly considered and recriminated— | yours ever | R B Sheridan

594. [To Colonel John McMahon]

Windsor MSS. 40959–60. *Wm.*· 1805

[*Oct. 1806?*]
Richmond
Sunday Evening.

My Dear Friend

I have been reflecting as I came in my chaise to this Place on what Tierney said and you so properly gave no answer to but that you would bear testimony that he had so said, and I think I was deficient in attention not to have offer'd the Proposition I now make. He said 'is there a friend of the Princes who will pay £4,000 for a seat[2] and I will ensure it to him?' Now I think I ought to have proposed this—I have relied on a *positive engagement* with our late excellent Friend Fox that *I* should have a seat free of expence. The Prince took this obligation off the hands of Government, and in point of fact I was return'd by *Him* for Stafford, at my last re-election without the smallest assistance from or obligation to Government. I understand both from Mr Tierney and Mr Calcraft[3] that Sir Christopher Hawkin[s]'s[4] reserve of *one seat* for an *unmentioned* Candidate was considered by them as the reserve for Shelly[5] and that certainly alone

[1] Downs?

[2] In his reply to S. of 'Tuesday' [18 Feb. 1806?], Fox wrote: 'I should suppose there are many Boroughs which might be opened for £2,000 or less. Now if Shelly would pay four considering two as part of what he is to pay at the general Election the thing might be done satisfactorily to all parties' (Osborn MS.). S. seems to have taken up this suggestion with the Prince, and Shelley paid out two sums of £2,500. He was duly returned for Helston in 1806, but lost the seat in Nov., and was not sent back to the Commons until 1816. He recovered £1,500 of his money from the Prince. See Windsor MSS. 42449–52, 42467–9; and *Leveson Gower Corr.* ii. 220–1.

[3] John C. Calcraft (1765–1831) was Clerk of the Ordnance, 1806–7.

[4] Sir Christopher Hawkins (1758–1829), M.P. for Grampound, 1800–7. He was patron of the boroughs of St. Ives and St. Michael's.

[5] Sir John Shelley, 6th Baronet

accounts for Mr Calcrafts telling you and me that Sir John Shelly's business was settled without the interference of the Treasury. What I propose is this. The Prince I think will not submit with temper to the scandalous breach of Faith on the part of Sir Christopher Hawkins and Sir J. Shelly will have every thing to complain of if his agreement with Mr. Fox is not fulfill'd. I am desirous to waive the assistance which Mr. Fox thought it most proper I should derive from the Transaction—and I will sustain the expence of my son's election at Stafford,[1] that is of *the seat I was promised free of expence*—and let Sir John Shelly's money which I answer for his making up £3,000 go to the purchase of his seat. The other £1000 will remain a matter of consideration as to the mode of obtaining it. However embarrassing this arrangement might prove to me I see no other mode of avoiding what I am sure the Prince will consider as ill-treatment of him, and what unquestionably Shelly will have great right to complain of. You have my full authority to communicate this and Shelly's letter. But have the latter back. | Your ever, | R B Sheridan

P.S. I send this by Downes who will be in Town to Night. Your Friendship will lead you to think that the arrangement I propose is hard on me, but I see no other course. I shall at least get time from the Stafford Electors who confide in me, unless for the first time this Treasury misunderstanding of the Persons employ'd in the Election arrangements, may have lost my son a seat He was otherwise sure of.—You will see that these my sentiments ought to be immediately communicated to those who take the lead in these matters | R B S

Downes has been at Windsor canvassing the Stafford militia for my son.—Mansel Phillips[2] having by these blessed misunderstandings and delays two Days start of him[3] at Stafford.

(1772–1852), was M.P. for Helston, 1806, and aide-de-camp to the Duke of Sussex. He is named in the list of S.'s supporters in *The Times*, 23 Oct. 1806.

[1] There Henry Clifford advertised that he had not asserted that S. had sold the Stafford Seat for 3,000 guineas. See *Staff. Adv.*, 1 Nov. 1806.

[2] Richard Mansel Phillips (*c.* 1768–1844) was the younger son of Sir William Mansel, 9th Baronet, and was M.P. for Stafford from 1806 to 1812.

[3] *The Times*, 21 Oct. 1806, reported that Tom S. had left town to canvass Stafford.

595. To His Sister-in-Law

Osborn MS. *Wm.*: 1805

[Oct. 1806?]

My dear Madam

You must not judge of the sincere Interest I take and shall ever continue to take in everything that relates to you and your Family[1] by the seeming negligence of my not answering Letters or writing to you when I have nothing pleasant to communicate. I am aware of and attentive to your situation, and you may depend on every exertion in my Power to relieve you from the difficulties you apprehend and which certainly ought previously to my poor Brother's death to have been prevented. | I am most sincerely | yours | R B Sheridan

596. To Viscount Howick

Grey MS. *Dock.*: Mr. Sheridan | Oct ye 13. 1806 | Rc: 14

13 Oct. 1806
Fenton's Hotel[2]
Monday near six.

My dear Grey

I have seen Lord Grenville[3] who will speak with you. He appears to see the matter entirely as I could wish—indeed I cannot say what my mortification would have been could it have been otherwise | Yours ever sincerely | R B Sheridan

Viscount Howick.

A Line will catch me here. I dine at Holland House.

[1] C. F. Sheridan died at Tunbridge Wells on 24 June 1806. His wife, Letitia, wrote to S. on 9 Oct. (Widener MS.) to say that she feared that her children might be totally destitute, and that confidence in S. was her only resource.

[2] The *Morn. Her.*, 6 Oct. 1806, reports: 'Arrivals at Fenton's Hotel St. James's Street: . . . Mr. Sheridan, Mr. and Mrs. T. Sheridan, from Winchester.'

[3] The decision to dissolve Parliament was taken at a meeting of the Cabinet on 13 Oct. Did S. now seek from the leaders of the administration a promise of support if he stood for Westminster? See p. 288.

597. To the Prince of Wales

Windsor MSS. 40767–8. *Dock.*: Mr. Sheridan | Octr. 14. 1806

Tuesday
October 14th. 1806

Sir

I trust the consequences of this Dissolution[1] will strengthen the Government your Royal Highness supports, and that particularly the number of Friends attach'd and devoted to you may be still more encreased. I fear Ministers have not been sufficiently prepared, but still I think the measure had become absolutely necessary.

Your Royal Highness will have heard of the king's visit to Bulstrode[2] etc. I believe there was among some of them a sanguine expectation that he would not consent to a dissolution. His doing so will have the impression with many, however contrary to the fact, that he has made up his mind to the administration as at present constituted, or that the others felt themselves too weak to undertake it, either of which will assist the support of the present Ministers. I dined yesterday with Lauderdale[3] at Lord Holland's—He was very angry, tho' goodnaturedly angry at the *timing* of the attack on Bolougne[4] and I really believe had there been much mischief done or Lives lost that He would have been in great Hazard.

I have been very much struck with a remark of your Royal Highness's as I understand that the dissolution should have been immediate. I hope there may arise no cause to regret the Delay.

[1] The dissolution actually took place on 24 Oct. The decision to dissolve (taken on 13 Oct.) was strongly criticized in the *Annual Register . . . 1806*, p. 262, on the grounds that even if peace had not been attained the ending of the negotiations was not known to the public, and that the administration had sought to bring this Parliament to an end because it was not constituted to its liking.

[2] The King visited the Duke of Portland on 11 Oct.

[3] Lauderdale had been trying to negotiate a peace with France but had now returned to London without having achieved Fox's aim.

[4] On 8 Oct. a British attempt was made to destroy the French flotilla at Boulogne. Three hundred rockets were discharged.

On the subject of your Royal Highness's absence from the Funeral I sent a short paragraph to the Herald[1] alluding to your Royal Highness's Letter to Lord Grenville which has been copied into the other Papers and has I find had a compleat good effect.

I have *this moment* received the Decisive answer of Government accepting in a very handsome way my offer of standing for Westminster. I look above all things to your Royal Highness's Protection and my own Friends will go also for Lord Percy.[2] Tom will set out for Stafford tomorrow.[3] | I have the Honor to be | Your Royal Highness's | Most faithful and dutiful Servant | R B Sheridan.

[1] 'A letter from his Royal Highness the Prince of Wales to Lord Grenville, on the subject of his attending Mr. Fox's funeral, is greatly spoken of by the few in the higher circles to whom it has been shewn. It is said to be as eloquent and affecting an appeal to the heart and judgment as ever was addressed to either, as well as a most beautiful record of his Royal Highness' affection and reverence for the Illustrious Statesman to whose remains he was so anxiously desirous to pay the last tribute of respect. The letter, full of duty to his Royal Father, was read by Lord Grenville to the King, and report states his Majesty to have been so struck with it, that had not important objections remained, his gracious approbation of the Prince's wishes would have followed.

'The Prince's regret has been strongly expressed that the solemnity of Friday should have been in part maimed, by denying to the solemn music its allotted place in the procession. We need scarcely say, that this was done entirely without Mr. Sheridan's concurrence, and we cannot but be of opinion, that as the conduct of the whole ceremony had devolved on him, and to which he paid the most indefatigable attention, his deliberate judgment in this respect ought to have had decisive weight.' (*Morn. Her.*, 13 Oct. 1806.) The King had forbidden the Prince to attend Fox's funeral for reasons of court etiquette: see *Dropmore Papers*, viii. 376–7, for the Prince's letter to Grenville, of 7 Oct.

[2] On 25 Oct. Lord Grenville wrote '. . . the Duke of Northumberland is so offended at Sheridan's standing, that he withdraws Lord Percy. I mean, if I can, to induce Sir Samuel Hood to offer himself . . .' (*Dropmore Papers*, viii. 400). The Duke of Northumberland's correspondence suggests, however, that he was much more offended by Grenville's allowing him to put up Percy and spend a considerable sum 'when his Lordship well knew all this would not give him a Seat as Parliament was not to meet again before the Dissolution' (Alnwick MSS., LXIII, f. 256). He had been offended at not being consulted when the administration had been formed, and this further lack of consideration only served to alienate him.

[3] To stand as a candidate. He had made a call there on his way home from Ireland, had spent the night at Horton's (24 Sept.) and dined with friends at the Swan Inn. See *Staff. Adv.*, 27 Sept. 1806, and p. 285, n. 3.

598. 'To the Worthy and Independent Electors of the City of Westminster'

Pub.: *The Times*, 20 Oct. 1806.

20 Oct. 1806

Gentlemen

It was not in my power to express, in terms adequate to the sensations in my mind, the gratitude I felt, when, at the Meeting of the 18th of last month[1] your partial kindness induced you to regard me as a person worthy,[2] through your confidence and choice, to succeed your late revered Representative, Mr. Fox. My motives for then declining the distinguished honour proposed to me must, I hope, have received, upon due consideration, the sanction of every unbiassed and reflecting mind.

The present general expectation of an immediate dissolution of Parliament, opens to me the course which every motive of duty, gratitude, and fair ambition calls on me to pursue; I earnestly solicit from each of you the honour of your support, and vote if necessary, at the approaching Election. I make no professions, I am confident you do not expect any from me. What I have been, I shall continue to be; the maintenance of the principles of Mr. Fox is now more than ever a sacred duty.

It is a solemn trust, bequeathed especially to those who shared his confidence, gloried in his friendship, and followed in his steps while living. Such efforts as I can make to execute my humble share in that trust, will, in my estimation, at all times be overpaid by the continuance of your protection, and approbation. | I have the honour to be, Gentlemen, | With the sincerest respect and devotion, | Your obliged servant, | Richard Brinsley Sheridan.

Somerset Place,
Oct. 20, 1806.

[1] At the Crown and Anchor, when S. withdrew in favour of Lord Percy.

[2] This is challenged in Add. MS. 27850, ff. 12–15, 22.

599. To [William] Horton[1]

Pub.: S.C., 14 June 1870, lot 771.[2]

Oct 20th [*1806*]

... Pleased at the handsome manner in which you mentioned my standing for Westminster.

600. To Lord Grenville

George Fortescue MS. Text from Dr. Arthur Aspinall's transcription.

Saturday, 25th October [*1806*]

I am extremely happy to learn that Sir S. Hood[3] becomes a candidate; you may rely on every exertion being made to save him from all fatigue or trouble, for which object we will all go to work immediately and I will wait on Sir Samuel to set his mind at rest in this respect.

601. To William Cobbett[4]

Pub.: *Hist. Westm. El.*, p. 194.

[*27 Oct. 1806*]
Monday evening, 8 o'clock

Sir, on my return to town this evening, I received your note, which gave me the first intimation of Mr. Paull's[5] intention to stand for Westminster. I admit your motives in making

[1] Founder of the shoe trade in Stafford, and a warm supporter of S. See Kelly, ii. 77.

[2] This catalogue prints the recipient's name as 'Horten', but it had appeared in S.C., 12 Dec. 1854, lot 314, as 'Horton'.

[3] Sir Samuel Hood (1762–1814), naval commander.

[4] S. had no reason to like William Cobbett (1762–1835) for he had made a sustained attack on S. as and in *The Political Proteus* (1804).

[5] James Paull (*c.* 1770–1808) had been a merchant in India and went into Parliament in June 1805. When he found that All the Talents would not impeach Wellesley for his treatment of the Nawab of Oudh, Paull joined the more radical Cobbett and Burdett. He was nominated by Burdett at the Westminster hustings of 3 Nov.

the communication[1] to be as frank and direct as you profess them to be, and I thank you for your attention in having made it.

602. To Sir Robert Barclay

Harvard MS. *Wm.*: 1802

Monday Evening
Oct 27 [*1806*]

My Dear Sir Robert

I am very sorry we did not meet to Day. I understood and relied on your being here with me at the Pi[a]zza.

I shall be sure of assisting in the business of late so interesting to you—but you must suspend Goldsmid's[2] for a *little time* and really not long—pray let us meet in the morning— | yours ever | R B S.

What say you now to Paul. I count on some rough work on the Hustings.—

603. 'To the Worthy and Independent Electors of the Borough of Stafford.'

Pub.: *Staff. Adv.*, 1 Nov. 1806.

28 Oct. 1806

Gentlemen,

It gratified me very much to find, from the best information I could receive from Stafford, that my intention to comply with the earnest and general request of the Electors of Westminster, that I should offer myself to succeed their late Illustrious Representative, as Member for that City,

[1] Cobbett stated that he had decided to do all he could to prevent S.'s return, but in his letter to S., published in *The Courier*, 15 Nov. 1806, he remarks, 'I am well assured Mr. Paull does not mean to be *considered as opposed to you*, and that if there should be any hostility shown between you, *the fault will not be his*, or *that of his friends*.' See also *Hist. Westm. El.*, pp. 185–9.

[2] Probably payment due to one of the financiers, Benjamin Goldsmid (1753 ?–1808) or Abraham Goldsmid (1756 ?–1810).

had been so favorably received[1] by you, Gentlemen, from whom no ordinary call should ever have separated me.

I should not have delay'd to express my sense of your kindness on this occasion, but that it was my intention to have left Town this very Day, in company with my Friend, Major Downs,[2] (who will deliver you this short address), in order to pay my respects to you, and solicit in Person for my Son, the continuance of that Support and Friendship which I have so long experienced, and I trust not undeservedly. The sudden and unexpected resignation of Lord Percy, has changed the whole circumstances of the Election here, which would otherwise have been over this Morning, and compels me to adopt this mode of returning you my sincere thanks for the past, and earnestly soliciting your present and future support of my Son, who is sufficiently known to you, to render it unnecessary for me to urge any thing in his favor. | I have the honor to be, | Your obliged and obedient Servant, | R. B. Sheridan.

Somerset-Place, 28th October, 1806.

604. To Sir Robert Barclay

Harvard MS. *Address*: Sir Robert Barclay | Bart— | Mr. Paul's | near Berkeley- | Square *Fr.*: R B Sheridan *Wm.*: 1805

[*Oct.–Nov. 1806?*]
Friday Night

Since we parted I have intelligence of the greatest importance—fail not to be with me before 9 in the morning. | R B S.

605. [To Colonel John McMahon?]

Harrow MS. Cf. Maggs Catalogue 166 (1899), item 1183.

[*1 Nov. 1806?*]
Saturday Night

My Dear Friend—

I have only this moment received the Bailiffs[3] Tickets—

[1] After his nomination as a candidate for Stafford, Tom S. 'refuted the charges of neglect and desertion which had been industriously circulated against his Father' (*Staff. Adv.*, 8 Nov. 1806).

[2] Downs set off for Stafford with Burgess and Finnerty on 3 Nov. See P. Finnerty's letter in *The Courier*, 15 Nov. 1806, and *Hist. Westm. El.*, p. 188.

[3] The High Bailiff of Westminster, who was in charge of the election? Cf. iii. 331–2.

do not impute neglect to me I have been worried to Death by the base opposition to my son at Stafford[1]—and more than all by my wifes being confined to her bed by a dangerous Fever.[2] My grateful Thanks to Mrs. Clarke and Mr. Gillingham. | Yours truly | R B Sheridan

606. To the Westminster Electors

Pub.: *The Times*, 8 Nov. 1806.

5 Nov. 1806

Gentlemen

Impressed with every sentiment of gratitude for the hitherto almost unsolicited support I have received, I beg leave to assure you, that I am not in the least dismayed at the present appearance of the Poll.[3] The circumstances of various kinds, which, from the day of the Dissolution of Parliament, have interfered with and delayed the necessary arrangements for a proper canvass[4] for this extensive City, as well as my own personal exertions, it would be, at this moment, an useless intrusion to detail to you; I only entreat you to attribute this seeming neglect to any other cause than the slightest want of respect, either on the part of my friends or myself towards Electors, who have it in their power to bestow the highest honour which political ambition can merit, or aspire to.[5] I have now the satisfaction to inform

[1] P. Finnerty's letter in *The Courier*, 15 Nov. 1806, makes it plain that on 2 Nov. S. had only just heard that his son was unexpectedly engaged in a contest at Stafford. Tom S. was crushingly defeated by R. M. Phillips.

[2] The *Staff. Adv.*, 8 Nov. 1806, stated under 'London Thursday', that 'Mr. and Mrs. Sheridan, who have been severely indisposed . . . were much better last night'.

[3] Sir Samuel Hood, James Paull, and S. were nominated as candidates for Westminster on 3 Nov., and at the end of that day S. had gained 178 votes to Paull's 327 and Hood's 161. On 5 Nov., however, the poll figures were S., 789; Hood, 1,281; Paull, 1,516 (*The Times*, 4 and 6 Nov. 1806).

[4] Lord Holland writes of S.: 'he thought, in his inordinate vanity, that he might defy the Court, the Aristocracy, and the Reformers; and such was his confidence in his own personal popularity and management, that he not only neglected but derided and insulted the clubs and committees through whose agency Mr. Fox's elections had been generally secured. He was bitterly deceived. Our party supported him very feebly . . .' (Holland, ii. 64).

[5] Wellesley wrote to Grenville on 3 Nov.: 'The general voice is most undoubtedly adverse to Sheridan; between whom and Pau[l] little difference of character is felt' (*Dropmore Papers*, viii. 421).

you, that a systematical arrangement of canvass is established, which, I doubt not, under your protection and indulgence, will speedily recover the ground lost by past omissions. I have greatly to regret, that the course I had entered upon, for paying as far as possible, my personal respects to you, has been interrupted by unexpected indisposition; and I trust to your kindness to make allowance for the cause.[1]

Of the ultimate success of a combined, zealous, and persevering exertion, I have no doubt. The accomplishment of my personal wishes, or ambition, is nothing in the great cause in which we are engaged; and to the maintenance of that cause, amply indeed to be affected by the event of the present contest, will I devote every energy I am capable of; while there is an Elector, who, with me wishes to defend it, left unpolled in this great and renowned City. | I have the honour to be, | With the highest respect and sincerest devotion, | Your obedient servant, | Richard Brinsley Sheridan.

Somerset Place,
Nov. 5th. 1806.

607. To Lord Holland

Holland House MS., S. 79. *Address*: Lord Holland | Holland House | Kensington

[*7 Nov. 1806*]
St. Albans Tavern
½ past one

Dear Holland,

The Committee which was supposed to meet here does not exist.[2] The St. James's Committee which sits here exclusively for Hood consider the advertisement[3] as a Trick

[1] *Hist. Westm. El.*, 1807, p. 53, prints a further sentence: 'I hope, to-morrow, to be able to resume my duty in this respect, as far as the state of the Election, and the difficulty of yielding to any preference in attention will admit of.'

[2] On 5 Nov. Lord Grenville wrote to Fitzwilliam: 'I have . . . I hope this day prevailed upon Sheridan's and Hood's committee to join . . .' (*Dropmore Papers*, viii. 427). Agreement was reached in the evening of 5 Nov. (*The Times*, 7 Nov. 1806.)

[3] Printed in the *Hist. Westm. El.*, pp. 53–54. It reports a meeting of the supporters of S. and Hood, and their resolution to form a central committee to meet at ten o'clock every day at the St. Alban's Tavern, in St. Alban's Street, St. James's.

and have sent up more Votes against me to day than any other Day! while my own committee is dispersed.

Mr. Willock[1] of this committee who received from Mr. Freemantle a[2] Letter exclusively for Hood has never received any other Intimation. No Soul has been here but Mr. Briton[3] who went into the St. James committee room and wrote my name on a few cards—the St. James never heard a word of any change and were much affronted—if all this is only neglect it is[4] strange indeed. They sent a message to Hood and the answer was that He knew nothing of any coalition![5] I am to be here at *8* this evening—and Hood. I earnestly entreat you to be in Town and say where I can see you. I cannot venture to comment on all this, but if such is to be the Conduct the cause is lost which could not otherwise fail— | Yours truly | R B S.

I would not trouble you so pressingly but I have had in this settlement no communication or reliance on any one but yourself[6]—all my People have been canvassing for Hood

608. To Lord Holland

Holland House MS., S. 82. *Address*: Ld. Holland *Dock.*: Sheridan | W. Election | Nov. 1806 *Fr.*: R B Sheridan *Wm.*: 1804

Friday
Nov 7 *1806*

Could you meet me at Lord Grenville's at 5? it may be of the greatest consequence—with common sense and fair dealing we cannot fail. | yours ever | R B S

but Mr. Booth[7] must not otherwise than he does.

1 A magistrate. He nominated Lord Cochrane at the Westminster election of May 1807. See *Bell's W. Mess.*, 11 May 1807.

2 W. H. Fremantle (1766–1850) was Joint Secretary to the Treasury.

3 *The Times*, 13 Nov. 1806, reports that Col. Britten congratulated at the hustings (on 12 Nov.) those who had voted for S.

4 S. has substituted 'is' for 'will be'.

5 Hood mentioned the union between S. and himself, from the hustings on 7 Nov. (*Hist. Westm. El.*, p. 93).

6 Lord Holland states that 'With great exertion I obtained for him some reluctant assistance from the Ministry; and he was with much difficulty brought in as second Member to Sir Samuel Hood . . .' (Holland, ii. 64).

7 Frederick Booth, vestry clerk of St. Martin-in-the-Fields? He was a solicitor for the Affairs of Taxes, and of 3 Lincoln's Inn.

609. To Lord Holland

Holland House MS., S. 83. *Address*: Lord Holland | Earl Spencer's | St. James's Place *Fr.*: R B Sheridan

[*7 Nov. 1806*]
Friday 8 O'clock

I beg your Pardon if I fail'd you at Lord Grenville's but seeing Lord Howick at 5 He told me you meant to meet me there after Dinner. I wish not to go out this evening, being really fagg'd and not very well—can you look in on me in your way to C. G.[1] or after? I wrote to you sanguinely this morning before I knew anything of the Poll[2]—but vex'd at the St. James Committee—I repeat my confidence in the result under the condition I then stated | R B S

610. To Lord Holland

Holland House MS., S. 95. *Address*: Ld. Holland.

[*7 Nov. 1806*]
Friday Evening

you have not got I surmise my note to you at Lord Spencer's—I am knock'd up but busy too in the extreme and I beg'd you to give me a call for 5 minutes going or coming | yours ever | R B S

611. [To Lord Holland]

Holland House MS., S. 89. *Dock.*: Sheridan's *Wm.*: 1805

[*8 Nov. 1806*][3]
Friday Night
two o'clock.

As you seem'd rather fidgetty on the subject of our using

[1] S.'s supporters held a dinner at the Shakespeare Tavern in Covent Garden on 7 Nov., with Lord William Russell in the chair. 'Mr. Scott, in the unavoidable absence of Mr. Sheridan, from indisposition, returned thanks' (*Hist. Westm. El.*, pp. 89–94).

[2] On 6 Nov. the poll figures were: S., 1,330; Hood, 1,927; Paull, 2,143. On 7 Nov. S. polled more votes than Paull but was still bottom. The figures on this day were: S., 2,054; Paull, 2,517; Hood, 2,723. See *Hist. Westm. El.*, pp. 71, 85–88.

[3] At two a.m.

Elliott's[1] name I enclose you my authority before I go to bed tho' I am weary enough. Moore's note is an answer to one of mine begging him to *see* Elliott and to tell me his Christian name, which explains his Parentheses,—I also enclose a note of mine which follow'd you to Lord Spencers in mitigation of my apparent unpunctuality—I am very confident but don't be at all dismay'd if I don't make an equally good stand tomorrow and on monday—make *my* excuses to Lady Holland if you kept her waiting | yours | R B S.

keep Moore's Letter—

612. To the Westminster Electors

Pub.: *The Times*, 10 Nov. 1806.

9 Nov. 1806

Gentlemen,

I trust you are now convinced that it proceeded from no light presumption in me, that in my advertisement of the 5th inst., acknowledging my gratitude for your past and almost unsolicited support, I have ventured to declare that I was not in the least dismayed by the then existing appearance of the Poll. The result of the two last days more than justifies the confidence I then expressed:[2] that confidence was founded on my knowledge of the good sense, the honour, the loyalty, and the patriotism of the Electors of Westminster. Of the success of the pretensions of any Gentlemen who appeared to assume that they did not possess these

[1] S.'s committee, under the chairmanship of Peter Moore, decided on 7 Nov. that the public should be invited to subscribe towards the cost of S.'s standing for Westminster. An advertisement in *The Times*, 8 Nov. 1806, gives the treasurers' names as Lord William Russell, Sir Robert Barclay, and John Elliot. The first two are named in the list of those who had undertaken to canvass or conduct the election for S. (*The Times*, 23 Oct. 1806), but Elliot's name is not there. He was 'a Brewer, a rank tory and Colonel of the Westminster Horse Volunteers' (Add. MS. 27850, f. 17); and had seconded the nomination of Earl Percy on 23 Sept. He stood for Westminster in May 1807, but withdrew on the eleventh day of polling.

[2] The poll figures for 8 Nov. were: S., 2,424; Paull, 2,658; Hood, 3,102.

qualities, I really never entertained any serious apprehension; such a Candidate could only obtain the appearance of a momentary triumph by others remissness. I am willing to take my full share of the blame on the present occasion, confident that a short perseverance will give complete success to our exertions in a cause which deserves and demands the exertions of every man who desires the preservation of the British Constitution. | I have the honour to be, with the utmost respect and gratitude, | Your faithful servant, | R. B. Sheridan

Somerset-Place,
Nov. 9, 1806.

613. To Lord Holland

Holland House MS., S. 80. *Address*: Lord Holland *Dock.*: Sheridan | W. Election | 1806 *Wm.*: 1805

[*9 Nov. 1806*]
Sunday Evening
near 7

Dear Holland

I am afraid I have kept your Servant—but I assure you sin[c]e 7 this morning till now I am come home I have been incessantly at work. My Friends have taken a little Panic—I have not. The great Rumour as of a Riot tomorrow—a Lord Mayor's mob[1] to meet Burdat[2] returning from Brentford at two o'clock and drawn up to the Hustings—all these things are exag[g]erated—mob enough I have no doubt there will be and bad votes press'd in the confusion[3]—| Yours ever | R B Sheridan

I shall certainly be on the Hustings.[4]

[1] The Lord Mayor's show was held on 10 Nov.

[2] Sir Francis Burdett (1770–1844) was the Radical candidate at the Middlesex election, which opened at Brentford on 10 Nov.

[3] See iii. 332.

[4] *The Times*, 11 Nov. 1806, reported that on 10 Nov., S. made his first appearance on the hustings since 3 Nov.

614. To Lord Holland

Holland House MS., S. 81. *Address*: Lord Holland | Holland-House | Kensington. *Dock.*: Sheridan | W. Election | 1806 *Fr.*: R B Sheridan *Wm.*: 1805

[*Nov. 1806*][1]
Somerset-Place
Wednesday 3 o'clock

It is suggested that a morning meeting of the Whig Club would do great good and I think a Line from you to Perry[2] Lowten[3] Gregory[4] and Clarkson[5] would be better than from me. Lowten I am informed does not mean to ask in future singly[6] as enclosed—but still I do not hear of Letters respecting me being sent to the *same Persons* as those respecting Hood were directed to. I am not a bit dismay'd if there is exertion and cooperation. But I wish we could meet this evening and I must not go to Day—tho' tomorrow I will be on the Hustings | Yrs | R B S

I mean it as particular important I should see you this evening

615. To Lord Holland

Holland House MS., S. 90. *Address*: Lord Holland etc etc etc *Fr.*: R B Sheridan *Wm.*: 1805

[*12 Nov. 1806?*][7]
Tuesday near
two

My Dearest Lord,

I could not avoid seeing many Friends to Night tho not

[1] Wednesday, 5 Nov. seems to be too early for S. to expect effective help from Hood's supporters. 12 Nov. is the more likely date, but S. was certainly on the hustings then. See the *Hist. Westm. El.*, pp. 144–5.

[2] James Perry. He spoke at S.'s dinner at the Crown and Anchor on 3 Nov.

[3] Thomas Lowton (1747–1814), solicitor and Clerk of Nisi Prius in the Court of King's Bench. He subscribed £5. 5*s*. 0*d*. towards a statue of the Duke of Bedford in 1802. See *The Times*, 12 June 1802, and *Annual Register . . . 1814*, p. 131.

[4] John Gregory was the treasurer of the fund instituted to pay Fox's expenses at his election in May 1796. See Alnwick MSS., LVIII, f. 178.

[5] Romain W. Clarkson was secretary of the Whig Club in 1806. He was an attorney of 39 Essex Street.

[6] A vote for Hood only.

[7] Wednesday, two a.m., Tuesday's

very good for me however I think it must have done me good. For they are most sanguine and resolute for going on —and there certainly will be no want of *supplies*.[1] More withdraws all idea of Elliott and is vehement for going on. Under these circumstances and what your Letter contains I beg you to assure Lord Grenville that I will shrink from no exertion but go on to the last hour to prevent the scandal and Danger[2] that threatens us. | Yours | ever | R B Sheridan

616. To William Cobbett

Harvard MS. Copy.[3] *Pub.*: *The Courier*, 15 November 1806.

[*12 Nov. 1806*]

Somerset-place, Wednesday Evening, Nine o'clock.

Sir,

The bustle of an Election day, and occupations fitter for me to attend to than any communication from you, have prevented me noticing the letter you have honoured me with till this moment.[4] I am very much amused by the folly of it, and very little provoked by its insolence. I shall not, however, be deficient in gentlemanly respect to the call of any man, and you will receive from me to-morrow such an answer[5] as I shall judge proper to give such a letter. | I have the honour to be, Sir, | Your obedient Servant, | R. B. Sheridan

W. Cobbett, Esq.

poll showed that S. was only two hundred votes behind Paull. He passed Paull's total on the following Friday. See the *Hist. Westm. El.*, pp. 135, 178.

[1] The Duke of Queensberry contributed a thousand guineas to the election fund. See Rhodes, p. 215.

[2] Of Paull's victory. S. received some subscriptions merely so that he might keep out Paull. See *Dropmore Papers*, viii. 439.

[3] In Cobbett's hand. S.'s original MS. may be that listed in S.C., 14 Mar. 1912, lot 17, though it is only signed by S.

[4] Cobbett referred to a report in the *Morn. Chron.*, 12 Nov. 1806, of a speech by S. in which Cobbett was alleged to have promised S. Paull's second votes if S. would stand neutral. Cobbett demanded that S. should either deny the report or print his letter. See the Harvard MS. and *The Courier*, 15 Nov. 1806.

[5] In the afternoon of 13 Nov. Cobbett approached S. on the hustings and repeated his question. S. stated he would reply by publishing Cobbett's and other letters, with comments, in the next day's newspapers. See *Hist. Westm. El.*, p. 163.

617. To Peter Moore[1]

Pub.: *The Times*, 15 November 1806.

Somerset-place, Thursday Nov. 13th. [*1806*]

Sir,

In compliance with your request, I send you Mr. Cobbett's Letters, and leave it to you and the Committee to decide whether they should be published or not. I have never suffered Mr. Cobbett's first Letter to me to pass from my desk; nor should I now consent to the publication of any Letter, not avowedly meant to be published by the Writer, but that you will perceive Mr. Cobbett himself calls for its publication; how discreetly for the cause he supports is his affair. I need not tell you how decidedly I have disdained to allow this letter, or that from Mr. Paull[2] to Mr. Finnerty,[3] and by him placed in my hands, to be used for the purpose of gaining me a single vote from the supporters of Mr. Paull. What their object was, and what advantage I might have made of it, had I been base enough to have stooped to profit by their advances, is too evident to require a comment. My conduct has been without disguise or reserve. It is known to you, Sir, and to the Committee, and to you and them I leave the vindication of it. | I have the honour to be, | Your very obliged humble Servant, | R. B. Sheridan

To Peter Moore, Esq.

[1] Moore (1753–1828) is best known as Thackeray's guardian. After fourteen years' service with the East India Company, he retired to England, and became Whig M.P. for Coventry in 1803 at a cost of £25,000. He was one of S.'s warmest friends, and was chairman of his committee in the Westminster election of 1806. His letter stating that the Cobbett correspondence ought to be published is in *The Courier*, 15 Nov. 1806. For his character, see W. W. Hunter, *The Thackerays in India* (1897), pp. 100–2, 105–9.

[2] It was written on 'Tuesday Morning' and contains the sentence, 'I am not opposing Mr. Sheridan.' It is given in full in *The Courier*, 15 Nov. 1806, and the *Hist. Westm. El.*, pp. 187–8.

[3] Peter Finnerty (1766?–1822) was a Whig journalist who was pilloried in Dublin in 1797, and imprisoned in London in 1811. He supported S. on several occasions between 1806 and 1808, and was a noted talker. Cf. *The Letters of . . . Shelley* (ed. F. L. Jones, Oxford, 1964), i. 23 *n*. 42 *n*.

618. To Peter Moore

Pub.: *The Times*, 15 Nov. 1806

Somerset-Place, Nov. 13, 1806.

Sir,

I have received a Petition from John Davenport, the man who assaulted me, as I left the Hustings, the first day of the Election.[1] It appears to me to be dictated by very artless and sincere contrition. He states himself to be very much intoxicated at the time, which I find to be true; and avers he did not know it was me he struck at. He further urges, that his wife, who has lost the use of her right hand, and a large family, might perish for want, if deprived of his support; and, on their account very penitently implores my forgiveness. I do very freely forgive him, and request you, Sir, with the approbation of the Committee, to take proper measures to procure his liberty, and to provide that his family may not be injured by his confinement. | I have the honour to be etc. | R. B. Sheridan.

To Peter Moore, Esq.
Old Shakespeare Tavern.

619. [To W. H. Fremantle]

The Lord Cottesloe MS. [Ph.] *Dock.*: Mr. Sheridan

[*Nov. 1806*]
Somerset Place
Thursday Evening.—

My Dear Sir,

I am very sorry to say that circumstances have been forced on my notice to night that compel me to believe that Mr Booth has been acting in direct violation of all that was settled this evening. I shall enquire more particularly and

[1] Davenport, a butcher, had aimed a blow at S. 'which, by testimony of four respectable witnesses, would probably have killed him on the spot, had not his weapon been arrested' (*Hist. Westm. El.*, p. 51). For his letter of thanks for his release see ibid., pp. 161–2.

send the evidence to Lord Grenville tomorrow. Nothing but Treachery or timidity can cause us to fail, but if a Person connected with Government[1] does in its effect the same for Mr. Paul, as to canvass for him, the struggle will be difficult indeed. | yours truly | R B Sheridan.

I beg you to send me a copy of the memorandum written by Lord Holland in the morning—of course you will rely on my discretion in the use of it.

620. To W. H. Fremantle

The Lord Cottesloe MS. [Ph.] *Address*: Private | W. H. Fremantle Esq. | Treasury Chambers | Whitehall

[*Nov. 1806*]
Thursday Night

My Dear Sir

I dare say half the names I send you are for foolish applications but the[y] are suggestions of committee Friends and jealous Partizans—and I have not time to look at them, and am tired to Death but very stout for going on for the real great object. What letters you think right to write send to me— | yours truly | R B Sheridan.

621. To the Duke of Northumberland's Agent[2]

Pub.: *Hist. Westm. El.*, pp. 215–16.

Somerset-Place, Sunday Evening,
Nov. 16 [*1806*]

Sir;

The impudent libel posted about the town this day, accusing me of having uttered on the Hustings yesterday, the most foul and illiberal abuse of the Duke of Northumberland,[3] and charging his Grace with having previously, by

[1] R. Birnie, chairman of Hood's committee, replied to a letter from S., and stated he knew of no 'influence. . . by the Duke of Northumberland . . . in this Parish on the part of Mr. Paull' (*The Times*, 17 Nov. 1806).

[2] J. Morris.

[3] *The Hist. Westm. El.*, p. 203, merely reports that on 15 Nov. S. said: 'I have to regret that I am not honoured with the Noble Duke's support, though undoubtedly Mr. Paull has it not.' Cobbett,

circular letters, done the same towards me, is really such a wretched expedient of despairing profligacy, that I can scarcely bring myself to condescend to notice it. There must have been, at least, a thousand auditors who heard every word I said yesterday on the Hustings, and who know that I did not then speak, as I never have in any other place, or on any other occasion, spoken one disrespectful word of the Duke of Northumberland. I was happy to have it corroborated from you today, that the assertion of the Duke having sent round such letters to the vestries as are described in this atrocious libel, or of his Grace's friends having for a moment thought of supporting Mr. Paull, was an audacious falsehood. I find your communication supported by the testimony of the respectable persons to whom you referred me, and whose averments, as far as time may allow, will, I understand, be published to-morrow; but really it is painful to be called on to answer such trash, or to approach to any degree of collision with the cowardly miscreants who deal in it. | I am, Sir, etc. | R. B. Sheridan.

622. To the Westminster Electors

Pub.: *The Times*, 22 Nov. 1806

21 Nov. 1806

Gentlemen,

The Communication made to me this day from the General Committee, who so kindly and disinterestedly undertook the management of my Election, and to whose exertions I owe eternal gratitude, has decided me to make very brief the public address, to which, on the close of the Poll,[1] I intended to have solicited no brief degree of attention; but, on re-considering all that has passed, and bending to the judgment of those whose opinion I ought to respect, I forego my first intention of refuting all foul and foolish

however, alleged that the Duke of Northumberland had written to say that he 'could not bring himself to consent to his son's standing with such a man as Mr. Sheridan', and that when S. was told of this, he answered that if 'the Duke of Northumberland were not an *old cripple and a dotard*, he would chastise him for his letter'. See the *Hist. Westm. El.*, pp. 244–6.

[1] S. was elected with Hood on 19 Nov. S. had 4,758 votes, Hood 5,478, and Paull 4,481.

calumnies which have been put forth against me, as well as of re-stating, with that proud confidence which I feel myself entitled to retain in my own bosom, my claims as a public man to the honour which I have aspired to, and which your justice and judgment have now conferred upon me. Why it has been urged to me, should I stoop to a controversy with scurrility and falsehood, proof against the shame of detection, and insensible to the contrast of gentlemanly manners? It is true, and so I leave the question. At the same time, I cannot but cherish a hope, that all respectable persons who have been arrayed against me, have not been implicated in or even informed of the baseness of the means by which their cause has been attempted to be supported; could I believe otherwise, I should feel that I owe it to the honour of the Citizens of Westminster, to declare to its Electors that we cannot be justified in desiring to remember our success as a triumph, without endeavouring to forget who were our opponents. One word more, Gentlemen, and I have done: I take to myself the greatest blame, and I must also include many of my friends for my admission, for the negligence, mismanagement and misapprehension, which attended the too long protracted commencement of my canvass. To enter into the causes of this, would be to enter into a detail not now of material interest, or easily to be explained. I only intreat you to ascribe it to any motive but a want of personal respect in me towards any one Elector of any degree amongst you; and that I am sincere in the profession, I shall endeavour to prove by the utmost assiduity, now the Election is over, to shew to you, individually and collectively, the gratitude, esteem, and devotion, with which I have the honour to be, Gentlemen, | Your faithful servant, | Richard Brinsley Sheridan.

Somerset place,
Nov. 21, 1806.

623. To ——

Yale MS. *Wm.*: 1803

[Nov. 1806 or May 1807]

Sir,

I am so convinced that my Friend Mr. Graham would

never recommend to me any one who would not be proper for me to respect, I very cheerfully subscribe to his Statement.[1] | R B S

624. To Peter Moore

Pub.: *Hist. Westm. El.*, p. 297.

Somerset-Place, Nov. 22, 1806

Dear Sir—The Committee, you inform me, wish that Mr. Paull's advertisement of the 29th of September last, so ardently extolling me, and especially my pretensions to represent Westminster, should be published, that the attention of the Electors, and particularly of his own supporters, might be calmly called to the contrast of the sentiments then deliberately avowed by him, and the language he and his friends have since thought proper to hold. To this I can only repeat the answer I gave to a similar remark at the Thatched House,[2] that I am far from being anxious to obtrude on the notice of the public Mr. Paull's praises of me, and still more reluctant to assist in circulating a very coarse, though impotent, attack on the Duke of Northumberland and Earl Percy.—And as to Mr. Cobbett, I must again beg leave to differ from the Committee. Believe me, there can be no use in continuing to detect and expose the gross and scurrilous untruths which his nature,[3] his habits, and his cause, compel him to deal in. Leave him to himself; rely on it there is not a man, woman, or child, in Great Britain, who believes one word he says. With regard to the passage respecting the

[1] This accompanies John Graham's note, which was written at the Piazza Coffee House on 'Friday Evening': 'Having taken the liberty to mention to Mr. Sheridan that you had it in your power to do him a great deal of Service in his Election for Westminster I leave a space underneath for him to state his request to you.'

[2] At a dinner in the Thatched House Tavern (on 19 Nov.) to celebrate his election, S. said that he had been asked why he had not republished Paull's fulsome compliments earlier in the election, and he had answered that he was ashamed of Paull's praise and 'would not contribute to libel the Duke of Northumberland' (*Hist. Westm. El.*, p. 269).

[3] But S. said on the hustings on 15 Nov.: 'though there is much in his notions which I abhor, there is something in his character which I respect . . . he has, by his own unassisted talents and energy, raised himself from a very humble condition to a situation of respect . . . and he has the manliness and good sense not to be ashamed to avow the fact' (*Hist. Westm. El.*, p. 204). See also ibid., pp. 280–90, 307–8.

scandalous words he continues to assert I spoke on the Hustings, notice of a different sort will be taken of that. | I have the honour to be, yours, very faithfully, | Richard Brinsley Sheridan.

To Peter Moore, Esq.

625. To His Wife

Pub.: Rae, ii. 229–30.

[*19 Dec. 1806*]

. . . The House of Commons began yesterday. W. Lamb[1] acquitted himself admirably, but I really cannot describe how incomparably Grey spoke,[2] or the decided credit he has acquired and confirmed to himself in every respect. It was a very trying moment and occasion, appearing for the first time as Minister and Leader of the House of Commons. Beside excellent argument and statesmanlike, he showed the greatest readiness in replying to every part of Canning's prepared speech, and that is the faculty that takes most with the House. There is but one opinion on the subject and that is, if possible, more favourable than even what I am stating. I assure you from my heart that this has given me the greatest pleasure, as I am sure it will you.

626. To Sir Robert Barclay

Harvard MS.

[*1806–7?*]
Polesden
Monday morning

My Dear B

write to me by tomorrows and wednesday's Post Pavilion

[1] William Lamb, afterwards 2nd Viscount Melbourne (1779–1848) and Prime Minister. In the debate on the Address on 18 Dec., Lamb pointed out that there was now little hope of an honourable peace with France and that the nation must be unanimous and vigorous in its dealings with Europe.

[2] Canning had followed Lamb on 18 Dec. and had stated that there had been too much delay in the peace negotiations and that the conduct of the administration towards Prussia had been rash and hasty. Grey answered him by saying that if the charges were accurate they should form the basis of an impeachment. He went on to defend the peace negotiations.

Brighton. I rely on your managing the Richmond business[1] for me—I see that my sitting down there comfortably will be of the greatest possible advantage to me in all my affairs. Mrs. S. is delighted with Lady B. and your Daughter not forgetting the cottage— | Yours ever | R B S.

627. To Sir Robert Barclay

Yale MS. *Address*: Sir Robt. Barclay Bart | Ivy-Cottage | Parsons-Green *Wm.*: 1805

[*1806–7*]
Somerset Place
Sunday

My Dear Barclay

Putting all things together—Mrs. Sheridan's health—Riding absolutely prescribed for her—the vicinity to the Park[2]—my nervousness at her riding on the road and the necessity of my being at present near London the absolute Danger of my own Boy remaining longer at Polesden the care of my Grandson[3] the means of accommodating Tom or Scott,—The vicinity of Mrs. S. dearest Friends and Relations, the handiness with which we can meet etc etc etc I absolutely find I must not mind £100 or two. So I beseech you close with the jew at all events—and I will immediately pay you the difference beyond my order. Pray don't be later with me than eleven tomorrow morning when I shall be most happy to find this done— | yours ever truly | R B S.

628. To Sir Robert Barclay

Harvard MS. *Address*: Sir Robt. Barclay | Bart. *Wm.*: 1804

[*1806–7*]
Somerset Place
12 o'clock.

My Dear Barclay,

Ill luck without my Fault made me too late for you at the

[1] Apparently Sir Robert was trying to secure a house for S. at Richmond through one S. Parsons. He is possibly Sam Parsons, auctioneer, of 41 Great Queen Street.

[2] Richmond Park?

[3] Richard Brinsley Sheridan (called 'Brinsley' in this correspondence) was born in 1806. He was known in later life as R. B. Sheridan of Frampton.

Cottage[1] I have sent after you to the city but it may miss you. My salvation for monday depends on my being at another Place two miles off precisely at two—but fix where I shall see you—I will come to the cottage at your own hour or if you can put off your engagement I will be home at 5 for see you this evening I must—

I have reduced what I want of G. to something so very safe and moderate that I trust there will be no difficulty | Yrs | R B S

629. To Sir Robert Barclay

Harvard MS. *Address*: Sir R. Barclay Bart. | Ivy-Cottage | Parson's Green | deliver at 8 in the morning. *Fr.*: R B S

[*1806–7?*]
Richmond
Monday

Dear Barclay

I missed you to Night, but saw Parsons—Mrs. S. is going tomorrow to meet her mother in Hampshire—I want to scrape together every shilling I can early in the morning to pay little things here. Send me by bearer what Parsons gave you—and mark dine here on saturday and on to Polesden sunday | Yrs ever | R B S

630. To Parsons

Harvard MS. *Address*: – Parsons Esq: | Church-Lane | Fulham *Fr.*: R B S

[*1806–7?*]
Tuesday
5 oclock

Dear Sir,

I find Mrs. S. means to go so early in the morning that I should be greatly distress'd to wait your coming. I therefore send a man with this and beg you will see Sir Rt: as soon

[1] Sir Robert's house, Ivy Cottage, Parson's Green?

as you receive it and send back that trifle by him, or Mrs. S. will be disappointed | Yours | R B S.

631. To Sir Robert Barclay

Shuttleworth MS.

[*1806–7*]
Richmond Hill
Tuesday—

Private and Confidential

Dear Barclay

I was going I confess to write to you in a Tone of warm expostulation this morning but after communication with Parsons I trust matters have not merely been misunderstood but misrepresented—Mrs. S. conceived herself to have been deliberately and systematically insulted on every side—and certainly if the reports of our Servants are to be credited not without great reason. Could anything be more strange than without the least previous intimation to find her maid refused admission to wash her a Gown in the Laundry I had made! and a little Fruit for a prize for the child denied from the Garden I rent as much as the House? For the idea of any Person having the right to enter it or to touch a leaf in it without my consent 'till my time is up is a Joke. Nothing hurts me so much as to see her worried and vex'd by these things to the degree she has been and I must wait 'till she is cooler before I can convince her that you have not encouraged them—on the subject of the Rent in making your arrangements you may reckon [on] the strictest punctuality on my Part.—

With regard to the business of so much greater importance, it is not a matter to be discuss'd by Letter—but I cannot but say that throughout I have shewn the most unqualified confidence in your fairness and integrity—this ought to be reciprocal—but we will discuss it fully when we meet—in the mean time I need not remark that I have and do hold it to be a matter of strict honor that *no Person whatever* should share our confidence respecting it.

I hope to see you at Richmond on saturday as Parsons will explain—but also you will find me in Somerset Place thursday morning really as early as you will | Yours truly | R B S.

4. 14. 6
4. 11
£9. 5. 6

Pray settle the small matter as Parsons will explain—Mrs. S. goes tomorrow for Hampshire and it is for her I want it.

PRINTED IN GREAT BRITAIN
AT THE UNIVERSITY PRESS, OXFORD
BY VIVIAN RIDLER
PRINTER TO THE UNIVERSITY